D1606534

For Labour and for women

For Labour and for women

The Women's Labour League, 1906–1918

Christine Collette

Manchester University Press
Manchester and New York
Distributed exclusively in the USA and Canada
by **St. Martin's Press**

Published by Manchester University Press
Oxford Road, Manchester M13 9PL, UK
and Room 400, 175 Fifth Avenue,
New York, NY 10010, USA

Distributed exclusively in the USA and Canada
by St. Martin's Press, Inc.,
175 Fifth Avenue, New York, NY 10010, USA

British Library cataloguing in publication data
Collette, Christine
For labour and for women : the Women's
Labour League, 1906–18.
1. Great Britain. Political parties.
Labour Party. Great Britain. Role,
1906–1920, of women
I. Title
324.24107'088042

Library of Congress cataloging in publication data
Collette, Christine.
For labour and for women : the Women's Labour League, 1906–18 /
Christine Collette.
p.cm.
Bibliography : p. 218.
Includes index.
ISBN 0-7190-2591-5
1. Women in trade-unions—Great Britain—History—20th century.
2. Women's Labour League (Great Britain)—History. 3. Women and
socialism—Great Britain—History—20th century. 4. Women in
politics—Great Britain—History—20th century. 5. Labour Party
(Great Britain)—History. I. Title.
HD6079.2.G7C65 1989
322'.2'088042—dc19

ISBN 0 7190 2591 5 *hardback*

Typeset in Great Britain
by Megaron, Cardiff, Wales

Printed and bound in Great Britain
by Anchor Press Ltd, Tiptree, Essex

Contents

Figures, maps and tables

Figures

Maps

Tables

Foreword

I have benefited from the advice of many people during the lengthy production of this book. Some must be mentioned: Les, who lived with it and earned our keep; women in the Oxford Women's History Group, especially Lyndal Roper, from whose discussion of feminist historiography I gained perspective; Victor Treadwell, who claimed me for academia when I was at Ruskin College; Sally Alexander, who examined an early draft; Tina Delves, who would take no payment for typing a later one, and Heather Kilminster who typed the final draft. June Hannam acted as my editor. The librarians at the Labour Party and at Ruskin College made research comfortable; Stephen Bird, Labour Party archivist, gave invaluable assistance. Labour Heritage women gave support. The Labour Party has allowed me to reproduce photographs; Mrs Helen Wilson, of Manchester, owns her mother (Annot Robinson)'s papers and has deposited them at Manchester Central Library for researchers. The Twenty Seven Foundation made me a grant to complete the book. My mother's lifelong interest in history was surely the first thread in its fabric: together, we made the first map. To all these and many more who gave assistance the book belongs. It is not a last statement of women in the early Labour Party; if it does its job, it will be a beginning that stimulates others to fill in the gaps which I hope will not, meanwhile, cause too much irritation.

Christine Collette
Oxford, summer 1988

Introduction

'The Secretary was empowered to destroy correspondence before 1912, and unimportant letters since that date' *(Women's Labour League Minutes*, 1916). Thus instructing Marion Phillips, the Women's Labour League seems, almost wilfully, to have hidden itself from history. Its president, until 1911, was Margaret MacDonald: her husband, Ramsay, burnt most of her papers on her death. As women formed Labour Party sections and councils after 1981, they worked without the benefit of the knowledge of the previous, separatist League, affiliated to the Labour Party for a decade before the new 1918 constitution organised women into a space which has never since been found adequate. The League has remained obscure and the attention paid it by historians even during a vigorous expansion of labour history, has been negligible. Early Labour women stalwarts, such as Lisbeth Simm, who organised League branches in the North-East, had entirely disappeared.

Fortunately, records have survived through devious routes. James Middleton (Labour Party assistant secretary and secretary for most of its first half-century), married to Mary, League secretary, was more careful of her papers. They descended, in due course, to his third wife (Lucy Cox) and, being deposited in the Labour Party archives, form the basis of the early League correspondence files. Some of Margaret MacDonald's papers found their way to the British Library of Political and Economic Science and some were deposited with Ramsay's in the Public Records Office. Gertrude Tuckwell's papers are available at the Trades Union Congress and she collected and preserved a myriad of press cuttings about the League.

These scattered records obviously present problems; for instance, the letters to a manufacturer are kept by the Labour Party, his replies are in the Public Records Office. As the role of women in the party has not, in the past, been a focus of interest, papers relating to the League have not been collected or referenced together. An additional, smaller problem is that Margaret MacDonald's handwriting is extremely difficult to read and the records are all in manuscript until 1916, when the minutes began to be typed. The London-based committees are, nevertheless, generally well documented: exhaustive enquiries have failed to unearth provincial records of any substance.

The scanty nature of the evidence is far from unique in Labour movement history, although this is sometimes written as if there were no omissions. The ready and confident acceptance that the lack of records proves there were no women Labour Party activists has not been sufficiently challenged. Constituency papers in particular are generally very poor. Mainstream Labour history, as opposed to biographies, accounts of Labour governments and the more dramatic, but extraneous, left-wing groups, is generally underwritten. The poor recording of Labour Party history has prompted the formation (1982) of an affiliated historical association, Labour Heritage, which, with its Women's Research Committee, aims to encourage interest in making, finding and preserving source material.

It is especially unfortunate that women activists have not been studied, since their place within the Party remains controversial. Women's tiny vote within the Party leadership is lamented as frequently as separatist organisation is denounced. Yet a limited and impotent separatism is countenanced as a way of increasing the decibels. The women's sections, councils and advisory committee now form a labyrinthine organisation, the result of sporadic attention and adjustment. Women are annually denied the right to vote for their own representatives on the National Executive committee and the ability to send resolutions from their own conference to the Party conference. The ears of the leadership are open to advice, but closed to instruction from the women's organisation. The arguments have now spread into representation for black people, without any solution to gender discrimination being available as an example. One way of elucidating the debate is to assess the brief, unique span of truly autonomous women's organisation: the Women's Labour League.

Such an assessment has its difficulties. It requires an historical understanding of instances of feminism and of socialism, in so far as the early Labour Party was connected to the socialist movement. Both feminism and socialism are emotive words, conveying a complex set of ideas. They include movements, which contain groups, whose theories vary. Feminism embraces the sisterhood of women who share a consciousness of oppression. It is more than this consciousness which, although vital, does not necessarily lead to action for its improvement. Feminism is an active faith, but it is more than the struggle for any one improvement, for any benefit is valued subjectively. Feminist action is underwritten by the belief that concepts of gender assignment and role are restrictive in all aspects of life. Feminism requires freedom from gender oppression for men and women: it seeks to enquire into the concept of female, or male, and to release people from the limitations that ensue from arbitrary gender designation. Feminism therefore seeks to transform society. I define feminism as the commitment to change society so that gender is not oppressive.

Particular theories on the means of transformation, the quality of oppression, abound in the heterogenous women's movement, from radical lesbian separatist to liberal reformist. It is important not to take back one view, but to look at past instances of feminism and their own particular theories: 'feminism is not consciousness in general but a particular ideology arising from economic and social forces experienced by women at a particular time' (Rowbotham *et al.*, 1979, p. 58); this is an historical understanding of feminism.

Socialism also requires a transformation of society. Its ideology is basically simple; common ownership of the means of production, distribution and exchange. Socialism is also a feeling of power within oneself and of comradeship with others. It can be revolutionary or reformist and gradualist; activity is directed by groups adhering to specific theories, specific instances in time of the basic ideology. Most people work in the main group of the labour and trade union movement that is, paradoxically, not socialist. The long experiment with constitutionalism, the parliamentary road, has become the respectable norm in British politics, edging revolutionaries, anarchists, communists, syndicalists to the periphery. Familiarity with this norm can mean that the examination of past instances of socialism and the early Labour Party is prejudiced in favour of the importance of the latter when it was but an agency, fragile and insecure.

In 1914, at the Women's Labour League conference, Ada Salter said:

> A tremendous transformation was going to take place on this earth; and the injustices of the ages, the misery of the oppressed classes, and the sorrow of the poor, and the tyranny of the wealthy were going to be swept away for ever. Nothing could stop the movement. When the trades movement fully realised that all workers, men and women, youths and maidens, were members one of another, then they would hear more than the rumble of revolution in the distance; the revolution would be here.

This is the ultimate goal of class and gender politics (the 'wild wish' of Mary Wollstonecraft, writing about women's emancipation at the time of the French revolution). Meanwhile, there are frequent and diverse attempts to begin the realisation of at least the nearer reaches of the vision, rubbings of the brass lamp in order to propitiate the genie, if not to bring forth its appearance. Evidence of such attempts can be found in the repeated allusions of the 1987 Labour Party General Election publicity to women's participation in decision-making and the necessity of public authorities being aware of feminine needs. In education, in health, the prevention of poverty, the 1987 Labour Party made the same sorts of proposals for positive discrimination that the Women's Labour League made before the First World War.

Socialist feminism, the genie of the lamp, is obviously a connection of the feminist and socialist concepts. Before the genie appears, we can only guess its guise. We grope towards an understanding of socialist feminism. It would be premature to begin the account of the Women's Labour League with one inflexible idea of socialist feminism; there are many definitions. The League history has to conclude with an identification of its own brand of socialist feminism, learnt from League theory and practice; on this the assessment of the League depends.

Socialist feminists can agree that women's emancipation, in order to live equally with men under the domination of the few with wealth and power, is as redundant as the liberation of workers into a community where women are subordinate. Beyond this, the relationship of class and gender politics is experienced and thought about in a number of ways, optimistic and pessimistic. The special contribution and skills of women are believed to be an essential element of class politics by some; in others' opinion, such distinctions lead to the entrapment of women in the maternal and domestic role. Some look for grass-roots connections and contributions within a mass movement. Others search for an enlightened vanguard. Some believe the connection is false and inevitably doomed.

The pessimists have, perhaps, been embittered by misogynists such as Belfort Bax, a prominent socialist theorist at the turn of the century. Bax wrote in 1906 (p. 297), 'The woman possesses the means of satisfaction, her body: and for allowing (the man) access . . . the law entitles her to demand a rent and dues in the shape of food, clothes, shelter.' Women were said by Bax to be inferior in muscular ability and constitutional vigour: hysterical, a lower evolutionary type, ranking between the child and adult male. Some men (and women) who do not indulge in such mysogyny nevertheless fear the diversionary effect of gender politics on the class struggle. Women reformers have been mistrusted as ladies interfering with working-class lives, their ill-formed philanthropy obscuring the will of their social class to mould, punish and restrict inferiors until they become model employees. 'At least she was no lady', was the chosen epitaph of one woman socialist writing in 1900 (Wilkinson, 1910, p. 28). Such prejudices beget their opposite. Some feminists distrust class politics as an attack on gender solidarity. Some believe any collaboration with men to be impossible while the Belfor Bax syndrome is extant.

There is an undercurrent to socialist and feminist historiography: a belief that the account is one of progress. The present government is therefore described as reactionary or regressive. The idea of progress is suspect and would not be so easily tolerated in other branches of history. Partly it is wish-fulfilment; we have paid attention to our brass lamp for a long while, dusting and polishing. The condition of the working class has improved; whether it has improved in relation to other social classes is not so sure. The willingness to engage in political or industrial action is not obviously greater now than in 1900. It is not at all clear that women's lives have improved in relation to men's. Descriptions of the separate, idle sphere that existed for middle-class women have been over-influential; the sofa never supported the supine form of the industrial woman; she does not share her social superiors' sense of escape from its confines. The belief in progress has, nevertheless, been proclaimed by politically active women (cf. Montefiore, 1927; Brittain, 1953).

Doubting the idea of such progress makes the study of the Women's Labour League especially pertinent and exciting. It was active at a time when the women's movement was sturdy and mature, when the Labour Party was new. In mills and sweated workshops, in the homes and factories of an industrialised society, women had fought for better conditions. They had accumulated vast knowledge, practical and theoretical. The historian could not assume that the Party would inevitably be male dominated and antagonistic to feminism from its inception. On the contrary, one could expect its leadership to have been aware of feminist thought and activity and to have debated the significance of the women's movement for their own party. In the gap between these expectations and the reality of women's small presence in the Party grew the Women's Labour League, deriving from the women's movement as much as from the socialist one. The League was an historical instance of the conjunction of class and gender politics; no-one has attempted, in any detail, the assessment of the degree of its success.

Hidden for so many years, the League is revealed as an organisation appropriate to its historical setting, the efflorescence of socialism and its impact on the established women's movement. The Edwardian era in which it existed was characterised by an impulse for social change shared by movements of high and low politics, in which there was space for experiments such as the League. Progressive opinion was oversetting the truths of a less erratic, but perhaps politically more sterile past age. As Britain was felt to be losing its mastery of the world markets, the attachment to the concepts of the established political economy weakened. There was growing awareness of the conditions of the industrial workers and of the causes of poverty. Knowledge of evolutionary theory impacted on the understanding of society. In parliament radicals were encountered on the Liberal government benches from 1905 and also in the ranks of the Unionists, while the presence of the new Labour Party was a reminder of the growth of trade unions across the work-force and of the proliferation of socialist societies. Women claimed their parliamentary voice, equal citizenship and assimilation to the ranks of government.

Measures of social reform brought about in this society were mostly *ad hoc*, in response to one or more of these stimulants to change. Contemporaries' attacks on the 1834 Poor Law, the introduction of old age pensions and of a national sickness and unemployment insurance scheme have a place in explaining the attractions of the League as a focus for organising labour movement women.

While discussion of the League operation as such a focus, and of its experience of class and gender politics are a continuous theme, the approach taken to recounting the organisation and activities of the League has been to give a chronological account. The reasons for this are first, that the League underwent a dramatic change in leadership in 1911 when both Margaret MacDonald and Mary Middleton died, and second, that operating in a time of profound political change, particularly Britain's entry into the First World War, affected the League's identity and activities. Under different leaders and in different situations, for instance, the space given to provincial branch initiatives varied, as did the League's relationship with the rest of the Labour movement and with the women's suffrage movement.

The League's origins are first discussed, followed by a detailed account of its formation. Chapter 2 describes the organisation of the League from its acceptance by and affiliation to the Labour Party (1908) until the death of Margaret MacDonald and Mary Middleton. In Chapter 3 the activity of the League before the First World War is discussed. Marion Phillips's leadership from 1912 and the changes that ensued are recounted in Chapter 4; Chapter 5 charts the effect of the war. The League then partly renounced its separatism, both for a closer connection with the Labour Party, which had become its banker, and because engagement in mixed gender groups administering the labour movement's contribution to the war effort made separatism an anachronism.

The experiment of autonomy was over. Walter Crane's picture, *Garland for May Day, 1895,* quoted Tennyson: 'The women's cause is man's, they rise or sink together, dwarfed or godlike, bond or free.' The Women's Labour League had come to accept this and made an offering of their organisation to the Labour Party in its 1918 chiliasm. The use made of the gift remains a controversial subject. At least the assessment can be made of the value of the League offering.

1 Origins

'The men's party' – Marion Curran, description of the Labour Party, 1908

A campaigning group of women, committed to the cause of Labour representation in parliament, organised separately, exclusively for and by women, the Women's Labour League from 1906 to 1918 is unique in Labour Party history. It partly derived from the same mix that enabled the Party's foundation and development, imagination inspired by the efflorescence of late nineteenth-century socialism, tempered by great determination to claim the right to participate in the constitutional process. Segregation of the sexes was characteristic of turn-of-the-century political activity; it is impossible to envisage that fertile vista without its ardent women campaigners, conspicuous precisely because they were collected separately, the agitated hats and flying cloaks of the female claimants to citizenship contrasting with staid male morning dress decorated by still and folded hands. Extraordinary to and ignored by the Labour historian, the Women's Labour League has been obscured to feminist historiography sated by the grand medley of consciously directed and well-defined groups that formed the turn-of-the-century women's movement, of which it was just one example and from which it equally derived.

Whether she decided to befriend young servants, campaign on behalf of prostitutes, promote women's emigration, work with women prisoners, a woman then could find a group of like-minded souls. Organising autonomously, women championed their society. Their success on various fronts had been remarkable; for instance, the persistent and meticulous campaign about women's legal status from 1839 entirely altered a married woman's position. Formerly her husband's property, with no rights over her children, after 1882 a woman was equal guardian of her children and had sole rights over her own property and earnings. Equally forceful was the challenge to social conscience on promiscuity, prostitution and child sexual abuse centred on the multi-faceted campaign to repeal the Contagious Diseases Acts of 1864, which had allowed the forcible treatment of suspected prostitutes in seaport towns.

In political life progress was more chequered. In municipal government women ratepayers were allowed to vote for and be elected to Poor Law Boards of Guardians (1834).[1] Women who had one year's residence in a municipal corporation could vote for its councillors (1869). Women were empowered to vote for and be elected to school boards (1870). From 1888 women could vote for the new county councils, but a legal decision the following year meant they were unable to stand for election thereto. Parish and district councils were created in 1894 and women could both vote for and be elected to them, but did not have the right to stand for the London borough councils created in 1899. In 1902, when school boards were transferred to local authority control, women lost the right to be elected to them.

All women were specifically excluded from the extended parliamentary franchise from 1832. In the House of Commons the suffragettes might be boxed into the Ladies' Gallery, but men's political clubs were matched by women's. As a Labour Party woman remarked, 'Political associations for women are, of course, no new thing. They were in existence long before women got the vote and, apparently, found extremely useful by the two older parties; for although women were not considered to be capable of understanding political issues, they were found to be extremely capable of understanding men and useful, accordingly, in an election.'[2] Conservative women organised in the Primrose League and Liberal women in the Federation (1886) and National Association (1892). These women's political groups did not exist merely for men's convenience, but to express women's own political commitment. Both Liberal women's groups were a form of individual party membership that predated such a concept in the Liberal Party generally. The National Association was set up to accommodate women who wished to challenge the political parties on women's suffrage.

When it challenged property and political rights enjoyed by upper- and middle-class men, asking for equality for women of the same social classes, the women's movement could be said to be acting in the bourgeois interest. The debate about discrimination, however, embraced all women. Although middle-class women preponderated because they could devote time and energy, the women's movement membership was drawn from all social classes. It is only recently that the lives of working women have become accessible and their participation in emancipatory campaigns has, perhaps, been underestimated. Marian Barry, for instance, came from Ireland to work in a London sweatshop and then worked for the Women's Trade Union League, which aimed to organise industrial women previously not represented and sometimes ignored. She moved to Jarrow when she married Pete Curran of the Gasworkers' Union, but remained politically active and became secretary of Jarrow Women's Labour League. With her experience of separate women's organisation, Marian Curran referred quite naturally to Labour as 'the Men's Party', although she campaigned on its behalf.[3]

Wage labour and housework did circumscribe the activity of women of the working classes. Hannah Mitchell, who left a record of her life, lamented her time-consuming domestic drudgery: 'Looking back on my life, I feel my greatest enemy has been the cooking stove.'[4] Having lived as a boarder, Hannah married for a home of her own, but found the price high – the loss of independence and ambition. When she went to a meeting she had to make elaborate arrangements with neighbours to carry out her chores, and after long absences was faced with a backlog of work. Her husband once, to her disgust, paid her fine rather than go without his home comforts during her imprisonment for suffrage activities.

Hannah Mitchell did find that occasionally visiting women speakers would exclude her from conversations in her own home. However, if sometimes insensitive, middle-class women were far from ignorant of the lives of women of the working classes. While some women had benefited from the gains of the last fifty years and equipped themselves with an education and organising skills that allowed them to be directly involved with working women, setting up agencies such as the Women's Trade Union League, engaging in social reforms or investigative surveys, others conducted pioneering social casework. Much of this work was unpaid and has sometimes been stigmatised as inexpert and ill-advised because it was voluntary. To dismiss such middle-class women's efforts as patronising or punitive would be to deny the real interest displayed in the functioning of discrimination. They were feminist in that they attempted to address the oppression of women in all kinds of social circumstances, the recognition of the kinship and common interests of women, at work or home, married or single, in comfort and poverty.

It was a keen interest in wage labour itself and the emancipatory nature of economic independence that linked women across class barriers and was common ground for the feminist and the socialist who addressed class discrimination. Women of the working classes, of course, always engaged in wage labour, as servants, on the land, in sweated work at home and in the many manual and mechanical tasks demanded by the workshops and factories of a nation in the process of industrialisation. Opportunities for waged work for middle- and upper-class women were less; from the 1850s the simple, basic philosophy of the women's movement had been that without work women were subordinated to the men who kept them, be they husbands or fathers. The demand for work had been clearly articulated by the group of educated and well-connected women (Barbara Bodichon, Bessie Rayner Parks, Emily Davies, Sophia Jex Blake) centred on Langham Place, London, where the Association for the Promotion of Employment for Women was founded and the *English Womens's Journal* printed. Census returns had demonstrated that there were not enough husbands to go round and that one in six women never married, supporting the women's movement argument that marriage could not be the universal women's career.

The turn of the century was a time of transition in the labour market. For men of the working classes seasonal, casual jobs were beginning to give way to more permanent and better paid employment, although workers remained highly mobile and were mostly employed in small, family-run workshops. Apart from pockets of textile and industrial trades, women of the working classes tended still to work at home, in sweated workshops or domestic service. Such women, if married, stayed at work until the eldest child was able to earn a wage; the double burden of paid and domestic labour was very heavy. For single, middle-class women work opportunities had grown as office techniques improved. The Civil Service employed more women, nursing achieved some respectability and elementary education (for girls and boys) was introduced. However, discrimination was practised against professional married women, who were often forced into resignation, and against women generally by the inequality of their pay. When they stopped work women of all classes found that management of the household budget was a poor return compared to their own financial independence. It was the position of women in the labour market as a whole that therefore attracted women investigators, the tasks undertaken, the rewards allocated and the management of the 'double burden'.

Social surveys proliferated in the late nineteenth and early twentieth centuries. For Beatrice Webb, beginning a life of social investigation and commitment to gradualist state socialism, a founder of the Fabian Society and the London School of Economics, this was the time of her apprenticeship. She gave four main reasons for the new interest in the human condition: first, the development of scientific method and the service of man rather than God; second, fear of the potential for revolutionary change amongst working men enfranchised in 1866 and 1884; third, middle-class recognition that industrialism had failed to improve conditions for the majority, amounting to 'the consciousness of sin', a 'collective or class consciousness'; fourth, the increasing participation of working men in state affairs so that they became recognisable individuals.[5] Investigations ranged from government commissions, and especially departmental enquiries, with expert participants and specialist witnesses, increasingly used in favour of select committees confined to Members of Parliament, to free-lance, quantitative surveys by people who set their own criteria and programme (Booth in London, Rowntree in York) or by concerned Civil Servants (Beveridge, the Toynbee Hall movement).

Progressive opinion was rethinking political economy (Marshall, Jevons, J. A. Hobson), developing social science and sociology (L. T. Hobhouse), and inspiring 'new' liberalism to countenance a greater degree of collective responsibility and state action for social reform. Darwinism formed an intellectual backdrop for the progressives, who used biological metaphors to illustrate explanations of society: people's changing ideas about state and community (which the reformers inspired) were described as part of an evolutionary process whereby society, itself a conscious entity, changed and developed. For the health of the whole social organism each individual, each component part, should contribute effectively according to capacity. It was a small step to eugenicism, breeding only from the fittest components, so that the contributions were the best possible. At a time of aggressive colonial expansion this was underwritten by concern about the military capacity of the recruits who proved so dismally inferior in the South African wars (1899–1902).

An example of those who wove the women's movement concern with work into the progressive philosophy was Clara Collett.[6] While never becoming a socialist, she provided evidence for trade unionists through her detailed surveys. A prolific writer and indefatigable statistician, fellow of University College, London, high-school teacher, Clara Collett was special correspondent to women's industrial conditions at the Board of Trade and contributed to Charles Booth's study of London. She was noted for her short (ankle-length) skirts, worn day and evening for comfort at work. She was appalled by the waste of talented young girls and the misery of some of the married women she had seen. She argued that there was a persistent 'underground expectation' of marriage which prevented young women from attempting to become efficient, and made women who should be in their prime, old, weary and disappointed. Branded a failure because she was not supported by a man, the working woman was discriminated against, low pay bedevilling even the well-educated. The economic emancipation of women which had begun at the bottom of the scale was undercut by upper-class women, who were so desperate for work that they accepted low wages and could not provide for their old age. Instead of being alarmed by the 'surplus' single woman, society should realise it could benefit by her activity; the single woman's continuity in the labour market would encourage her to join a trade union and fight for better pay, so all women's wages would improve. Clara Collett believed women's tastes differed from men's, as did their intellectual and inherited experiences and emotional nature; women had a specific contribution to make. She saw that whatever their social background, women were discriminated against and undervalued.

The appointment of women to serve on the Royal Commission on Labour in 1892 was a rare event. In the previous decade there had been thirty-three Royal Commissions and women had been appointed to one only, that on secondary education. The appointment of Clara Collett, May Abraham and Margaret Irwin as Lady Assistant Commissioners to enquire specifically into the effects of women's industrial employment on health, morality and the home was, in part a recognition of the experience the women's movement gained in the facts of women's work. It was also, perhaps, an acknowledgement that women had a special contribution to make in understanding and interpreting these facts. The Labour Commission as a whole was to enquire into 'the relations of employer and employed and the conditions of labour raised in trades disputes', and to report on any legislative remedy for the evils that might be disclosed.[7] The twenty-seven male Commissioners included the future Conservative Prime Minister Balfour and the Socialist Tom Mann. The Commission Secretary, Geoffrey Drage, took the opportunity to employ university women as clerks to the Commission.

May Abraham had been secretary to Lady Dilke, President of the Women's Trade Union League and then became treasurer to that organisation. Margaret Irwin was a Scots trade unionist, secretary of the Scottish Council for Women's Trades, and investigative body which also promoted legislation on behalf of women and children. Unfortunately, the Conservative administration which set up the Committee felt it necessary to award one of their supporters a place, despite her relative lack of knowledge of women's industry. Eliza Orme was appointed Senior Lady Commissioner; she was to countersign each report. Margaret Irwin, in particular, found it difficult to work with Eliza Orme and felt her investigations were hampered: reports went missing and misleading footnotes were added. Part of the problem appears to have been that the Scottish Council had not affiliated to the Women's Trade Union League and Eliza Orme was a friend of Lady Dilke.

The terms of reference also posed a problem for the investigators in that they implied bias against women's work. Inevitably during their investigations, horrifically bad conditions of work were exposed in many trades and the difficulties of combining dangerous work and domestic chores and the adverse effects of heavy work on pregnancy, childbirth and child care were revealed; the women Commissioners wanted improvements in all these areas. On the other hand, they were reluctant to 'prove' that women's work in any specific trade was a social danger and to jeopardise the independence of women wage-earners. The women interviewed seem themselves to have recognised the dilemma, denying obvious grievances and refusing to complain about the most harsh and demanding labour.

Whether from resentment of their inferior status or in order not to deny women's right to work, the investigative women Commissioners decided not to include any specific recommendations, but to let the facts speak. They divided trades and regions between them and surveyed hours, health and safety, the availability of rest and refreshment, sleeping accommodation, sanitary arrangements, trade union activity and wage rates. The volume of work and their commitment to it was tremendous. For instance, as she was responsible for investigating shops, Margaret Irwin had often to call after 10.00 p.m. at night to interview shop assistants in private and to find if they had been released from work (shop hours were meant to be no longer than 8.30 a.m. to 9.30 p.m.). Apart from making available a mass of evidence to the women's movement and the trade unions, one positive result of the Labour Commission was the founding of the first women's factory inspectorate. May Abraham and Mary Patterson were the first women factory inspectors (1893). Nevertheless, on her marriage to the Liberal Member of Parliament, Tennant, May Abraham had to give up her own work and be content to preside over Liberal Party dinner tables.

Liberalism remained the political home of many in the women's movement. However, progressivism was the philosophy that for others paved the route from gender to class politics, from social reform and investigation to the socialism that effloresced in the late nineteenth century into a proliferaton of small, town-based groups. Progressivism was a different understanding of society than socialism, the latter's economic base more structured, defining people in terms of their relationship to the means of production and in struggle with each other, while the progressives preferred to think in terms of the contribution of the individual. Liberal progressives and socialists, however, worked comfortably together in groups like the Rainbow Circle or the editorial board for the *Progressive Review*. Professional women had their own experience of gender solidarity in the women's movement and their interest in work itself to underwrite their connection with the socialist movement, while others in the women's movement were working women whom the socialists would have naturally sought to attract. Particularly empathic to the women's movement had been the 'new life' socialism of the 1880s, which engaged in living out the quest for an immediate microcosm of experience in a socialist society, without fear or oppression. Christianity was a popular analogy for the loving kindness of the 'new life' ethos. Not just work, but everyday arrangements were to change into a culture where men and women equally pursued individual development, living a simple life without servants, sharing domestic work, wearing practical clothes.

One example of the interaction of the women's movement with political ideas that lent towards socialism was the newspaper *Shafts* printed from 1892 for 'Women and the Working Classes'. *Shafts* advocated the education and enfranchisement of women; its front cover bore the design of a woman aiming shafts of wisdom, truth and justice into the world. It reported various women's groups' activities, particularly those of the Pioneer Club, a forum that brought together women of the middle and working classes and discussed a wide range of social and political ideas. Although it was bound by no creed or class and was not party political, *Shafts* expressed solidarity with the working classes by reporting industrial news. There was always a column, 'What Working Women and Men Think', carrying snippets of news and discussion of issues such as arbitration to settle a strike. The inauguration of the Independent Labour Party was reported at length in September 1893. On 16 March 1894 Eleanor Marx Aveling (an active socialist campaigner) was to lecture in the office on socialism for women. Socialism was welcomed as the solution to the 'Woman Question' by offering food, clothes and leisure for all; it would give the opportunity to enlarge minds and expose genius.

The International Congress of Women, called in 1899 by the various national women's councils, was a second example of the women's movement concern with work breeding familiarity with socialist and trade union ideas.[8] The Congress had been founded in 1888 in Washington 'for the promotion of unity and understanding between all associatons of women working for the common welfare of the community'. It was suggested that Esperanto be adopted as a common language. The National

Union of Women Workers of Great Britain and Ireland modified its constitution to become the British National Council of the Congress.

The Congress was not party political. The delegates in 1899 included progressive Liberals such as Mrs J. A. Hobson, who spoke on the ethics of wage-earning and the discontent of economically dependent women. Others were Fabian gradualists, such as Beatrice Webb, who roused delegates to angry debate by defending wage legislation for women and claiming that free collective bargaining would lead to a deterioration in women's wages. Socialists were represented by women such as Margaret MacMillan, who spoke on the importance of the child's environment to its physical and mental well-being. There were about thirty meetings in all, with eight papers read at each. Lady Aberdeen (President of the Scottish Council for Women's Trades) presided: in her opening speech she referred to the contemporary gender division in political activity, of women 'bonding together apart from men', and feared that ultimately this would prove detrimental to society: 'in most cases a temporary expedient . . . It must not be allowed to crystallise into a permanent element in social life.'

It was their acceptance of socialism that led some women out of single-sex groups into mixed ones. Such women had already studied the causes of their own oppression and formed ideas about the remedies that should be sought. Instead of tagging their feminism on to ready-made socialist dogma, these women could participate in directing the philosophy and organisation of the new parties that coalesced from the diversity of 'new life' and town-based socialist groups; they could invent their own socialist feminism. Such an interaction of gender and class-based politics heralded the Women's Labour League.

Socialism thrust into the twentieth century. Ideology was refined, the 'Woman Question' much discussed. A fairly common approach was the simple equation of capitalism and patriarchy. The economic mode of production, especially the holding of private property, was given as the direct reason for women's oppression. There was no attempt to explain why capitalism should be patriarchal and it was taken for granted that patriarchy did not exist outside capitalism. Glorious were the descriptions of a past 'golden age', when women had been included in decision-making and respected for essential work. Engels's theoretical work (*The Origin of the Family, Private Property and the State*) may have been particularly influential in this respect.

In practice, the socialist movement was as diverse as the women's movement; organisation and constitutional structure grew around particular interpretations of the basic belief in the necessity for common ownership as the means of production, distribution and exchange. The variety of opinion in both women's and socialist groups allowed differing fusions between them. The value of women's separate organisation was remembered in some groups, forgotten in others. It is useful in considering the origins of the Women's Labour League to discuss the gender politics of some of the early feminists and contrasting socialist groups. The Independent Labour Party, the Social Democratic Federation and the Co-operative Women's Guild repay attention in considering the landscape from which the Women's Labour League was built.

The Independent Labour Party encouraged mass membership to achieve representation for the mainstream of working people on local bodies and in parliament, being constitutional whilst keeping alive the idea of the 'new life'. The tensions of a constitutional approach and an ethical foundation were never resolved. The Independent Labour Party carefully avoided the word 'socialist' in its title, fearing to arouse distrust, but drew its members from those who wanted to transform society and redistribute wealth. The ILP was not a centralised organisation. Its conference was, in theory, the prime policy-making body. As a prominent few became insulated from challenge by years of received adulation, conference lost power in practice. The ILP Executive, however, continued to be named the National Administration Council to indicate that its role was merely the implementation of conference decisions. Local branches of the ILP were free to act on their own initiative and were supported by paid organisers and by regional federations.

The Independent Labour Party perhaps got off to a bad start in that *women* founder members cleaned the hall prior to its inaugural conference, decorating the trestle with a red cloth. Trade union women, however, joined the ILP, as did women involved in suffrage activity. Seats on the National Administration Committee were regularly won by women at the annual conference, for instance by Isabella Ford, Mrs Pankhurst and Katherine Bruce Glasier. Katharine, formerly Katharine Conway, was the only woman on the 1892 committee appointed by the Trades Union Congress to organise the conference of labour and socialist organisations which became the ILP in 1893. Enid Stacy, a Bristol socialist and agitator amongst women trade unionists, who lived for a while in a Lake District 'new life' community, challenged Keir Hardie for the ILP chair in 1898.

Enid Stacy had suggested the formation of an Independent Labour Party women's association in 1894, but no action was taken. There were local ILP women's sections and guilds which discussed gender politics and women's participation in the Labour movement. However, at national level there is no evidence of this debate being continued. In 1896 an opportunity of giving women national support and a central forum was lost. Christian socialist speaker and organiser Caroline Martin died and the National Administration Committee had to decide between the merits of remembering her by appointing a women's officer or by investing in a van and publicity fund. They chose the van. More remarkable were fears for the chastity of the male ILP officers: on 3 July 1896 the National Administration Committee resolved: 'for the benefit of the general and assistant secretaries, no typewriter (female) be employed until she had attained the age of thirty at least and is otherwise respectable'. There was debate about the wisdom of a parliamentary policy, including challenges at conference and attempts to reverse policy back to grass-roots organising, but the fact that a parliamentary policy might alienate disenfranchised women was not addressed. Neither was the problem of how the ILP could attract female recruits, although the lack of these was deplored. Women's exclusion from Salford ILP meetings held in a men's club (decorated for the occasion by Sylvia Pankhurst) was a motive for the formation of a separate women's group, which became the Women's Social and Political Union.

The Independent Labour Party expressed its views through *Labour Leader*, edited on behalf of the National Administration Committee. Initially, *Labour Leader* was Keir Hardie's paper; he was editor and writer of most of the copy, in various guises, including a women's column under the pen name 'Lily Bell'. Later, John Bruce Glasier was editor (from 1905) and on his death Katharine took over. Keir Hardie seemed to enjoy romantic serials which had stock characters (the 'rake' or the 'coquette'), despite having presumably written the July 1899 article which deplored 'bowdlerized melodrama' and reminded the leadership that the new woman was in a minority and 'it is on the sweat worn pennies of Demos that the enormous circulations are built'. There was little to challenge fixed ideas of womanhood; the romances usually portrayed women at home; if they escaped into drunkenness or promiscuity the 'heroines' were lost in degradation.

A feature of *Labour Leader* that contradicted accepted standards of morality, however, was space given to advertisements for abortafacients – Dr Davies's or Dr Towle's pills for removing obstructions. Also advertised were pills to restore 'lost vigour' in men. Sometimes snippets of news were given about women's rights, for instance, reporting the 1899 International Congress of women or deploring that Ruskin Hall (the new Oxford College for working men) was not to provide accommodation for women. However, the column of Independent Labour Party branch activities was headed 'chronicle of the sayings and doings of young *men* in a hurry' (my emphasis).

Katharine Bruce Glasier wrote a woman's page in *Labour Leader* under the pen name 'Iona'. She regularly reported on the drudgery faced by working women and how difficult it was for those in poverty to keep a home together. The best work of all, in Iona's opinion, was the creation of a comfortable home; she believed this was women's work as a man would lief as live in a tent. Women's groups were often reported as makers of tea and arrangers of socials. Much of the material was condescending, but there were occasional attempts at a more leisurely discussion of issues such as militarism, dress and appearance, as they affected women. In May and June 1906, for example, Iona gave lengthy consideration to stoutness, which she claimed to be the result of women's hereditary oppression, rather than dietary excess. 'What courageous, big hearted and gallant creatures some men are', commented Iona, expressing a longing to see a 'before and after' photograph of a husband reported to walk beside his wife only if she wore stays.

Isabella Ford was a prominent member of the Independent Labour Party, a parish councillor for Adel and worker for women's trade unionism.[9] She believed that socialism 'insists on a moral regeneration of society of the most complete and lasting kind, in order to make a lasting foundation for social and political change'. The many gains of the women's movement – measures of domestic and industrial reform – in Isabella Ford's opinion, helped prepare for the best type of socialism. The socialist movement enhanced the struggle for reform by introducing the idea of common ownership. Women's and socialist groups, existing separately, could stimulate each other and gain from each other's membership. Immediate aims were held in common, such as decent housing, a good water supply and equal pay. Isabella Ford acknowledged that there had been prejudice in the past against bourgeois women reformers, but founding socialists were bourgeois men; besides, 'Labour has swept into its current followers of all classes.'

One lesson Isabella Ford insisted that socialist women must learn: that however right a reform, however just a claim, the initiative for change must come from women of the working classes themselves; they must think and act in their own interests. In all her many pamphlets, tracts and novels Isabella Ford emphasised 'intelligent discontent, mental revolution'. The humility and patience that the philanthropists who read the Bible to factory women sought to inspire was useless, as industrial women must control their own lives as a prelude to the collective bargaining which would alone bring improvement.

Ethel Snowden was also a constitutional, reformist socialist and applauded women reformers for their personal example of organisation and social service.[10] The object of feminism was that women were as free as men and both as free as possible. Society limited personal liberties and assigned to women the role of childbirth, a role far exceeded by women's energies and talents. In Ethel Snowden's opinion the true feminist was of necessity a socialist. Feminists wanted economic freedom, which could only be assured if society was organised in such a way as to provide food and necessities for all, through political evolution and economic change, the public ownership of land and industry. For its part, socialism stood for equality and opportunity for men and women in every department of human activity where sex did not impose a barrier.

In contrast to the views of Ethel Snowden and Isabella Ford were those of revolutionary socialist women such as Lily Gair Wilkinson of the Socialist Labour Party.[11] This syndicalist inspired group, influenced by De Leon (a Marxist syndicalist active in America) and some disaffected erstwhile Social Democratic Federation members, believed (and believes) in revolution through consensus, countenancing parliamentary action, but refusing to compromise its principles of revolutionary change. The class struggle was the prime, urgent issue, to which all energies would be directed, the goals social ownership, the means industrial unionism. The Socialist Labour Party took the classic line that women were therefore best served by subsuming their feminist activities and working for socialism. Lily Gair Wilkinson, nevertheless, set out to examine how far feminism and socialism were in sympathy and how far they were antagonistic. She concluded that the reforms gained by the women's movement were illusory. Women capitalists, in Lily Gair Wilkinson's opinion, were every bit as bad as male oppressors. If there were freedom from industrial disease there would be no need for doctors, if there were no property arguments lawyers would be redundant. Women could not benefit from entering the men's world, whose terms were those of slavery: 'Woman's emancipation is not to be attained apart from man's emancipation, nor for that matter, man's apart from woman's, but, being slaves together, they will gain true emancipation when they strive together for freedom.'

Despite this conclusion, Lily Gair Wilkinson did acknowledge common interests amongst women of all social classes: 'Social restrictions prevent the full, free and natural development of nearly every woman that is born.' The poor woman was always cheaper goods than her brother, partly because of myths about the debilitating effect of menstruation. The rich woman sold herself into bondage to serve a man's pleasure; he owned her carriage and her jewels and fed and clothed her. The woman's body was always the commodity on sale: 'All these women enter bondage by selling their bodies, selling them for man's pleasure or selling them for the profit of an employer, but always selling that sacred thing, a woman's body.' Being a willing slave was the more humiliating and Lily Gair Wilkinson rejected that stigma: 'If anyone should compose for me an epitaph, I wish it may be written, "At least she was no lady."'

Isabella Ford, Ethel Snowden and Lily Gair Wilkinson all emphasised that oppression at home prevented women from being active in the class struggle. They debated domestic roles and lifestyles. 'New life' socialism had experimented with communal living. The experience of women of the working classes, like Hannah Mitchell, was not necessarily that of kinship group households. Jane Hume Clapperton devised a new housing scheme as a remedy for emancipation from domestic pressures.[12] In her 'unitary homes' domestic work would be shared and time found for study and debate. She wrote that true love was not superficial but very complex; communal, free personal relationships would allow a woman to seek fulfilment, intellectual, material and sexual. She would have the advantage of living with a variety of people, yet could still be supported within a traditional family unit, within the unitary home, if that were her wish. Jane Hume Clapperton advocated birth control and equal licence as the principle of marital harmony and perfect equality between sexes as the only route to a pure and happy monogamy. Meanwhile, Isabella Ford wrote that 'men and women stand in a false position of unequality to each other and that falseness spreads, as a fungus spreads its evil growth, into their relationships to others'.

Most important to the Social Democratic Federation was the education of the workers in the class struggle. The Social Democratic Federation, although a vanguard organisation (a group at the forefront of the workers' movement, enlightening the consciousness of the whole body), did have a programme of reform and stood candidates at local and parliamentary elections. Candidacies for and membership of school boards and poor law boards were especially valued, intrinsically for the reforms that could be achieved and because of the propaganda opportunities afforded. These candidacies were often undertaken by SDF women. Women's membership of the SDF was not large. Some women did manage to win prominent positions, being sent as delegates to international gatherings and serving on the executive committee. There were never more than two women on the executive committee and often none; Mary Gray and Edith Lancaster had seats in 1896; Mary Gray served for seven years. Mrs Blochan was on the parliamentary committee in 1897 and Mrs Bridges Adams of the Greenwich school board on the education committee in 1906. Dora Montefiore, an ardent follower of Jane Hume Clapperton, served on the executive in 1904 and Rose Jarvis in 1905 and 1906.

It was not until Dora Montefiore reached prominence that attempts were made to involve women more fully; through her suffrage work and membership of the Clarion Club she had a thorough grounding in women's and socialist organisations. There were women's groups in the Social Democratic Federation, but they had no constitutional recognition; in 1904 Dora Montefiore successfully proposed the formation of a woman's branch, which became the women's committee with affiliated women's circles, the purpose first, to make women socialists and second, to get them to join the SDF. The perception of women's groups as a temporary training ground was, of course, very akin to that of Lady Aberdeen's at the International Congress of Women and should not be seen simply as the inevitable result of women operating within a vanguard organisation. In fact, rather than receiving training, women ended up ensconced behind the SDF urns: the 1908 conference report included the immortal lines: 'a section of the Women's Committee have continued their labours in providing the refreshments served'. Dora Montefiore resigned from the executive in 1905 for that reason.

Despite arguments over editorship, we may take *Justice* as largely representative of the opinions of prominent Social Democratic Federation members. There had been a great debate on 'the Woman Question' in its columns in 1895. One main topic was whether there should be reforms affecting women's position, so that they could increase the effectiveness of the class struggle by participating, or whether personal politics should be ignored until that struggle had succeeded. The problem was, as Belfort Bax wrote (12 January 1895): 'the curious fact about the sex question is that it seems to entirely obliterate the usual class and party landmarks'. Margaret Hicks, for instance, wrote (6 April 1895) of the difficulties of organising women who were not free to make their own decisions; as fifty per cent of working women were under twenty-five and only partially self-supporting, they were subject to pressure, as a work force, from the men who maintained them: the SDF should, therefore, support the unionisation and politicisation of women; it was no good waiting for the class struggle to make everything right for women, else they would all be dead and buried.

A leader writer ('International Notes', 7 December 1895) commented that socialism embraced every human condition, the sex relationship in marriage being a factor in social economics, relationships free from oppression benefiting children. The opposition came mostly from 'Topical Tattle', who wrote (22 June 1885) that women were not subjected, merely socially and economically dependent and content so to be. He was supported by correspondents who believed women to be intolerant, tyrannical, a source of cheap labour, reactionary once elected to reformist positions. A constant theme was that now women could keep their own property they could leave their husbands destitute, while the man still had to support his wife, that a husband could not compel a wife to cohabit, but would still be penalised by payments under a separation order if he refused to live with his wife. Although several correspondents wrote that such opinions only applied to middle-class marriages, the male columnists kept up the lament about men paying for women's keep. Eleanor Marx Aveling and Belfort Bax debated the comparison of women to the proletariat, Eleanor Marx Aveling maintaining that women did most of the work of the world despite having the least strength, while man treated woman as a capitalist treated labour, withholding subsistence and forcing her to accept terms. Bax quoted Proudhon as the authority for his opposition and finished his contributions (23 November 1895) with a phrase that summarised the Social Democratic Federation attitude to personal politics, at once restrictive and libertarian: 'It is . . . the best thing for members of the SDF to shut up their bedrooms when going out to party meetings.'

Belfort Bax, it must be admitted, remained a misogynist; there is ample evidence in his essays 'The Monstrous Regiment of Women', 'Feminism in Extremis' and 'Some Current Fallacies on the Woman Question' (*Essays in Socialism New and Old*, 1906): 'I think from a survey of the facts given', quoth Bax, 'every unbiased person must admit that women, far from being oppressed, are steeped to the teeth in sex prerogative.' He had a particularly nasty tolerance of wife-beaters: 'if all the husbands were sent to jail for trivial assaults on their wives, there would not be enough prisons to maintain them'. Indeed, Bax did not believe women were wholly human: 'woman had no artistic achievement and was a stranger to morality, justice and truth'.

Many women's groups, perhaps reaffirmed by acquaintance with socialists like Belfort Bax, remained single-sex groups. The Co-operative Women's Guild, for instance, although it promoted the interests of women of the working classes who preponderated at branch level, never embraced a socialist, or, indeed, any political party. Women had actively influenced the spirit of co-operation since the time of Robert Owen and his vision of people living and working collectively in disciplined communities. There were obvious connections between co-operation and later experiments in 'new life' socialism. The Guild was extremely successful at organising women, having 32,000 members in 611 branches by 1914. The Guild was founded by women as a separatist organisation; although ultimately responsible to the Co-operative Union (the governing body of the

Co-operative Societies), it did not emerge as a subordinated group and retained complete autonomy over its own members. Indeed, for a period of four years the Guild was denied the annual subsidy by the Union because it persisted in supporting relaxation of the divorce laws.

Women participated in the Co-operative Societies directly, as purchasers and consumers, channelling the household budget to a retail outlet that catered for their needs, and offered an extension of their financial control by giving them a voice in wholesale purchasing policy. The societies were also large employers of women, in shops and food factories. However, women could not claim to be fully represented in decision-making; the women present at Co-operative conferences were usually spouses or daughters of male delegates. It was women's dissatifaction with this passive role that had led to the formation of the Women's League for the Spread of Co-operation, renamed the Co-operative Women's Guild in 1883. Members were organised hierarchically in branches, districts and sections and governed by the central committee. As a single-sex organisation, the Guild was effective in bringing together women of different social backgrounds. Margaret Llewellyn Davies was General Secretary from 1889 until 1921, very much the leading figure. Guild campaigns covered all aspects of women's lives, encouraging them to join trade unions and taking up such issues as bad housing, sanitation and maternity and child welfare.

The interaction of classes and gender politics was complex, as a comparison of the Independent Labour Party, Social Democratic Federation and Co-operative Women's Guild shows. The activity of the reformist and progressive woman outside class politics continued, including involvement with trade union work; meanwhile, female socialists were not necessarily feminists. Many areas of possible dispute were left unresolved and the tensions facing women in socialist groups were not properly addressed. However, there was a practical and theoretical understanding of socialist feminism by 1900, when the Labour Representation Committee was formed as an agency to achieve the direct representation of working people. The relative success of Independent Labour Party electioneering contributed to its founding and men prominent within the ILP (Keir Hardie, Philip Snowden, Ramsay MacDonald), with a grounding of gender politics, were amongst its initiators, Ramsay MacDonald was elected Labour Representative Committee secretary and worked from home, in company with his wife Margaret. She was president of one of the women's movement organisations which campaigned against sweated work, the Women's Industrial Council. They worked surrounded by their babies and children. Clara Collett was a correspondent.

Not specifically socialist itself, the Labour Representation Committee drew its class politics in part from the socialist societies but also, and more substantially, from the trade unions, so that it was reformist and gradualist. It would obviously not attract the revolutionaries such as Lily Gair Wilkinson or Dora Montefiore, but an Isabella Ford or an Ethel Snowden might have been expected on its executive committee. There was more reason to expect the Labour Representation Committee to attract such prominent women members in that it aimed at constitutional reform, parliamentary representation of an aggrieved section of people who trusted in citizenship and the workings of democracy to meet their needs. This attention to constitutional redress exactly matched that of the contemporaneous women's movement, wherein suffrage was becoming an obsession. There was no political reason why the Labour Representation Committee could not have drawn members from the socialist feminist theorists, the constitutional and progressive reformists of the women's movement. It could have escaped description as 'the Men's Party'.[13]

There were, however, organisational and functional reasons for the masculinity of the Labour Representation Committee. First, organisation. It was not possible to join as an individual member. The LRC was both the simple agency of organisations running candidates, independent from the existing political parties, to represent working people in parliament and a more complex gathering, the political committee of their combined forces. Five seats on its executive committee were set aside for socialists; there was no restriction on class or dogma; theory was left to be debated later, along with discipline and finance. Some groups stayed aloof, such as the Co-operative Societies; others soon left, like the Social Democratic Federation. The size of the damages claimed in 1901/2 against the railway unions, after the Taff Vale strike and the legal judgement that the unions were responsible for their members' actions, made political action even more attractive: trade union affiliations doubled, so that the great bulk of membership providing the finance were trade union men. As its agency, the LRC reflected the masculinity of the labour movement; the ordinary woman member was therefore a rarity.

There were exceptions; Margaret Bondfield, who had supported the 1899 Trades Union Congress resolution to join with socialist organisations in order to achieve direct labour representation, was one of the first to affiliate (30 October 1900) in the name of the predominantly female shop assistants' union, 7,000 members at 10*s* per head. Margaret Bondfield represented one of the few sizeable groups of union organised women; the Labour movement was almost inevitably male dominated because of women's position in the work force. Separated into the poorly paid and badly organised trades, women's trade union membership remained extremely small outside the cotton industry. Table 1 shows the female

Table 1 *Female membership of all trade unions, 1914, compared to membership in 1918*

Union	*Women members, 1914*	*Women members, 1918*	*Women members, 1918 (%)*	*Date women first admitted*
Miners	140	10,000	1	1897
Metal	1,041	11,000	1	1906
Textile	288,630	423,000	60·3	1880s
Clothing	25,858	119,000	56·4	1880s
Transport*		54,000	6·0	1915
Printing	8,285	39,000	27·5	1904
Furnishing/woodwork	568	5,000	5·2	1911
Chemical	325	3,000	13·7	1906
Pottery	1,804	20,000	60·6	1906
Food and tobacco	3,317	7,000	15·8	1895
Distribution	18,357	62,000	41·9	1890s
Clerical	15,459	83,000	24·3	1890s
General labouring	25,534	216,000	19·6	1890s
All	357,956	1,086,000		

Note: * National Union of Railwaymen, Women admitted 1915; London and Provincial Vehicle Workers, Women admitted 1916; Amalgamated Tramway and Vehicle Union, Women admitted 1915.
Source: Barbara Drake, *Women in Trades Unions* (London, 1920).

membership of all trade unions in 1914 and the dates women were first admitted; in seven trades only is the date before 1900. The executive committee of the Labour Representation Committee remained all male because it was drawn from the executives of its affiliated bodies, maximising the difficulties of women's participation. The prominent women activists were therefore missing from its leadership.

By 1906, when the Labour Representation Committee was renamed the Labour Party, indicating that it had developed from an agency into a body with its own separate identity, assisted by the growth of local LRCs which formed resolutions debated at its annual conference, it was still not possible to overcome the masculine bias of its organisational structure. There was a further confusion in that local LRCs might be dominated by the Independent Labour Party or Social Democratic Federation (even after the latter's secession nationally) and reflect the gender politics of that group.

The masculinity of the Labour Party was also functional. It existed to get men into an all-male parliament for which only men could vote. In its early years it evaded the cause of women's suffrage. This was, in part, because the campaign for women's enfranchisement, albeit devoted to one issue, was organisationally diverse; it was a spirit, uniting women, rather than a body controlling them; there was no single head to the body to speak to the Labour men. More importantly, although both the Labour Party and women's suffrage organisations professed single and limited aims, each had a much more general and diffuse unstated programme. Women's suffrage meetings and journals tended to address women's oppression on a variety of counts and to articulate opinion about discrimination in general. Manchester and Salford District Women's Trade Union Council wrote perfectly reasonably in 1902 to ask Ramsay MacDonald what benefits membership of the Labour Representation Committee would bring women, and whether female representation was part of its programme.

Apart from its immediate aims, Labour Party identity and politics were obscure. For instance, in an essay on 'The Labour Party', printed in 1909 in W. T. Stead's *Coming Men on Coming Questions*, Ramsay MacDonald described its function as: 'Representing trades, representing the working classes and representing a coherent body of fundamental labour opinion; the Labour Party has hitherto refused to compile a programme, for the sufficient reason that a party is created not upon a programme, but upon a point of view.' This obscurity of function meant that socialist feminists were addressing not clearly stated objects open to debate, but a more complex, almost mystical consensus, arrived at by the masculine body.

Within parliament the Labour Party separate identity was difficult to establish, members co-operating from 1906 with a Liberal government encouraged by substantial members of progressive supporters to countenance *ad hoc* measures of limited social reform such as old age pensions and sickness and unemployment insurance. Until 1903 Labour Representation Committee policy had been to co-operate with other parties willing to provide legislation for labour, and in that year Ramsay MacDonald reached a secret pact with the Liberal whip to co-operate in election arrangements. The trade unions' criticisms of the Labour members acting as junior Liberal parliamentarians grew, culminating in a special conference in 1914. Fragile, defensive, obscure, the LRC/Labour Party was unlikely to jeopardise its remaining support by addressing the functional and organisational problems which excluded women from participation.

Very few women were sent as delegates to Labour Representation Committee/Labour Party conferences. Isabella Ford was an ILP delegate. In 1904 she deplored the absence of women from the executive committee, but said that 'nothing could be done unless the women pressed the matter in their various committees'. When women started to act autonomously, however, the obvious step, given the current political climate, was to set up their own separate organisations. This mirrored the activity of women in the Liberal and Conservative Parties, in the Co-operative Society and in the women's movement generally. It conflicted with the experience of the earlier, mixed-sex socialist groups, the Independent Labour Party, Social Democratic Federation and Socialist Labour Party. Getting the balance right between participation in the Labour Party and reflecting the experience of the women's movement was a complex process. The first attempt at a Women's Labour Representation Committee, formed in 1903 by Mrs Pankhurst after her experience of exclusion from the Salford ILP meetings, was an example. The name of Mrs Pankhurst's group was changed before its first meeting to the Women's Social and Political Union because it was intended to conduct, in addition to political work, 'social work' such as the provision of maternity benefits and to emphasise the demand for women's enfranchisement. The cause of votes for women almost immediately became the overriding concern of the WSPU.

The second attempt was pioneered by Mary Fenton Macpherson and resulted in the foundation of the Women's Labour League.[14]

Mary Macpherson was a linguist who translated at international labour movement conferences and wrote a 'Women's Corner' in the *Railway Review* under the pen-name Margery Daw. The *Railway Review* was the organ of the Amalgamated Society of Railway Servants which was complemented by a women's organisation, the Railway Women's Guild. Membership of the Guild was open to women in a railworker's household, who could join in order to organise and educate themselves politically. Mary Macpherson's idea was to set up a similar sister organisation to the Labour Representation Committee, a female agency to match the male agency. Through an organisation that was autonomous, equal, yet an integral part of the overall body, she thought it would be possible to attract not only merely women already in membership of trades union or socialist bodies, but the many women in unorganised trades or unemployed. This would have been a new synthesis of the women's and labour movements, allowing maximum participation while retaining the benefits of autonomy.

The next step was to get the Labour Representation Committee to debate Mary's idea. She wrote to Ramsay MacDonald in December 1904 to say she was thinking of the best way to progress; she would approach LRC affiliated organisations, such as Margaret Bondfield's to submit a resolution to the LRC executive. Although local groups were already acting on her suggestion and she had her own executive's support, Mary was strict about not committing the Railway Women's Guild before its conference agreed, and would act merely in a personal capacity. The Stockport Railway Women's Guild was addressed by Mr. Wardle, the local Labour parliamentary candidate (sponsored by the railway unions, Member of Parliament from 1906) who advocated a women's committee to help the LRC at elections. As Margaret Bondfield was unable to help, Mary asked Ramsay MacDonald to raise the issue of women's representation himself, which he did, being instructed to refer to the scheme very briefly in the LRC executive report to conference. There was much debate at the 1905 LRC conference on consitution and membership, but very little comment on the final executive recommendation, which was that where the LRC was standing a candidate, a local women's organisation should be formed. A client organisation or subordinate female supporters was entirely contrary to Mary's idea and instead of accepting the compromise, she worked within her own organisation to pursue her original suggestion.

Urgency resolutions, arising from her comments on Wardle's speech in her annual report to the Railway Women's Guild made the position clear:

> This conference is strongly in favour of the true principles of Labour representation on all local governing bodies and in the House of Commons and pledges itself to do all in its power to return direct representative of Labour. This conference requests the national L.R.C. to take immediate steps to form a NATIONAL LABOUR WOMEN'S COMMITTEE and directs our secretary to send these resolutions to the L.R.C. (my emphasis)

Ramsay MacDonald seems to have wanted to ensure maximum support for his reply, because he channelled it through the political hierarchy of first the Independent Labour Party (whom Mary had not addressed), and then the Labour Representation Committee. Both bodies met on the same day (4 October 1905), but it was the ILP which first drafted the reply which reached Mary; the LRC

> was willing to address the political organisation of women in every way that was practicable. It desires to point out, however, that women are eligible for membership of all local LRCs and that they may be elected as representatives to its annual conference and may sit on its executive committee. Some of us think that women ought to make more use than they do of these opportunities to take part in our work.

Willing to countenance subordinate, local, female support groups, the LRC seemed to reject the traditional remedy for women's exclusion from masculine political bodies, separate organisation: there was no discussion by either the Independent Labour Party or Labour Representation Committee on what contribution a separate women's organisation might make, or why women were not taking up their opportunities, no appreciation of the functional and organisational reasons for women's exclusion.

Ramsay MacDonald had advised Mary in 1905 'to continue to push matters on your own lines'. Accordingly, she went about setting up a women's body on her own, forced back into the usual pattern. Inevitably and immediately, the problems of relationship to the Labour Party were encountered. A leaflet was drafted stating that a national Women's Labour League in connection with the Labour Party had been formed with a central committee for organising and advisory purposes. The committee would like to encourage local branches to be formed and brought to the notice of trade unions, the Independent Labour Party, the Social Democratic Federation and the Co-operative Societies. The object was to organise women for labour representation; membership was open to women members and wives and daughters of members of societies affiliated to the Labour Party. If there were no local branch, individuals would nevertheless be welcome to an inaugural meeting to be held on 9 March 1906. Ramsay MacDonald wrote that the Labour Party executive objected to the words 'in connection with the Labour Party' as outsiders might presume an official connection, and asked that they be changed to imply nothing more than that the Women's Labour League would work with the Labour Party. Perhaps the Labour Party was defensive because the leaflet addressed socialist societies; Mary's women's group, emphasising the agency nature of the Labour Party, seemed to threaten its development as a separate party in its own right. The inaugural meeting was held at Margaret MacDonald's home, after extensive press advertisement. James Middleton, Labour Representation Committee assistant secretary, proved helpful, running off the agenda and advising about chairing the meeting. Mrs Cawthorne (from Hull) seconded Mary's resolution to the meeting, 'that it is desirable to form an organisation of women to work for Labour Representation on the lines of the Labour Party' and the Women's Labour League was formally constituted, Margaret MacDonald acting as chair and Mary as secretary. A temporary executive committee was elected and dues set at 2*d* per year payable to the local secretary for the central organising fund, the amount of subscription to the local branch to be determined locally. These dues were intended to bring membership within the reach of women of the working classes; in 1906 the popular socialist *Clarion* newspaper cost 1*d* per week.

It is at this point that contemporary and subsequent interpretations have obscured the provenance of the idea of the Women's Labour League. Margaret MacDonald became heavily involved in the League from 1906, and many accounts attribute its formation either to her, or to Ramsay MacDonald acting through his wife. Ramsay MacDonald's biography of his wife emphasises her part in the League's creation, although the 1911 and 1912 versions differ slightly, as does Lucy Herbert's biography (*Mrs Ramsay MacDonald*, 1924); an undated typewritten note in Ramsay MacDonald's papers (Public Records Office, London, PRO/30/69/1366/214) credits Ramsay with approaching Mary Macpherson in 1906 and asking her to contact his wife about starting an organisation for women. However, the early correspondence between Mary Macpherson and Ramsay MacDonald indicates that far from being a client organisation, the Women's Labour League was set up in defiance of Labour Party criticism. Its creation followed the normal pattern of contemporary political activity, women organising separately in their own interests. The gains Labour made in the 1905 General Election (twenty-nine Members of Parliament elected) may have made the idea of a women's support organisation more attractive to men in the party; the divergence of the Women's Social and Political Union and the support it attracted may have made Labour men fear that potential women supporters and existing activists would be tempted away. Yet to credit men with the energy to form women's groups demands a denial of historical experience. Margaret MacDonald's role in relation to Ramsay's position as secretary of the Labour Party is unclear; there is no record of her involvement in the Women's Labour League before the meeting in her flat; perhaps the greater success of the Labour Party encouraged women already active in the Labour movement to demand fuller representation.

The account given of the League's formation in its own magazine (*League Leaflet* no. 12, December 1911), while acknowledging the MacDonalds, confirms that the League was set up by women, for women: 'the Railway Women's Guild resolution was sent to Ramsay MacDonald in 1905 . . . who, however, did not think the time opportune for taking this decisive step until after the Labour Party victories at the polls in 1906 . . . then, after a long consultation with Mrs MacDonald, the executive committee of the Railway Women's Guild called a preliminary meeting of women'.

A public meeting held to inaugurate the Central London branch of the League on 9 April 1906 roused much press interest and was important in serving as an occasion when individual Labour men could give support, among them Keir Hardie, always a friend to the League, and Wardle, who had helped at the outset. Mary said that although there were women in existing socialist and labour societies, large classes of women remained unrepresented. Margaret Bondfield asked that meetings be held at convenient times for women who had children and homes to look after. Ramsay MacDonald announced himself a warm supporter and said that to be successful the League must cover the whole field of women's interests, responsibilities and duties. Plans were laid for the first conference.

Disappointment had been expressed at the inaugural meeting about the lack of Labour Party support, although it was accepted that an official connection could not be claimed and Ramsay MacDonald was asked to approve the wording of the invitation to conference: 'you will see on the enclosed agenda the "object" of the Women's Labour League is formulated as being "To form an organisation of women to work for independent labour representation in connection with the Labour Party." I trust there will be no objection to that statement.' Ramsay MacDonald replied with his goodwill and hearty congratulations: 'if it is within my power to give the Women's Labour League a friendly lift at any time, I shall be delighted to do so. I am afraid I must bar public speaking – you must apply to the other members of the household for that.' In fact, he had been obstructive until 1906, was still denying organisational connections and was now telling Mary that he had no intention of giving public support as an individual. That the unofficial, separate organisation Mary was able to create differed from her original conception is illustrated by the fact that the Railway Women's Guild did not yet affiliate to the Women's Labour League.

The first League conference was held in Leicester in 1906. Branches represented were Central London, Bow and Bromley, Leicester, Hull and Preston; over one hundred women attended, including Isabella Ford, one of the first members. Resolutions covered a variety of subjects; medical inspections, free compulsory secondary education, registration of women workers. The objects of the League were resolved, as Mary had stated them, but with a clause inserted as the result of an amendment successfully moved by Isabella Ford: 'and to obtain direct representation of women in parliament and on local bodies'. This was a clear distinction from Labour Party policy at that time (which was to obtain full adult suffrage) and firmly set the League on its course, for Labour and for women.

No women's organisation formed in the decade before the First World War could ignore the suffrage question, as the League's leaders perhaps hoped to do. The lack of a clear commitment to women's suffrage in the original wording of the League objects had drawn adverse criticism. Marion Coates Henry, for instance, wrote to Margaret MacDonald before the first conference: 'It is dreadful to me to think that all the many women you appear to have interested are contented with that one meek and mild objective, and

WOMEN'S LABOUR LEAGUE LEAFLETS. NO. 1.

Why Women want a Labour League.

IT HAS ALWAYS BEEN THE PRIDE OF THE LABOUR PARTY THAT ITS MEMBERS STAND FOR THE EQUAL RIGHTS AND DUTIES OF WOMEN AND MEN AS CITIZENS.

Why then do women want to start a special League in connection with the Labour Party? Why are they not content to sit on the same committees and do work at the same time as the men?

First, let there be no misunderstanding. The women have not started the League with the idea that those who have the opportunity will work less with the men than before. On the contrary, they mean to use the League to give them fresh inspiration and fresh knowledge for their duties as active members of the whole Labour Party.

The League will meet some of the special needs of women and use some of their special powers.

It will enable wives and mothers and home keepers generally to meet at times convenient to themselves. At these meetings they can discuss subjects which directly affect the home life of the workers.

For instance, during the few weeks of the present Session, Members of Parliament have been discussing such questions as Feeding of School Children, Old Age Pensions, Inspection of Factories, Workshops and Laundries, Wages of Women engaged on sewing coats and trousers for soldiers and postmen, etc.

Much of the work of Town Councils and Boards of Guardians is a sort of municipal housekeeping.

The teaching of the children is of particular interest to their mothers.

The problem of the unemployed weighs as heavily upon the women as upon the men, but in a different way.

All such things our women would like to discuss amongst themselves, and their opinion and experience is of special value.

Fig. 1 Women's Labour League *Leaflet* no. 1: 'Why Women Want a Labour League'
Source *Women's Labour League Secretarial Papers and Related Correspondence*

make no provision for the representation of women by women.' Isabella Ford's amendment gave the League credibility in the eyes of the women's movement. The League constitution also resolved in women's favour the organisational problems which excluded women from the Labour Party by allowing for individual membership. In successfully moulding function and organisation to enable women to participate fully, however, the League enhanced its differences from the Labour Party with its affiliate membership and its object of returning working men to parliament.

Unlike the women's movement groups it resembled, the League continued to seek a closer connection with 'the Men's Party'. Affiliation was the chosen method of expressing an identity of interests; this would have meant the League was one of the bodies which the Labour Party served as agent and political committee and would, to an extent, have redressed its masculine bias. By 1907 the League had headed notepaper on which to explain to the Labour Party that it was a combination of women drawn from exactly the same sections as the Labour Party drew its strength, that the League 'gives a channel for the expression of the special knowledge and experience of women of the party'.[15] The women's movement identification of women's special character and experience was thus reflected. Mary had become ill and Mary Middleton took over as secretary, Margaret MacDonald as president. These were, respectively, wives of the assistant secretary and secretary of the Labour Party, but that did not help them win affiliation. A Labour Party fraternal delegate was invited to the 1907 conference; John Hodge, British Steel Smelters, Iron and Tinplate Workers' secretary, was chosen to go, although he had been the only member of Labour's executive to vote against the gesture: he demonstrated his reluctance: he did not wish to add to, or duplicate the present number of exchanges, he did not know where the conference was to be held, it was one of his few open Saturdays, could not someone else go? Finally he assented, explaining, 'I was not sure if it was the other crowd or not.'

Affiliation was the first business discussed at the 1907 conference, resolved upon and duly sent to the Labour Party together with resolutions urging initiatives be taken on inspection in dangerous trades and free school meals. Mary Middleton thought no objection would be raised and John Hodge, won over, said he could vouch for every Labour Member of Parliament being heart and soul with the

League; however, he pointed out that the Labour Party constitution would have to be amended to allow the affiliation of the League. In the event, the Labour Party executive 'declined to comment on letters from societies not already affiliated'.

The executive's intransigence did not reflect rank and file opinion. Locally, *de facto* recognition had been achieved. The League sent delegates to local party meetings, arranged joint events, shared platforms at public meetings. The League proved its worth at local elections. The executive finally agreed to recommend the necessary constitutional changes to the 1908 Labour Party conference. The League staged a coup; its conference was held at the same time, January, and in the same place as the Labour Party (Hull). Rooms were requested and granted, although Ramsay MacDonald found it necessary to write to each executive committee member for their opinion; Pete Curran replied angrily that of course the request should be met and there was no need to ask. The League events were not advertised on the Labour Party agenda, but proved a huge success. On the Saturday evening before the conferences started the women held a social; John Hodge sang. Katharine Bruce Glasier, presiding, said: 'they were hoping as a League that their relationship with the Labour Party would, with that conference, have passed beyond the dubiously delightful stage in courtship known as a friendly understanding . . . into a definite engagement, soon to develop into a life-long union for mutual service'.

Keir Hardie spoke in favour. William Robinson of the Beamers' and Drawers' Union was the Labour Party fraternal delegate and commented that the sooner the women were in the Labour Party, the greater their effect would be. However, with everything set for affiliation, the Central London branch successfully moved a resolution that must have put it in jeopardy; the League resolved to accept in membership societies of women not eligible for membership of the Labour Party. This was a clear indication that women's interests remained a major concern of the delegates.

The outcome was a compromise. The Labour Party conference report commended the League election work. The much amended and heavily scored draft report shows that the exact nature of the recommendations for League recognition was the subject of intense debate. The League was to contribute to the general, but not the political fund and consequently not to vote on the latter. As the Party executive committee was elected by trades union and socialist societies, the League could not take part in its election: 'and we could not very well give it a representative of its own'. No record survives of debate about why the League should not have its own representative. The uncomfortable conclusion is that it was dismissed out of hand. Without representation on the executive committee the League was excluded from any real power within 'the Men's Party'. However, League women were to be allowed to send representatives to the Labour Party conference. 'Should a national organisation of women accepting the basis of this constitution and the policy of the Labour Party be formed', continued the proposal, perhaps diplomatically ignoring the fact that it was at least two years out of date, 'it shall be eligible for affiliation as though it were a trades council.' (This was before the spate of trades council affiliations in 1910/11, so the recognition granted to the League was more unique than appears at first sight.) The League accepted the terms.

On 21 March 1908 Ramsay MacDonald was able to write to Mary Middleton: 'I placed your letter . . . before the executive and it was the unanimous decision to accept the affiliation of the Women's Labour League.' Part of Mary Macpherson's idea, the formation and acknowledgement of a national women's committee, had been achieved and the Railway Women's Guild now affiliated to the League. Equality and integration had not been won; paradoxically, through its obstructiveness, its caution and delays, the male-oriented Labour Party had been led to countenance an autonomous women's organisation. As the League wrote in the trade union journal *Woman Worker* (no. 8, April 1908), 'we are only free lances making our way and trying to justify our existence'. The League could now enjoy Labour Party recognition, while enjoying the benefits and experiencing the pitfalls of separatism.

Notes

1 E. Halévy, *A History of the English People,* Epilogue, vol. II, 1905–15 (Ernest Benn, London, 1934), p. 504: contains a summary of womens' electoral rights with full references to relevant Acts of Parliament and legal judgements. This information is, surprisingly, missing from many later suffrage histories.

2 Averil Sanderson-Furniss, 'Citizenship of women' in Labour Party Publishing Co., *The Book of the Labour Party: Its History, Growth, Policy and Leaders,* vol. II (London, 1925, p. 248).

3 Marion Curran. See Appendix 1.

4 Hannah Mitchell, *The Hard Way Up* (London, 1968).

5 Beatrice Webb, *My Apprenticeship*, vol. I (Pelican, 1938), p. 206.

6 Clara Collett's publications include: *Statistics on the Employment of Women and Girls* (1894); *Changes in the Employment of Women and Girls in the Industrial Centres, Part one, Jute and Flax Mills* (1898); *Money Wages of Indoor Domestic Servants* (1899); *Problems of Marriage for Women* (n.d.) cited, p. 20; *The Economic Position of Educated Working Women* (London, 1890). A sketch of Clara Collett is given in Duncan Crow, *The Victorian Woman* (Allen & Unwin, 1978).

7 *Royal Commission on Labour*, PP, 1892, c. 6894, XXIV. See also *J. R. MacDonald and M. E. MacDonald Papers*, PRO/30/69 (Public Records Office, London), 1375, Letter from Margaret Irwin to Margaret MacDonald.

8 Countess of Aberdeen (ed.), International Congress of Women, 1899, *Transactions* (London, 1899), *The Gertrude Tuckwell Collection*, 1890–1920, 347/8 (Trades Union Congress Library, London).

9 See Appendix 1. Quotes from *Women and Socialism* (London, 1904), pp. 4, 6, 9, 43.

10 See Appendix 1.

11 Lily Gair Wilkinson: Socialist Labour Party. Writings include: *Revolutionary Socialism and the Women's Movement* (Glasgow, 1910); 'Women's freedom' in S. Fleming (ed.), *Women in Rebellion*, Square One Pamphlets, no. 6 (Independent Labour Party, 1973), cited, pp. 16, 17, 28.

12 Jane Hume Clapperton. Writings include: *Margaret Dunmore, or a Socialist Home* (London, 1888); *Scientific Meliorism and the Evolution of Happiness* (London, 1889).

13 For the formation of the Labour Party and its early correspondence and reports of meetings see *Labour Representation Committee Papers* (Labour Party Headquarters Archives, London).

14 For Mary Macpherson's attempts to form the League from 1904 see *Labour Representation Committee Papers* and *MacDonald Papers*. Cited: correspondence Macpherson/MacDonald (1904), LRC/17; Railway Women's Guild Resolution, LRC/24/284; ILP and LRC resolution on women's organisation, LRC/24/285; correspondence Macpherson/MacDonald 1905, LP/GC/27/4; League inaugural meeting, LP/GC/1/344; Central London Branch inaugural meeting, *MacDonald papers*, PRO/30/69/1366/214.

15 1907 and 1908 correspondence Middleton/MacDonald, LP/GC/14/385; correspondence about fraternal delegate, LP/GC/13/283/LP/GC/13/285; affiliation request and rejection, LP/GC/14/342; conference rooms request, LP/GC/21/208; acceptance of affiliation, *Women's Labour League Secretarial Correspondence and Related Papers* (Labour Party Headquarters Archives, London), WLL/77.

2
Consolidation

'The free lances' – *Woman Worker*, 1908

The League had established its free-lance role as a sister organisation to the Labour Party through struggle and persistence. There is no doubting its impact. Recruitment was on a scale that would be envied by the present-day Labour Party, membership rising 500 per cent from the 100 women at the first conference in 1906 to the 5,000 credited in Labour Party *Annual Reports* of 1913 and 1914. The League success was part of the efflorescence of socialism in town and village throughout Britain; it was a time of frequent by-elections and three general elections (1906, January and December 1910) when the attention of both the Labour and the women's movements was directed to political activity. The free-lance role was played out in full spate of enthusiasm until 1911, Mary Middleton remaining as secretary and working in close partnership with Margaret MacDonald, League president. Both these women died unexpectedly in that year and it was a tribute to their energy that the League survived, to become a more professional organisation under the leadership of first, Margaret Bondfield and then, Marion Phillips. The Middleton/MacDonald years were characterised by an amateur style that succeeded because of its vigour, an enabling, rather than a controlling leadership, which allowed plenty of scope for autonomous branch life. In return, branch strength had given the League credibility in establishing itself nationally and encouraged the free-lance spirit to prevail.

The League was able to claim 5,000 members when sending delegates to a 1911 conference of women's organisations on the National Insurance Bill proposed by the Liberal Government. The number of members in each branch varied a great deal and the record of their subscriptions was haphazard, but would seem to indicate a total of 250 League members by 1907 (£2 1*s* 8*d* at 2*d* per member) and a total of 770 by 1908 (£6 17*s* 10*d*). This was a substantial membership for a new body, at its highest probably equal to that of its contemporary, the militant suffrage Women's Social and Political Union.

The Middleton/MacDonald League was an heterogenous body. Dorothy Lenn of the Central London branch wrote in *Labour Leader* (23 August 1908) of the diversity of women who joined, from Civil Servant to social worker, industrial worker to schoolteacher, married and single women. Reflecting the women's movement, belief in the goals of the League enabled a cross-section of women to co-operate. (Appendix 1 gives biographical details of some of these women.) Professional women were attracted (Ethel Bentham, a medical doctor and Sister Kerrison of the Seaman's Hospital, Greenwich) and women trade unionists were well represented (Mary Macpherson, Margaret Bondfield, Mable Hope of the Post Office Clerks and Mary MacArthur of the National Federation of Working Women). As was reported in *Women Worker* (January 1908):

> We feel the women's side of the movement will be incomplete unless we have all classes represented; each makes their own contribution, the seamy side of experience was helped by the educated one to put the case clearly and plan the detail of remedies, whilst book learning and enthusiasm are very empty qualities without the experience of the realities of life.

Comparison with the social composition of the membership of the Labour Party is difficult because the Party consisted of the members of its affiliated organisations – largely the trade unions, whose white collar representation was extremely low. There were the craft unions whose members could, perhaps, be loosely termed middle-class in habit and the general unions whose membership was overwhelmingly men of the working classes. Labour Party activists probably matched the League in social class, while the leadership of both League and Labour Party were nearly all middle-class, by the lifestyle that accompanied their political involvement, if not by background. Deliberating on the exact milieu for any individual within the Labour movement is an invidious task, as the movement formed its own social structure.

Moreover, as the Labour movement was, to some extent, a self-contained world, it facilitated relationships between its members, thus making their social classes more difficult to fathom. When League women married Labour men, the surviving records tend to reflect the positions won by the men within the movement, rather than the more sporadic activity of the women. This lays the League open to the charge levelled against it in 1912 by Theresa Billington Greig, of consisting 'chiefly of the wives and daughters of labour men who use it to voice their husbands' opinion or to please their fathers' (*The Consumer in Revolt*, London, *c.* 1912). While there were many single League women who led independent lives (Margaret Bondfield, Sister Kerrison, Mary MacArthur, Maud Ward, Ethel Bentham and Marion Phillips, the charge must be answered because some of the League leaders were, indeed, the wives of prominent Labour men (Marion Curran, Margaret MacDonald, Katharine Bruce Glasier and Mary Middleton). It is obviously difficult to know what pressures were brought to bear domestically, and the accepted accounts of the League's origins have credited Ramsay MacDonald with masterminding the League.

There are four reasons to refute the charge of male direction. First, as chapter 1 relates, the League's origins were, in part, rooted in the women's movement and it was founded despite Labour men's obstruction. Second, as the chapter on activity will show, the League had a separate life from the Labour Party, with its own codes, interests and methods of operating. Third, Theresa Billington Greig was not a totally reliable witness. She placed women's enfranchisement above all other political activity, resigning from the Independent Labour Party for this reason and was not, therefore, entirely in sympathy with League objectives; she also had difficulty working within an organisation, resigning in succession from several (the ILP, the (admittedly insensitive) Women's Social and Political Union because of its autocracy, the Women's Freedom League, from which she had resigned in order to study the way women operated as consumers by the time she wrote her comments on the League). Fourth, stating to what extent personal relationships affect political activity is an impossible task; it indicates prejudice to assume without evidence either that men dominate their spouses politically, or that no such domination exists. It might as easily be claimed that League women influenced their spouses as vice versa. Theresa Billington herself, Katharine Conway, Marion

Barry and Margaret Gladstone were already Labour movement activists in their own right before marrying Messrs. Greig, Glasier, Curran and MacDonald. There is no reason to suppose a change of name indicated a change in a commitment already proven. As Theresa Billington Greig wrote to Margaret MacDonald in defence of her use of both her own and her husband's surnames: 'The identity of a woman should not be necessarily sacrificed because she marries.'[1]

Margaret MacDonald's personality refuses to emerge from the past. She was from an upper middle-class background, enjoyed a private income, but showed a social concern from the time of her schoolgirl essays. Margaret was deeply religious, although not belonging to a conventional church, and saw her work as God's purpose. She lived in chaos, papers, babies, visitors all milling around in the Lincoln's Inn Fields home. 'Come back to my rooms', Margaret Bondfield begged, 'then I can be sure of getting your attention! What with babies, telephones and callers, etc. that is impossible at your home.'[2] Margaret Bondfield was sometimes appalled by Margaret MacDonald's appearance when she accompanied deputations; notorious was the occasion when she wore a new blouse, especially urged on her by the other petitioners, back to front. Margaret MacDonald was one of the main speakers and propagandists for the League, acting as parliamentary correspondent, encouraging local branches to obtain Bills for study such as those on the Treatment of Juvenile Offenders, Sweated Industry, Unemployed Workmen or reports of parliamentary committees such as that on Infant Life Protection. This was an invidious task: Ethel Snowden, asked to undertake it, told Margaret 'I refuse to watch the dullest of all parliaments through its unutterable drawlings and drivelings in order to supply reports to secretaries';[3] no-one else undertook the job after Margaret's death.

The League was not Margaret MacDonald's first priority. She was involved in many organisations and campaigns: state registration of nurses, police matrons for women prisoners, sweated work, school meals – and researched her subject and tended to channel the work through whichever organisation seemed most appropriate. Until 1909 the Women's Industrial Council perhaps received most of her output; her papers at the British Library of Political and Economic Science are mainly devoted to the Council. Her papers at the Public Records Office are largely unsorted, as muddled as they were at Lincoln's Inn Fields and were partially destroyed by Ramsay MacDonald shortly after her death.

Margaret's husband eulogised her. He wrote and rewrote her memoirs and designed a huge memorial statue of her in bronze with arms outstretched around a band of children, set on a marble plinth with a wooden seat. Unfortunately, this was unveiled in Lincoln's Inn Fields in 1914, when Ramsay's denunciation of the declaration of war had caused a revulsion of feeling against him, so that only the memorial committee attended. We therefore lack the more balanced obituaries that hindsight might have produced on the occasion. Lucy Herbert's 1924 biography (*Mrs Ramsay MacDonald*) closely follows Ramsay's earlier work and is sycophantic. This veneration of Margaret after her death has obscured the way contemporaries reacted to her. Some felt uncomfortable; Margaret Bondfield, for instance, at first disliked her aristocratic manners. Sylvia Pankhurst, writing twenty years after Margaret's death, retained a strong antipathy, remembering an occasion when Margaret had refused to succumb to Pankhurst pressure to abandon a prior claim for support from a Labour Member of Parliament who had won a place to introduce a Private Member's Bill. Sylvia Pankhurst described Margaret's 'amiable, babyish tones, showing her small, childish looking white teeth, with a space between each one'.[4] Mary Middleton, on the other hand, was a close personal friend, arranging to be at the same hotel for conferences and to make holiday visits.

Margaret's involvement in the liaison between George Belt and Dora Montefiore argues a busy, moralistic side to her nature.[5] George Belt, local full-time organiser for Hull Independent Labour Party (paid 25*s* per week), was married to a factory worker, but entered into a relationship with the wealthy socialist and suffragist Dora Montefiore. They met when both toured with the Clarion Van, which was funded by the *Clarion* newspaper to take the socialist message into the countryside. Mrs Belt intercepted their correspondence and passed it to the Hull ILP secretary, which led to George Belt's dismissal. Margaret showed the correspondence to Lady Aberdeen, president of the International Women's Congress in 1899, so that Dora Montefiore had to resign as acting recording secretary. Dora maintained that free, personal relationships were an intrinsic part of socialist philosophy and sued Margaret for libel. Ramsay MacDonald settled out of court and never forgot the incident, referring to it obliquely in Margaret's memoirs and refusing in 1906 Labour Representation Committee backing for George Belt's candidacy for Hammersmith in the General Election.

It was as a leader, one of the elite in the Labour movement, that Margaret seemed to perceive herself, despite her personal modesty. She was a self-effacing heroine, but not one of the rank and file. Margaret could occasionally be autocratic and insensitive and knew how to fight her own corner. She fell into dispute with the Women's Industrial Council in 1909 over the issue of minimum wages, which she did not support on the grounds that they would establish low fixed rates in a trade; first Clementina Black, who supported minimum wages, resigned from the Council to undertake her survey into women's work on a private basis and finally, when the survey (and Clementina Black with it) was about to be reinstated, Margaret resigned, taking all the League members of the Council with her. In 1907, when Margaret was to chair the League conference after a prolonged absence touring the Colonies with Ramsay, she returned to find that her own branch, Central London, had submitted a resolution to make the League aims more specifically socialist by adding, 'By the education of working women in the principle of socialism, to endeavour to hasten the overthrow of the present capitalist system of production.' Mary Macpherson thought the resolution 'a pity, as our sole object is to work with the Labour Party, so we ought to keep in step – but it is always dangerous to stifle debate. Do you not think discuss it on its merits'. This was the time of the League feeling its way to the free-lance role and perhaps fearing to offend; Margaret, however, appears to have considered asking her branch to withdraw its resolution, as she wrote to Mary Middleton,

> we may as well let it go as it stands. Of course, I do not mean to stifle it in any case, as it would be on the agenda, and would be discussed by branches and anyone could move it, even if Central London didn't . . . I thought discussion might be confusing to our female intellects, however, I daresay we will muddle through.[6]

The League's own memorial to Margaret of a children's ward in Leicester Infirmary and the pioneering baby clinic set up in memory of both Margaret MacDonald and Mary Middleton were much more in keeping with her outlook than Ramsay's bronze and marble. Margaret's recorded speeches stress the wife and mother imagery of the League contribution to the Labour movement.

Typically, on the occasion of a fund-raising sale in Mary Macpherson's home, Margaret, baby Joan in arms, spoke of the League giving the children of the future a better chance. Margaret Bondfield's autobiography (*A Life's Work*, London 1949) records the League as Margaret's scheme: 'to help the wives of trades unionists, Labour men and co-operators see the best way to look after their homes was to take an interest in the life of the community'. That the League was merely for Labour wives has already been refuted. There are two other implications; first, that the issues of home and children should be discussed politically and addressed by the Labour Party and second, that these were women's issues.

The underlying belief that even the Labour Party would remain ignorant of the domestic drudgery caused by poverty and borne by women of the working classes, unless this was firmly brought forward by the League, reinforced the belief in women's special characteristics. It was not the leisured middle-class home with which the League was concerned, but the work-place where heating water, cooking food and cleaning demanded greater powers of organisation in proportion to the diminution of the power of the purse. The League continually stressed the need for women who had experience of an issue to present it: for instance, Margaret MacDonald wrote in *Labour Leader* (January 1911) that it must be women themselves who discussed the double burden of waged and housework: 'it is most difficult to get reliable evidence . . . theorising leads one astray'. As women coped with the problem, argued the League, women had acquired distinct skills and had a special contribution to make in the planning of remedies. Thus Katharine Bruce Glasier, in the chair at the 1908 conference said: 'the League could teach the men of their needs as women, of the needs of the children, and of the needs of the homes of the people if they really were to be homes and not merely work kitchens and sleeping dens'. Such opinions were directly inherited from the women's movement and the women social investigators who had made attempts to understand the burdens borne by women of the working classes.

Ramsay's biography claims that Margaret's belief in distinct female characteristics was her reason for organising the League and an object of the League's existence. The 1911 biography stated: 'It was from a deep purpose arising from her views of women and the home that she started the League.' Ramsay further defined these views: 'She liked neither "women on a manly pattern" nor "the anti-woman man".' Obvious self-interest caused Ramsay to continue the argument: 'she had seen the husband in public service drifting from his wife in purdah'; 'Through (the League) she was to supply him who toiled in the Labour movement with a wife who helped him in all his doings, who understood him, who was not misled by false ideals. She was to build up Labour women in the solid foundation of sympathy, of common cause, of hand in hand effort.' We cannot debate with Ramsay MacDonald his definition of Margaret's opinion, but she does seem to have accepted fairly standard gender roles in her speeches, if not in her lifestyle. We can see from the records that the League was not a subordinate male support system. Men, as spouses needing comfort, do not feature in the League records; no woman writes to organise support for her husband or makes his approval a condition of her activity.

On the contrary, the belief in women's separate powers and special contribution led the League straight into organising in a separatist way typical of the contemporary women's movement. It was because women were distinct that their autonomy was appropriate, in the League's opinion. *Woman Worker* (January 1908) reported on this very clearly:

> Women have always belonged to (the Labour Party) in absolute equality with men through their trade union or co-operative societies . . . it is not a case of a man's party admitting a women's organisation to membership on a less representative basis. The purpose . . . is simply to give our women's organisation a special representation . . . because the Labour Party recognises the need for women's demands for separate organisation in order to fully utilise their special powers is sensible and practical.

Having, as Margaret MacDonald forecast, rejected the Central London branch resolution in 1907 to make the League objects more specifically socialist, 'in order to stay the same as the Labour Party', the League, in contrary spirit, resolved on accepting into membership societies of women not eligible to join the Labour Party. This indicates both the difficulty women faced in joining the Labour Party and that the League was very clearly committed to working for women, with women. Special powers and special issues were not the only reasons given for continuing to organise separately. Lisbeth Simm wrote in the *Northern Democrat* (June 1910):

> there still seems an idea that if women are working in a distinctly women's organisation, that they will be deprived of opportunity for working with the

men. Experience proves the contrary . . . (women) cannot fail to see how small a proportion of time and attention is devoted to matters of special importance and particular interest to women. There is not time, for one thing, and too few women members for another.

The continued absence of women members justified the continuance of the League. The Labour Party was described as 'lopsided' at the 1907 League conference because women were excluded; in April 1908 *Woman Worker* expressed the fear that the Labour Party 'might grow too exclusively on the side of the male members and thus be one sided and incomplete'.

Not only did the League redress this imbalance, it was a friendlier alternative to the Labour Party. Branches made a conscious effort to ensure their meetings were congenial to women. Some branches welcomed children at meetings, St Pancras, for instance, which reported a meeting 'with four babies and three children to make it homelike'. Many branches alternated evening and afternoon meetings. At the 1908 conference Margaret Bondfield suggested women should arrange a rotating crêche. Women perhaps had different expectations from their meetings than did men; at a Newcastle Labour movement gathering held to welcome Keir Hardie from a foreign tour in June 1908, which was immediately followed by a concert, Lisbeth Simm detected 'much disappointment . . . comrades from outlying districts had not an opportunity of speaking with their friends . . . (I wonder if the men arranged it?)'.

Dorothy Lenn wrote in *Labour Leader* (23 March 1908) that women only occasionally attended Labour Party meetings and 'although a few bold spirits join the ILP, how many hundreds shrink from taking the plunge into the world of men and ideas?' She claimed the Labour movement 'sister' role for the League, writing that no other organisation shared the League's aims of 'bringing the Party influence to bear practically'. This view of the League as a nurturing ground for women politicians encouraged some women, like Margaret Bondfield, echoing Lady Aberdeen in 1899, to believe separate organisation to be a preliminary step to competent involvement in the mixed organisation. Others believed the League was essential to counter male resistance to female activity. Lisbeth Simm reported in 1908 to Mary Middleton, 'some women have hardly begun to think that (socialism) stands for women also; some old trades unionists are afraid we shall spoil the homes by taking women out to meetings'; 'the great answer up here is "women's

Fig. 2 Women's Labour League Conference, Newport, 1910 (Mrs Robinson's baby on the table)
Source Labour Party library

Fig. 3 Women's Labour League Conference (?1909), with Labour Party delegates (Sister Kerrison centre back)
Source Labour Party library

place is in the home" – women have heard it so often that they have begun to believe it now'.[7]

A single identity, a uniform outlook, should not be imposed in hindsight onto the heterogenous Middleton/MacDonald League. In theory, policy-making was conducted by the annual conference, to which each branch sent a delegate for every twenty-five, or part of twenty-five, members. No men were allowed to the early conferences so that women would learn to manage for themselves. After 1908 conference was always held to fit in with that of the Labour Party, the League day and a half beginning a week of Labour activity in the chosen venue. The local branch hunted out cheap lodgings and provided a social gathering. The conference arrangements allowed maximum branch participation; resolutions were submitted to the executive committee beforehand and circulated to branches so that amendments could be sent to the executive agenda committee which arranged the final agenda. A decision would be taken at conference on which resolutions should be forwarded to the Labour Party conferences and a delegate to that body was elected. The outgoing executive committee gave its report and elections were made to the new committee from nominations submitted beforehand.

Mrs Harrison Bell reported in the *Northern Democrat* (March 1911) on the last conference held (at Leicester) under the Middleton/MacDonald leadership. On arrival, with six other delegates, she was taken home by Councillor Mrs Riley, 'who fed us and saw us made tidy . . . The treatment meted out to the prodigal son pales in heartiness to the fellowshipping which took place at that evening's reception.' Conference began at the Queen's Hall, Silver Street, the next morning, thirty-one branches being represented by forty-one delegates 'who sat themselves down anyhow'. There was no platform, the chair's table being on the floor amongst the delegates. London delegates preponderated. Scrutineers, the credential committee and the standing orders committee were appointed. Fraternal delegates from the Women's Co-operative Guild and the Labour Party were welcomed. In the morning there were debates on armaments, the Osborne Judgement (which made the trade unions' sponsorship of the Labour Party illegal), divorce laws, the franchise, a Labour ministry, women on juries and retirement age. 'The photographers were a terrible bore.' The afternoon was 'devoted to home and the child' and a discussion on workers' co-operatives 'which brought out general instances of a kind of tentative co-operation going on in many places'. Mrs Harrison Bell's summary was: 'We were very earnest and at times angry in our hearts and very serious, but dull never unless by chance a delegate got out of harmony with the conference.'

The similarities with the Labour Party conference which followed were many; the appointment of scrutineers and conference committees, the welcome for fraternal delegates, conducting business by debate and moving and seconding resolutions. Perhaps the hospitable welcome could be identified as sisterhood in action, and the scope of business was certainly broadened by allowing one whole afternoon to home and children. In other respects the League conference was a duplicate of that of the Labour Party, its sole distinction being that it was for women. This duplication was inevitable when some women perceived their conference as a training ground for participation in the mixed event, when the League identified itself as a sister organisation to the Party and when the women's movement was concerned with constitutionalism. The proceedings of other women's bodies to which League delegates might have belonged, notably suffrage groups, offered little experience of alternative ways of working.

Every new executive committee met immediately after conference, and thereafter every two months, at the MacDonalds' home in Lincoln's Inn Fields. The executive committee was drawn largely, but not exclusively, from the London brannches. Table 2 shows the women who were elected in each year from 1906 until 1918. Sadly, little biographical information has survived even for the League leadership. In the first two years many women joined the new venture and were not re-elected thereafter; of Mrs Bell, Mrs Bellamy, Mrs James, Mary Muir and Margaret Smith there is no further information in the records. Of the longer-serving members more personal details have emerged, and these are mostly recounted with the discussion of their contribution to the League's work. There remain a few women not central to the story of the League's development, about whom some information should be given.

Sister Kerrison (elected 1907–17) was born in 1850. She was a member of the Independent Labour Party, had been elected to West Ham Poor Law Board continually since 1897, and became a West Ham Councillor. Margaret MacDonald may have met her in

Table 2 *Women's Labour League executive committee*

Name	*1906*	*1907*	*1908*	*1909*	*1910*	*1911*	*1912*	*1913*	*1914*	*1915*	*1916*	*1917*	*1918* (part)
Bertha Ayles					X		X	Until June					
Mrs Jennie Baker									X	X	X	X	X
Miss Bell	X	X	X										
Mrs Bellamy	X												
Ethel Bentham					X	X	X	X	X	X	X	X	X
Margaret Bondfield				X	X	X	X						
Katharine Bruce Glasier			X	X	X	X	X	X	X	X	X	X	X
Marion Curran				X									
Charlotte Despard	X	X											
Mrs Louise Donaldson								X	X	X	X	X	
Mrs Gawthorpe	X	X											
Florence Harrison Bell								X					
Mabel Hope	X	X	X										
Mrs F. James				X									
Sister Kerrison		X	X	X	X	X	X	X	X	X	X	X	
Mary Longman										X			
Eveline Lowe								From June	X	X	X	X	X
Mary MacArthur	X	X	X	X	X	X	X						
Margaret MacDonald	X	X	X	X	X	X							
Miss McKenzie	X	X											
Clarice MacNab											X	X	X
Mary Macpherson	X	X	X	X	X								
Mrs Macrosty						X							
Mary Middleton	X	X	X	X	X	X							
Mary Muir	X	X											
Minnie Nodin		X	X	X	X	X	X	X	X	X	X	X	X
Marion Phillips						X	X	X	X	X	X	X	X
Mrs Rigby	X												
Ada Salter						X	X		X	X	X	X	X
Mrs Scholefield								X	X	X	X	X	X
Lisbeth Simm			X	X	X	X	X	X	X	X	X	X	X
Margaret Smith		X	X										
Maud Ward						X	X						

Sources: Women's Labour League *Secretarial Correspondence and Related Papers; League Leaflet; Conference Reports* (Labour Party Headquarters Archives, London).

1906 when she became interested in the campaign for state registration of nurses. She can be identified in League photographs by her nurse's bonnet. Minnie Nodin (1907–18) lived with her husband Phillip in Surrey; she became an invalid before the First World War, but served on the League memorial baby clinic committee until her death in 1936. Charlotte Despard (1906) was born in 1884, had been a member of the Social Democratic Federation and the Independent Labour Party, joined the Women's Social and Political Union, but left in 1907 to become President of the Women's Freedom League. Mary Gawthorpe was only twenty-five when elected (1906, born 1881); she was an Independent Labour Party member and lived in Leeds. Mabel Hope (1906–07) was secretary of the Postal Telegraph Clerks Association. Miss Mackenzie (1906–07) was a member of the National Council for Adult Schools Association. Mrs Rigby (1906) came from Preston and left the League in 1907 to join the Women's Social and Political Union.

During the Middleton/MacDonald period the most frequently elected executive committee members were these two and Mary MacArthur (six times each), Sister Kerrison, Minnie Nodin (five times each), Margaret Bondfield, Katharine Bruce Glasier, Mary MacPherson and Lisbeth Simm (four times each). Leadership was fairly diversified, twenty-seven women in all being elected to the executive committee during this period. The chair should have rotated but, after 1910, was nearly always held by Ethel Bentham. The executive committee received reports, debated policies and controlled organising and propaganda work. There were *ad hoc* executive sub-committees, (for instance on sweated work and medical inspection of school children), and standing committees (general purpose and literature/publicity).

The literature committee undertook most of the written propaganda by producing leaflets on subjects ranging from pithead baths, women and the Labour movement, medical inspection of school-children to advice on the work of a Poor Law Guardian. All the socialist press was used, for instance, *Clarion* and *Labour Leader*. *Woman Worker* kept a page for League notes until 1909, when there was a dispute with the editor, Mary MacArthur. This was the time of Margaret MacDonald's disagreement with the Women's Industrial Council over minimum wages, which Mary MacArthur supported, so presumably the controversy in one body spilled over

Fig. 4 Women's Labour League executive committee
5th row, far right: Mrs Ayles. *3rd row, centre*: Sister Kerrison. *2nd row, 3rd from right*: ?, Margaret Bondfield, Katharine Bruce Glasier, Margaret MacDonald, Mary Middleton, ?
Source Labour Party library

to spoil League relationships with the Women's Trade Union League. The non-socialist press, in particular local newspapers, gave reasonable coverage to the League, the contemporary (and invaluable) habit being to report meetings almost verbatim. Some editors were late in noticing the League's existence; the *Westminster Gazette*, for instance, reported on 22 October 1908 that 'a female Labour Party' was 'the latest idea'.

The League maintained separately an organising fund and a general fund. The former was financed by donations and spent on election work; the latter was financed by a hotch-potch of delegates' fees, concerts, bazaars, sales and the affiliation fees. Each branch had to forward to the general fund 2*d* per member per year, which was usually raised by a local subscription of 1*s* per year. The general fund was spent on publication, printing and postage, office equipment and conference arrangements. Margaret MacDonald contributed generously. In January 1909 individual Labour Party Members of Parliament and candidates were asked for financial help, and then Labour Representation Committees in constituencies where Labour Party candidates were standing were asked to contribute. As the Osborne Judgement had resulted in the diminution of their own funds, only two were able to help. The League eventually received a direct grant from the Labour Party in 1910.

As she was a major contributor to its funds and housed the League executive meetings, Margaret MacDonald was in a strong position had she wished to dominate League activities. The spending of the general fund and production of propaganda were under the control of the executive committee, women whom she knew well. However, while many committee members were personal friends and might have been expected to be open to Margaret's influence, they were firm, sometimes inflexible characters who would have resisted any attempt at their subordination. Katharine Bruce Glasier, for instance, loved Margaret and missed her dearly when she died, but had her own distinctive outlook on women in the Labour movement and space to express it as editor of the woman's column in *Labour Leader*. Similarly, Mary MacArthur organised the Women's Trade Union League according to her own principles and came into occasional conflict with the League. Sister Kerrison, Minnie Nodin and Mary Middleton may have been more amenable to suggestion. In the event, administration was not Margaret MacDonald's forte, and the haphazard way directions were given to branches considerably lessened the scope for centralised control. The records abound in postcards sent in haste from president to secretary with reminders of tasks to be performed or confessions of duties left undone. In fact, Margaret MacDonald seems to have been content to allow branches to develop in their own way.

Although strong in London, the League was by no means confined to the capital, and the provincial branches were far from the leadership's sphere of influence. The League was very weak in the Home Counties, but gained substantial support in the north-east industrial regions and in the Lancashire and Cheshire area of the North-West. South Wales was also well represented. Some cities, such as Birmingham and Manchester, had several branches. Map 1 shows the distribution of branches; one branch was formed in each location, except for towns with several branches, numbered in brackets. Appendix 2 gives full branch details in table form, with information on the secretary and dates of activity; it indicates whether a branch returned an executive committee and whether a parliamentary general election was fought by the Labour Party in the constituency. The total number of known branches, drawn from conference reports, League correspondence and the executive committee minutes was 201, but these fluctuated and perhaps half were active at any one time. An address book compiled in 1910 records eighty-six branches and the *League Leaflet* of 1911 reports 100. Of the branches recorded in 1910, nine are known to have been formed in 1906 and 1907, ten in 1908 and eleven in 1909, indicating a small, but resilient, core of continuity. After 1908 the Railway Women's Guild was affiliated; this had eighty-eight branches by 1911 and therefore doubled the area of League influence.

The beginnings of a League branch were very much a local affair, an evolution from the local Labour community. The Labour Representation Committee or Independent Labour Party would hold a meeting, sometimes asking a national League woman, perhaps Katharine Bruce Glasier or Margaret MacDonald, to speak. Following such a meeting of twenty-five women, for instance, the Birmingham branch was formed. An executive committee of seven was chosen and Margaret Fiorci was elected secretary; she wrote to twenty-seven women in socialist societies such as the Labour Church, the Socialist Centre, the *Clarion* cycling club, delivering the letters by hand to save postage.[8] Birmingham Trades Council was asked for the names of women overleaf >

Map 1 Location of Women's Labour League branches*
Note *One branch was formed in each location, except for cities with several branches, numbered in brackets, e.g. Birmingham (4).
Sources *Women's Labour League Secretarial Correspondence and Related Papers*, WLL 1-172; Women's Labour League Conference Reports; League Leaflet (Labour Party Headquarters Archives, London).

trade unionists and, having to report there was none, was very receptive to the idea of a League branch. At the formal opening of the Jarrow branch in 1907 Lisbeth Simm gave an address on 'the Labour Movement', which was followed by a character sketch from *Nicholas Nickleby* performed by some of the younger members. The secretary took names and it was decided to meet on alternate Tuesdays: 'some of the women present said they knew little about Labour politics', reported the *Northern Democrat* that October, 'but their husbands had voted for Curran (the successful Labour candidate) so they had come to learn further'.

Response was not always as good as in Birmingham and Jarrow, Manchester Central's initial lack of enthusiasm illustrates how dependent the League was on the Labour community.[9] In 1906 Manchester Central Independent Labour Party decided to let the League letter about starting a branch in the town 'lie on the table'. Mrs Pankhurst was at the meeting and may have been opposed, fearing a rival for the Woman's Social and Political Union. Sam Robinson, propaganda secretary, said, 'our women are fairly well organised for our purposes', and was supported by Adela Pankhurst. In 1908 a subsequent League letter asking for information about medical inspections in Manchester schools was also ignored. It was not until 1909 that Sam Robinson (newly married to a feminist) persuaded the ILP branch to petition the local Labour Representation to donate £5 towards the foundation of a League branch.

Birmingham and Jarrow branches were League inititatives, as was Manchester. The efforts of George Kerr, Independent Labour Party organiser, could be said to have cancelled out the lack of Sam Robinson's: George Kerr addressed a meeting attended by Brechin factory women on 'the aims and objects of the Women's Labour League' and formed a women's circle, which he hoped would eventually become a League branch.[10]

SCOTLAND
ULSTER
IRELAND
WALES
Northumberland
Cumberland
Durham
Westmorland
Yorkshire
Lancs
Cheshire
Derbys
Notts
Lincs
Staffs
Salop
Leics
R'd
Norfolk
Hunts
Warks
Northants
Cambs
Suffolk
Here-ford's
Worcs
Beds
Glos.
Oxon
Bucks
Herts
Essex
Mdx
Wilts
Berks
Surrey
Kent
Somerset
Hants
Sussex
Devon
Dorset
Corn-wall

Map 1 Location of Women's Labour League branches

ENGLAND

Cheshire
Altrincham
Crewe
Eccles
Hyde
Macclesfield
Warrington
Wallasey

Cornwall
Liskeard

Cumberland
Whitehaven
Workington

Derbyshire
Derby

Devonshire
Newton Abbot

Gloucester environs
Bristol

Hampshire
Selbourne
Portsmouth

Kent
Chatham
Gillingham
Rochester

Lancashire
Accrington
Barrow-in-Furness
Blackburn
Blackpool
Bootle
Broughton
Burnley
Bury
Clitheroe
Colne
Earlestown
Eccleston
Golborne
Lancaster
Manchester
 see *Manchester environs*
Oldham
Nelson
Preston
Rochdale
St Helens
Wigan (3)

Leicestershire
Leicester

Lincolnshire
Holbeach
Lincoln

London
28 branches

Manchester environs
Ardwick
Ashton-in-Makerfield
Gorton
Haydock
Leigh
Manchester (5)
Pendlebury
Swinton
Tyldesley

Norfolk
Norwich
Walsingham

Northumberland and Durham
Benwell
Birtley
Bishop Auckland
Blyth
Boldon Colliery
Consett
Crook
Darlington
Felling
Gateshead
Hebburn
Jarrow
Newburn
Newcastle upon Tyne
North Shields
Shildon
South Shields
Stanhope
Stanley
Sunderland

Nottinghamshire
Long Eaton
Nottingham

Somerset
Taunton

Staffordshire
Hanley
Hutcheson
Smethwick
Stublands Cross
West Bromwich
Wolverhampton

Suffolk
Ipswich

Surrey
Annerley
Croydon
Sutton
Thornton Heath

Warwickshire
Birmingham (5)
Coventry

Westmorland
Bowness

Yorkshire
Armley
Brighouse
Halifax
Hull
Keighley
Kirkdale
Leeds (7)
Middlesbrough
Sheffield
Shipley
Shripley
Throckley

WALES
Aberdare
Abergavenny
Abertillery
Bargoed
Barry
Briton Ferry
Cardiff
Cwmavon
Ebbw Vale
Gorseinon
Griffithstown
Merthyr Tydfil
Nantyfflon
Newport
Ogmore Vale
Pontypool
Rowtynm
Swansea
Tondu
Wrexham
Ystalyfera

SCOTLAND
Aberdeen
Brechin
Bridgeton
Clydebank
Coalburn
Douglas
Dundee
Edinburgh
Glasgow (2)
Govanhill
Kilmarnock
Kirkintilloch
Larkhall
Leith
Lochgelly
Partick
Pemberth
Shettleston

IRELAND
Belfast

Evolving to meet a need of the Labour community, League branches met the same mix of help and hostility that the national organisation had found. The Labour Party's 1908 decision to accept League affiliation somewhat clarified the local position, but it was still very much left to the individual branch to establish its own space. In some areas women were already active in the Labour Representation Committee and possibly resented League attempts to separate them out, feeling their participation would be diminished; the Leeds branch reported: 'We have at Leeds a number of women attached to LRC branches which operates against us somewhat.' On the other hand, some local Labour parties appear to have formed women's groups which were not affiliated to the League. This may have been a failure of communication, or it may have reflected policy differences which would be of interest had the records survived to illustrate them.

It was hard work organising women where women were most isolated, for instance, in rural colliery districts, where women had traditionally been excluded from politics. Lisbeth Simm wrote to Mary Middleton (her emphasis): '*Where branches seem to be most needed*, as say, the mining villages where women are almost an unknown quantity, there it is most difficult.'[11] Although they may not have addressed the problem sufficiently well in the past, socialist men were often helpful to the League when it began to organise in such localities. Hebburn Independent Labour Party, for example, put back its meeting half an hour so that the League could meet in its hall from 6.30 p.m. to 8.00 p.m., before the ILP meeting. In towns such as Jarrow and Preston the opportunity existed for more practical assistance; in Jarrow the local Labour Representation Committee lent its rooms free of charge to the League and in Preston the Weavers' Union made a room available. Gateshead men acknowledged they 'had not been able to win their wives over' and hoped the League would be more acceptable. The League was a reinforcement to the local labour community and League branches benefited from organisational strengths that community had already established – access to the local press, to accommodation and to the homes of local Labour personalities.

The League had to coexist with the other Labour movement women's groups, for instance, Independent Labour Party women's sections, Social Democratic Federation women's circles and the Co-operative Women's Guild. ILP women were, perhaps, nearest the League in spirit. As befitted its notion of itself as a sister organisation to the Labour movement, the League contained many ILP women. To some it must have seemed that the League was the national organisation they lacked, their women's ILP. William Anderson wrote in *Labour Leader* (11 July 1912) that the creation of a separate ILP women's organisation 'lay fallow' until the League was founded to meet the need. Of course, the League had no responsibility to, and no direction from, the ILP leadership, although, as we have seen, branches locally were dependent on the ILP's good opinion. Annot Robinson at the 1910 ILP conference submitted a resolution condemning the leadership for failing to support adequately women's enfranchisement or the Women's Labour League. Yet when Margaret MacDonald wrote an account of the British section women's organisation for the 1907 Labour and Socialist International Congress of Women, she wrote on behalf of the ILP, leaving Mary Macpherson to submit a much smaller report from the Women's Labour League. Had the Labour Party not grown into a separate party, the story of the League would have been different; it was intrinsically bound to the accident of the Party's development.

There is evidence of some difficulty in distinguishing how far a League branch of Independent Labour Party women was, or was not, part of either organisation. Katharine Bruce Glasier spent much time convincing Lancashire ILP women that they could join the League without sacrificing their standing as a local ILP women's group: 'they ought and deserve to have a national life and they have not got one yet'.[12] She found 'when my back is turned their men seem to dissuade them'. There was also the problem that, having subscribed to the ILP and, in some cases, the Women's Social and Political Union or a local suffrage society, women had no money left to pay League dues. Cardiff ILP women's section affiliated to the League at 2*d* per member per year and were to get the privilege of a League branch, on condition that recruits were accepted who wished to join the League, but not the ILP. Islington League secretary admitted free women members of the ILP and of trade unions until told to charge the usual amount. Co-existence with the ILP was, as it seems another matter that branches resolved individually, with occasional admonitions from the executive committee.

The vanguard Social Democratic Federation was less congenial to the reformist League. The bad feeling between Margaret

MacDonald and Dora Montefiore (caused by Margaret's interference in Dora's affair with George Belt) never dimmed. Although some League women (Margaret Bondfield, the Burnley League branch which seceded to the SDF in 1911) were, or had been SDF members, League contact with the SDF was small and there was no organisational connection.

The Social Democratic Federation had attempted to give more attention to women members. At the 1905 conference the SDF was faced with the problem of distributing a pamphlet that had been designed for women members, as these were so few. *Justice* became more receptive to issues of personal politics: for instance, on 15 September 1906 a leader on 'Puritanism and the Social Evil' condemned moral outrage against prostitution used as titillation to sell popular newspapers; the only remedy was said to be the economic emancipation of women: 'under socialism prostitution and capitalism will equally melt away as the mists of the night before the risen sun'. From January 1907 'Jill' wrote a women's column. She was keen on promoting women writers and women's participation in the arts and applauded any attempts to widen women's interests; she believed women's needs were as great as men's and that women ought to receive a fair wage. However, she also wrote that women who asked for equal pay and equality in marriage 'must be very short sighted or courageous to excess' (18 June 1907).

By 1908 there were thirteen women's circles and two leaflets to be distributed. By 1909 the number of women's circles had risen to twenty-two and an annual conference of the Women's Committee had been organised. Mrs Murray Leyton's proposal, that the Women's Committee be merged with the general committee and its members be subject to election by branches, indicated some resistance to women's separate organisation, but was defeated. The debate revealed that it had been appreciated women could gain confidence within the circles. Women's education was believed to be particularly important, as women were the mothers of the future generation of socialists and endowment of motherhood and state maintenance for pregnant women became part of the Social Democratic Federation reform programme. SDF women were active in Socialist Sunday Schools and Rose Jarvis went as far as to write in *Justice* (8 October 1906) that it was socialists' duty to adopt children. This emphasis on women's education led to the renaming of the Women's Committee as the Women's Education Committee in 1909.

More difficult to understand than the distance from the Social Democratic Federation, with its half-hearted attitude to women's organisation, was the lack of sisterly attention the League paid to the Co-operative Women's Guild. The Guild attracted many more members than the League, over 30,000 in 600 or more branches, and was by far the largest group of Labour movement women. Its organisation was similar to the League, autonomous, affiliated but not subordinate to a mixed-sex but male-dominated parent body. In its provincial network of branches and its activities the Guild was so similar to the League that the lack of contact was extraordinary.

This may merely be the failure of the records; contact may have been so natural and so frequent that no-one bothered to write anything down. However, there is evidence that contact was limited for political reasons. The Co-operative Societies stayed aloof from the Labour Party and no Guild branch affiliated to the League, despite the latter's 1907 decision not to make its objects more specifically socialist and thereby alienate Co-operators. Margaret Llewellyn Davies wrote when the League was formed that it would be discussed at the Co-operative Women's Guild conference, but although there were many trade unionist and socialist women in the Guilds, there were also many Liberals.[13] Nevertheless, as the Guilds invariably took a Labour point of view and worked for the Labour Party in elections, Margaret Llewellyn Davies was of the opinion that League women should become Co-operators, rather than starting a separate organisation; they could then attempt to convert the Guilds to Labour. The Guilds, she wrote, had the advantage of an established organisation and carried out practical work attached to the Co-operative Societies. If the League was primarily intended for election work, she believed it must continue as a strictly separate organisation.

There was some suspicion of the League as a competitor. Edith Macrosty wrote to Margaret MacDonald that Mrs Gasson (a Guild president) would speak at a League meeting 'provided we can prove to her that the Women's Labour League has no intention of capturing the Guild'. Mrs Bellamy wanted to set up joint committees of League and Guild: she had been asked if Guild members could attend League meetings and replied that although there would be no objection to their attendance as non-voting members, it would be better if they joined the League and could be involved in active work. Once again, branches seem to have directed local connections to their convenience; however, the League was very definitely party political, the Guild was not and no formal national connection was made.

Many League branches worked locally in support of women's trade unions, for instance, amongst the dressmakers and staymakers of Portsmouth on short time and low wages, the card room workers at Preston, the laundry girls at Liskeard who were intimidated from joining the Federation of Women Workers. The tailoresses at Birmingham gave in their names to the Tailor, Machinist and Pressers Union at a League meeting addressed by Mrs Pankhurst.[14] Birmingham, Keighley and District Trades Council had a mere 1,500 trade unionists from 45,000 'in this benighted town' and was optimistic that the League would help redress the balance. In Wigan *Labour Leader* reported (27 April 1911) that the League was organising the pit-brow girls to become members of the Miner's Federation. During the great wave of industrial unrest of 1911 the Hull seamen and dockers went on strike (*Labour Leader*, 31 July 1911); League women set up a relief committee. Mrs Hill, Hull League president, was caretaker of the local Independent Labour Party hall which the women used to organise relief. They separated themselves into ward committees and made house-to-house visits.

The industrial agitation of 1911 was also vigorous in South Wales. Women and young girls employed in cigar-making bottling and laundry work came out on strike and Mrs Scholefield, president of Cardiff Women's Labour League, assisted by Margaret Bondfield, met them to give advice: 'We went into the highways and the parks, holding odd meetings in odd places', reported Margaret Bondfield in *Labour Leader* (4 August 1911). The laundry workers got together and organised a committee; Margaret Bondfield drafted a Laundry Workers' Charter with them. The employers set up their own association and met representatives of the laundry workers; the Charter was agreed and the employers 'came to terms'. The Workers' Union were so pleased at this success that they signed up Mrs Scholefield temporarily. She held meetings at Barry Docks on women and children and the effects of the strike.

The League did have contact with the National Union of Women Workers. This was rather misnamed, being an organisation of philanthropic and religious women rather than of industrial trade unionists. However, it was affiliated to the Labour Party, unlike many of the smaller women's trade unions. The legal position affecting the payment of political levies after the Osborne Judgement made it difficult for such unions to consider affiliation. Margaret MacDonald had been a member of the National Union of Women Workers' executive council since 1896. Lisbeth Simm was a guest at the NUWW 1911 conference and read a paper on education and women of the working classes. The Scottish Council for Women's Trades kept in touch with the League, Margaret Irwin writing frequently to Margaret MacDonald about sweated workshops and the conditions of women's employment. The National Federation of Women Workers was in close touch with the League while Mary MacArthur sat on its executive, but did not affiliate. Neither did Margaret Bondfield's former union of shop assistants.

League women had to be careful not to tread on the toes of the women's trade unions. In Hull, for instance, despite their work to relieve distress, the League branch was 'flatly told we were not wanted to help organise women workers'. Lisbeth was careful to ensure that the League executive committee did not send Mary MacArthur, who, as secretary of the National Federation of Women Workers, obviously had an interest in the 'intelligent and not easily humbugged' dressmakers and weavers amongst whom she was organising in Glasgow: 'we really have no right to bring in a trade union organiser to the women, they are competent to choose organisers for themselves and would certainly resent us sending one to them'.[15] This problem can only have been worse after the argument of the Women's Industrial Council over minimum wage legislation. Beforehand, at national level, there were some joint projects, for instance a 'Women's Labour Day', a 'Grand Labour Fête' and a 'Carnival and Reunion' at Earl's Court on 17 July 1909, which included a 'symbolic industrial pageant of Women's Trades'. Some actions did stretch friendly relations, such as the sheets of signatures collected by branches in support of a full dinner hour for Co-operative women jam workers, which were sent by the executive to Margaret Llewellyn Davies with a letter deploring the jam workers' low pay.

How women discriminated in their political activity in the early twentieth century is perhaps obscured from us by our adoption of different sets of values. The way we distinguish between vanguard and mass organisations and between revolutionary and constitutional action has been influenced by the fortuitous development of the Labour Party as a single, reformist body from which separate

WOMEN'S LABOUR LEAGUE LEAFLETS—No. 9.

Women's Labour League and Trades Unions.

The Labour Party's membership consists mainly of Trades Unionists; therefore the Women's Labour League ought to be in close touch with the Women's Trades Unions, and help to see that the women wage earners are organised both industrially and politically.

In those trades and districts where there are strong Trade Unions amongst the workers

Wages are higher and conditions better

than in the trades or districts where there is little or no organisation.

Thus the strongly organised

Miners, Compositors, or Engineers,

are better paid and have shorter hours than the partially organised

Shop Assistants, or the unorganised
Agricultural Labourers.

In Lancashire 96,000 Women Textile Workers are members of the Textile Trade Unions, and **are paid at the same rate as men for the same work.**

In Blackburn, where the Union is very strong, a **four-loom weaver** on full time receives **from 24/- to 30/-** weekly.

Compare this with the unorganised
Jam and Pickle Workers in East London, who often receive **as little as 4/- weekly,** and **seldom more than 10/- weekly.**

Fig. 5 Women's Labour League *Leaflet* no. 9: 'Women's Labour League and Trades Unions'
Source Women's Labour League Secretarial Papers and Related Correspondence

socialist societies have been gradually excluded. A mass membership party and constitutionally-oriented class politics have become the relatively respectable norm in Britain, the vanguard party and revolutionary tactics the prerogative of peripheral extremists. We have also come to distinguish industrial agitation from the parliamentary road because the Labour movement separated into distinct direct action and parliamentary wings. Gender politics have been perceived both as alternative and as subordinate to the varying manifestations of class politics.

Boundaries were not so clear before the First World War. In this climate the relationship of a women's group to a particular socialist society was more fluid. This was especially so with the Labour Party, created as an agency for various groups and to act politically for the industrial wing. As late as 1911, for instance, Keir Hardie and Hyndman of the Social Democratic Federation, whose politics in practice diverged, collaborated in a socialist children's book. Katharine Bruce Glasier spoke to SDF and Independent Labour Party meetings. It seems that the general tendency was for SDF women to limit themselves to that body, whilst Labour Party and ILP women joined the League and were active in their unions. Coordinated efforts, such as the 1911 campaign to include women more fully in the national insurance provisions, were conducted on an *ad hoc* basis through personal contact.

There had been attempts at a more formal connection. There was a sizeable British contingent to the 1907 Labour and Socialist International Women's Congress held in Stuttgart, at which member groups were instructed to organise more coherently amongst women. Clara Hendin, Social Democratic Federation women's circle secretary, proposed a national socialist women's committee 'to carry on a campaign of socialism amongst women and to keep in touch with our sisters from abroad'. There was little response at home from Labour movement women, who were perhaps wary of being educated by the SDF. International contacts, however, continued to be made. It is difficult to think back past the boundaries arising from the First World War and to realise how keen was the Labour women's international perception. Trips to America (Margaret MacDonald, Margaret Bondfield, Mary MacArthur, Annot Robinson, Dora Montefiore) and within Europe were relatively frequent. The International Congress of Women was still in existence, Lady Aberdeen still president, although for

Labour movement women its role had rather been taken over by international gatherings supported by the British Trades Union Congress. Labour and socialist women met every three years; the 1910 International was held in Copenhagen and although delegates from Italy, Spain and France found the journey prohibitive, British women attended, together with women from Poland, Germany, Norway, Sweden, Holland, Austria, Switzerland, America and Russia.

The 1910's women's meeting was held two days before the full International. Unfortunately, the British delegation used the occasion to display domestic differences.[16] The debate on suffrage took up most of the two days, the British delegation coming under fierce adverse criticism for supporting limited women's enfranchisement. This must have been particularly irritating for the League women in the delegation, as they did not support the limited franchise and as four League motions on other subjects failed to be discussed. Ethel Bentham, Marion Phillips and Mrs Despard had been chosen as speakers for the British delegation, but in the event, Clara Zetkin, in the chair, called on Dora Montefiore to speak. Dora, despite being a member of the Social Democratic Federation, did support limited enfranchisement and had been a member of the Women's Social and Political Union; she had refused to pay taxes and rates, had been imprisoned and was attacked in *Justice* for her beliefs. 'For the sake of letting things go smoothly', reported Margaret MacDonald, '(we) put up quietly with much more of Mrs Montefiore than is justified by her influence or representative character in the British movement'. However, League patience was finite and the ten League delegates walked out of the Congress during Dora's speech.

The Copenhagen International recommended that a women's council be formed in each constituent country and the Women's International Council of Socialist and Labour Organisations (British Section) was duly formed, open to all women representatives of socialist societies and trade unions. Clara Hendin dissolved the Socialist Women's Bureau in its favour. The League affiliated and Margaret Bondfield became chair of the council. Clara Hendin and Mary MacArthur were vice-chairs, Ethel Bentham treasurer and Mary Macpherson international correspondent. Margaret MacDonald became secretary. The Independent Labour Party, Social Democratic Federation Women's Education Committee,

Co-operative Women's Guild, Fabian Women's Group, Women's Trade Union League and Railway Women's Guild all sent delegates. Quarterly meetings were held, but no record of League correspondence or connection with the council survives for this period.

The main thrust of the League, however, was local and national constitutional action; change by parliamentary means, the use of the ballot box as the agent of reform. One cannot equate feminists, or socialist feminists, with suffragists. Suffragism is a particular political position. Revolutionary socialists, for instance, were opposed to constitutional amendment; Lily Gair Wilkinson wrote: 'If all the ballot papers in the world were at my disposal, the only use I should put them to would be to build a great bonfire of them and call for the people to come round and watch while I set them ablaze.'[17] It might have been expected that the reformist and constitutional League would give wholehearted support to the cause of women's enfranchisement.

Although this cause had become such an obsession, it was extremely controversial and divisive. There was a substantial body of opinion supporting the demand for full adult suffrage as opposed to women's inclusion on the existing electoral registers. The Labour Party before 1911 fell into this group; it was obviously in Labour's interests and an integral part of its political philosophy that working people should be able to vote. Those who failed to qualify on the grounds of property ownership, however, often failed to meet the alternative residence criteria because of their enforced mobility in search of work. Perhaps sixty per cent of working people had become disenfranchised by 1914. There was support within the Labour Party for a policy of achieving some immediate redress for women; Keir Hardie, for instance, was strongly in favour and there was much argument about the social class of women who would qualify to vote under the existing regulations; The Labour Party was not as intransigent as the Social Democratic Federation, which condemned the women's franchise campaign as an oppression of working people.

A further complication was that the campaign for women's enfranchisement was split between two groups; the older and larger National Union of Women's Suffrage Societies (suffragists) and the newer and smaller Women's Social and Political Union (suffragettes) represented the opposite poles. The Women's Freedom

League and Sylvia Pankhurst's East London Federation were groups which had both broken away from the WSPU and were similar in action and intent, although more democratically organised. There were a host of suffrage societies identified by profession, religion or geography. The NUWSS was a council that encompassed many of these societies; it had many Liberal women in membership, but also Labour women such as Lisbeth Simm, a member of the North-Eastern Society for Women's Suffrage. NUWSS women were dedicated activists, but did not follow violent methods. Many refused to pay local rates and taxes; they organised meetings and demonstrations and lobbied Members of Parliament. The groundswell of support for women's enfranchisement among Liberal back-benchers, the introduction of private members', and later, government bills on the issue indicated some success.

There were about 50,000 people affiliated to the National Union of Women's Suffrage Societies by the end of the Middleton/MacDonald period of League activity. There was no policy of opposing Labour candidates, although the NUWSS was working for immediate, limited women's enfranchisement. Occasionally League leaders joined the NUWSS in deputations, all petitioners agreeing to say nothing about the machinery of extending the franchise to women, but restricting themselves to the simple demand for the vote.[18] The number of NUWSS women who were League members (most of the north-east activists, for instance) indicates that there was no insurmountable reason for friction between the NUWSS and the League.

The Women's Social and Political Union also retained bonds with the Labour movement in its early years, as Mrs Pankhurst (WSPU leader)'s address to the Birmingham meeting for the League indicates. Margaret MacDonald's own branch (Central London) joined a WSPU suffrage demonstration in 1907. League policy differed from that of the Labour Party before 1911 in that League objects explicitly supported women's enfranchisement: Isabella Ford had moved an amendment to that effect at the first conference. It had been decided that the League would not work for Labour Party candidates who opposed women's enfranchisement.

Given its *modus vivendi* with the National Union, one must look further than opposition to limited women's enfranchisement to explain why the Women's Social and Political Union was less compatible with the League. First, in its early days when it addressed a whole range of grievances expressed by women in the Labour movement, the WSPU was a direct competitor: Manchester Central Independent Labour Party's lack of interest in the League is an example. Second, as the WSPU pursued increasingly aggressive militant tactics, dramatic in intent and costly to produce, it needed an autocracy antithetical to the League concept of branch autonomy. Its style alienated the WSPU from the League mainstream. Lisbeth Simm, for instance, was appalled at the amount of money the WSPU managed to collect in distressed areas; she went to one of Mrs Pankhurst's meetings and 'wished I'd my shilling back'.[19] (The entrance fees were 6*d*, 1*s* and 2*s*: 'most ILP-ers had complimentary tickets, but a great crowd had to pay'; the hall was full and a collection was taken which raised a further £30, perhaps two years' wages for local working women.) Lisbeth felt the WSPU organisers had little idea of the poverty of the region or the hardship their fund-raising would produce and lamented: 'we have to be content if a dozen join and never mind about raising funds'. She disliked the style of the meeting: 'How very theatrical they are.'

An example of the way the Women's Social and Political Union aroused increasing antagonism in a Labour movement that was, initially, reasonably supportive, was the Cockermouth by-election of 1906. The Labour candidate was Robert Smillie of the Independent Labour Party, secretary of the Miners' Union and supported by them. The ILP had been divided about limited women's enfranchisement; at the 1909 ILP Conference Mary Muir and Jennie Baker (both League members) had taken the adult suffragist position. The Pankhursts, however, were ILP women. Mrs Pankhurst had argued within the ILP that a consensus of all people must be obtained before socialism could be achieved by constitutional means. *Labour Leader* reported regularly on women's suffrage activities and on the court appearance of ILP women involved, usually Theresa Billington Greig and Christabel Pankhurst. These two went to Cockermouth during the election and conducted a campaign of votes for women; the ILP perceived this as hostile to Robert Smillie, who was resoundingly defeated. Thereafter, a distinct change in reporting became obvious: John and Katharine Bruce Glasier's *Labour Leader* comments were painfully adverse to the suffragettes; letters accused the WSPU of being financed by Tory gold; demands were made for the resignation or expulsion of Theresa Billington Greig and Christabel.

These two were members of the Manchester Central Independent Labour Party branch, which gave them a chance to reply.[20] Christabel reported that they had written to the local ILP for accommodation during the election which had been refused as the local ILP-ers were more concerned to maintain friendly contact with the Liberals. She denied that the WSPU campaign had hurt Smillie, and stated that his agent thought it might have helped. After full discussion, the Manchester Central ILP branch confirmed its confidence in the two women. However, the breach was not healed nationally; ILP National Administration Committee opinion hardened against suffragette activity. Suspicion of the WSPU, of course, spread to the Labour Party which was devoted to the electoral interests of trade unionists and ILP-ers. Ramsay MacDonald, in particular, disliked aggessive militancy, which he called 'criminal, vain and stupid'. Mrs Pankhurst and Christabel wrote to Manchester Central ILP resigning their membership in 1907; Mrs Pankhurst was 'still a socialist and in sympathy with the objects of the party', but Christabel thought her position as a WSPU leader made it necessary for her to renounce party politics.

Nevertheless, the Women's Social and Political Union did raise its funds and continued to be attractive to some League members. There was the advantage of committing oneself to immediate action, thereby stating one's freedom from stereotypical ideas of femininity. There was the bond of sisterhood in collective and sometimes dangerous efforts. There was excitement, a call to arms and a 'Joan of Arc' to follow.* Many Independent Labour Party and Labour Party women remained WSPU members and others, who were ardent suffragists, whilst not choosing violence, would not condemn the WSPU. Philip Snowden, for example, had been converted to the cause of votes for women by his wife and threatened to resign his Independent Labour Party membership unless firm support was forthcoming, complaining that Ethel Snowden's hugely successful suffrage speeches were not recorded in *Labour Leader*. As late as 1911, Margaret MacDonald was correcting a proof of a pamphlet by the WSPU's Mrs Pethick-Lawrence on the value of the unpaid labour of the wives of wage earners.[21]

*I am indebted to one of my students, Debbie Thomas, for discussion of the Joan of Arc imagery and its use by the Pankhursts.

Ramsay MacDonald perhaps exaggerated when he wrote that the League was 'nearly split asunder' on the suffrage issue (crediting Margaret with his own view of antipathy to selfish middle-class and upper-class women), but there certainly was controversy within the League. Some League members did want to make votes for women the main League concern. Ethel Snowden, for instance, resigned her League membership because of its deficiency in this respect; she was vice-president of the Free Church League for Women's Suffrage. Her resignation was the result of consideration; she believed that while suffragettes might not be socialists, it behoved socialists to support all measures of enfranchisement because of their commitment to democracy. She acknowledged that immediate female enfranchisement might delay the beginnings of a socialist society and that suffragism and feminism were not necessarily the same thing.

The President and general committee of the Preston branch resigned from the League on the suffrage issue, leaving a debt of £3; however, there had already been dispute within the Preston branch over campaigning for secular education.[22] All of Selina Cooper's Nelson branch resigned the League; Selina Cooper organised amongst women textile workers and believed their enfranchisement to be a prerequisite to better pay and conditions. Mr Rigby of Preston, Charlotte Despard and possibly some of the other women not elected after 1907 resigned from the League executive committee because it failed to give adequate expression to their commitment to women's enfranchisement. In 1907 when Theresa Billington Greig was facing expulsion from the Independent Labour Party, she addressed a meeting arranged by Gateshead ILP, together with Adela Pankhurst; Lisbeth Simm, no Pankhurst fan, chaired the meeting and enthusiastically endorsed the resolution, taken with only four dissensions, 'to enfranchise the women of this country in the next session of Parliament'.

Lisbeth attempted to resolve the difficulties and disputes presented by the suffrage movement in an article she wrote for the *Northern Democrat* (October 1908) on women's suffrage activities during the 1908 Newcastle by-election:

> One of the most interesting features of a by-election nowadays is the part taken by women who enter heartily into the fight in order to bring the suffrage question into the front. During the Newcastle contest women suffragists addressed dozens of meetings and made hosts of converts.

Wherever the politicians harangued an audience or waited for an opportunity there were the women also, preaching and teaching – generally with most interested crowds.

The National Union of Women's Suffrage Societies and the Women's Social and Political Union 'carried on their distinctive and separate campaigns'. Lisbeth acknowledged 'there is much divergence of opinion as to the wisdom of the different methods'. She was gratified that 'women are awakening to their conditions' and that 'Men . . . are acknowledging the justice of the claim and . . . public opinion is being moulded in a progressive way.'

Lisbeth's considered support, acknowledging the problems, was echoed in many branches. As with relationships with the Labour movement, branches were left to come to terms with this women's movement activity. There were a whole range of activities undertaken by branches, which meant there was room for agreement even when suffrage had become a controversial issue. Within the League women were politically involved, so the sense of exclusion from politics which aroused so much suffragist and suffragette anger was perhaps dimmed. Several branches worked on measures to achieve the passage of the Local Authorities (Qualification of Women) Act, which gave women the right to stand for all municipal posts, and the executive committee corresponded with the Women's Local Government Society which was promoting the Bill. In 1910 the executive committee declined to consult all branches on H. N. Brailsford's proposals to introduce a Conciliation Bill to enfranchise women. Brailsford was a National Union of Women's Suffrage Societies member and a Liberal Member of Parliament who condemned his government's inactivity. The executive committee did supply Brailsford with a list of branches so that he could make his enquiries directly. In early 1911 it was decided not to send a delegate to the International Women's Suffrage Conference in Stockholm.

Throughout this period suffrage became increasingly controversial as the suffragettes' activities won them greater notoriety; the dispute within the League came to a head in 1909. Margaret Bondfield was the League delegate to the Labour Party conference. She was president of the People's Suffrage Association, dedicated to adult suffrage; she had been a member of the Social Democratic Federation and had little sympathy with propertied women. She had tried unsuccessfully to persuade the League executive committee to affiliate to the People's Suffrage Society, although the League conference had voted against this in 1908 and 1909 (Mary Macpherson seconded the 1909 motion). As its delegate, Margaret Bondfield had to move the League motion on suffrage at the 1909 Labour Party conference. This read:

> Believing the active participation of women in the work of the government is in the best interests of the nation, and in view of the Reform Bill promised by the government, this conference demands that the inclusion of women shall not be left to the chances of an amendment, but that it shall become a vital part of the government measure; and further declares that any attempt to exclude women will be met by the uncompromising opposition of organised labour as to the whole Bill . . .

The executive merely minuted that Margaret reported on the conference and that her action on amendment was endorsed. In fact, joining forces with Arthur Henderson, Margaret had deleted the vital last phrase 'to the whole Bill' without authority and according to her own account, had to face a 'storm of criticism from certain members of the executive'.

By the end of the Middleton/MacDonald period the League was resolving the dispute in favour of the adult suffrage position. At the January 1911 League conference (Lisbeth Simm in the chair) there was much discussion of this issue. Mrs Harrison Bell moved a resolution in favour of the full enfranchisement of men and women. Annot Robinson moved the women only amendment, arguing that to pursue full adult suffrage was not practical politics. The amendment was lost by thirty-two votes to four. Interestingly, Ethel Bentham, Maud Ward and Marion Phillips all said they had changed their position to adult suffrage since the last conference; Ethel Bentham said that it was futile to demand anything less. Later that year the League attended a meeting of working women to demand the vote, perhaps indicating that its identity as an organisation for class politics had given the lead in settling the dispute over women's enfranchisement.

The controversy over the suffrage issue was, perhaps, another reason for the autonomy enjoyed by League branches. The leadership was sometimes divided about what directions to give, while the branches pursued their own priorities. Rather than the single issue of suffrage, it was a multitude of activities that the League leadership wished to stimulate; branch inititative was therefore more important than branch obedience.

The partly unofficial endeavours of Lisbeth Simm were the most sustained attempt at organising League branches into any coherent pattern in the Middleton/MacDonald period. Lisbeth lived in Newcastle with her husband M. T. Simm, who was North-East Region Independent Labour Party organiser. She initiated a cluster of branches grouped into regions. Lisbeth's husband edited the *Northern Democrat* in which she wrote a regular women's column. She therefore had ready-made channels of publicity and advertisement. For instance, in August 1908 she asked for names of women who felt 'disposed to join' a League branch in Newcastle, promising that work would be arranged to meet member's needs and that there would be both educational and social meetings. Men, who had learnt to appreciate women's work at election times, were asked to forward names. 'The subscription is very small, the mutual help of organised women is very, very great.'

Having set up such a branch, Lisbeth wrote 'voluminous correspondence' if it lacked business. She suggested a consecutive pattern of work for branches to follow and also the need for the central leadership to follow up new branches quickly. One of her recruiting methods, which she used in Jarrow and recommended in *Labour Leader* (13 September 1911), was that each member, 'by persistent persuasion, visitation, leaflets and personal talks', would recruit one other member in the year. Nursing mothers, she suggested, could be reached by means of a cup of tea and talk about the care of babies.

Lisbeth also advertised the League by speaking at open-air meetings. This could be extremely hard work. She rejoiced when the 'open-air season' was over after the 'wintry summer' of 1909 (*Northern Democrat*, October 1909). In September 1908 she had spoken at twenty-five open-air meetings and had felt unwell and unhappy. She would have liked to have taken a holiday, but her husband's commitments meant it would have been a solitary trip. Perhaps it was time with her husband that she missed: there was a whole network of friends and acquaintances to provide hospitality on her organising tours. These took Lisbeth around the colliery districts where she had been born, to the Durham Miners' Gala, Independent Labour Party conferences and into Scotland. In early 1911 Lisbeth spent a week in the Glasgow district, where she tried to get joint meetings of interested women from the town and surrounding areas. She wrote in *Labour Leader* (17 March 1911) that this should be the pattern for League recrutiment for all big cities. Later that month she was in Edinburgh and then travelled to Leith. In the latter stages of this trip she joined her husband who was on an organising tour for the ILP.

Lisbeth felt bitter that, unlike the Women's Social and Political Union, she could not offer the tea and entertainments so conducive to winning members. Indeed, she had to use her housekeeping money as League petty cash and was reluctant to claim her expenses. She wrote to Mary Middleton in June 1908 that she had meetings in Durham and would have to stay over: she had little cash in hand and had been using the housekeeping money; £1 or so would do, but £2 would be better if it could be spared.[23] The problem was that Lisbeth had no friends in Durham and would have to lodge. Also, she had to pay someone to do her housekeeping while she was away. Eventually a scheme was worked out whereby Lisbeth was paid a fixed sum for each meeting and travelling expenses; if she had to stay overnight, the fee would be increased and Lisbeth would undertake some visiting.[24] Knowing these details illuminates Lisbeth's courage in facing the daunting task of going into a city where she was unknown, travelling by train, seeking out a lodging in a strange house, in order to publicise the Labour movement amongst working people. It is noteworthy that where Lisbeth's network did exist, it consisted largely of Independent Labour Party members.

To hold her cluster of branches together, Lisbeth initiated district meetings in the North-East. She gave Margaret MacDonald three months' notice of such a meeting, open to the public, and tempted Margaret to speak: 'The WLL is much discussed up here now. Once we show we are able to do things our cause is won.'[25] Many of the women coming to Lisbeth's meetings were new to the Labour movement, so Margaret need not feel there would be a strictly Independent Labour Party audience. (This would surely have been a drawback only if Margaret felt herself redundant, or wanted to publicise the Labour Party rather than the ILP.) 'The branches must be linked', Lisbeth wrote, 'and we think this is the best way.' She hoped she had not offended but 'the executive committee give me such a free hand that if I have exceeded the limits of my duties I don't think I am to blame'.

One such district gathering at Gateshead was reported in the June 1909 *Northern Democrat*. Branches of the Women's

Co-operative Guild were represented and there were delegates from the Independent Labour Party and the Shop Assistants' Union. There were also 'a number of visitors of the sterner sex'. The determined relegation of the Labour male to visitor status was as characteristic of Lisbeth as her catholic approach to women's Labour organisations. The first resolution of the conference called for taxation on large unearned incomes in order to enable local authorities to reduce school class sizes, improve playgrounds, provide school nurseries and give medical aid at school medical inspections. Newcastle had a day nursery where women could leave their babies at a charge of 4*d* per day, and it was noticeable that 'so many of the babies so left had improved by the care and feeding they got'. The Sunderland delegate thought 'day nurseries must be a boon to mothers on washings days and such like, but they must feel the wages question was at the root, for a mother ought to be given the opportunity of minding her own baby'. Another delegate reiterated that 'Fathers and Mothers should be given the right to work.' This encapsulated the debate about maternal child care and women's right to work that was to occupy the women's movement for a generation after the First World War; League women were unanimous in demanding local authority child care provision for those who wanted it. Other resolutions included the Truck Acts, whereby the Shop Assistants' Union hoped to demolish the punitive system of fines and fees that diminished the shop workers' low wages, the Labour Party Right to Work Bill currently before parliament and the call for an eight-hour day. Mrs Shaw of Newcastle addressed the provision in the Old Age Pensions Act (1908) which disqualified a British woman married to a foreigner, an instance of sex discrimination in a measure into which its creator had been concerned to breathe an indiscriminate spirit.

By July 1910 the North-East meeting had developed into official annual reunions and a district committee was elected (Florence Harrison Bell (Newcastle), Miss Potts (Jarrow), Mrs Mills (Gateshead), Mrs Waldie Cairns). Branches decided to pay 2*d* per member per annum to a district committee fund. Several branches had made red and white banners behind which the conference delegates marched through Bolden Colliery, the 1910 venue: 'We were "played" through the lanes to a pleasant field, and there a lorrey (sic) formed our platform.' In 1911 district conferences were held at Hebburn and Gateshead.

Lisbeth Simm was both indefatigable and modest, an early example of the Labour Party woman stalwart, working without the sound of trumpets, status or salary, but drudging for the cause of deep conviction and loving kindness. She acknowledged herself to be 'afraid of the swells' such as Margaret MacDonald, but had a good relationship with Mary Middleton, to whom she signed herself 'in lovingest greetings', 'in loving haste'. It was developments in the executive committee perception of the organiser's job which laid the basis for a change to a more professional organisation and made possible some continuity after Mary Middleton's and Mary MacDonald's deaths. Lisbeth wrote to Mary Middleton in August 1908: 'when I see little bits in the *Woman Worker* about London WLL I think our branches must be very elementary, as yours seem so well advanced'. This was not the case, as perhaps should have been acknowledged. Lisbeth worked in a very much more difficult area than London, had less funds and more miles to cover. She had good ideas about arranging League work which were not paid enough attention and consequently she was undervalued. Also, her Independent Labour Party connections were perhaps seen as a threat, a distraction from the direct support it was hoped the League would give to the Labour Party.

The 1909 League conference was held in Portsmouth. Lisbeth did not attend because the fare was prohibitive and she therefore missed the meeting of the new executive committee, which was held, as usual, immediately at the close of conference. Maybe Lisbeth was also weary and sensed antagonism from the 'swells'. The new executive committee (27 January 1909) decided, in her absence, that because of her travelling difficulties, Margaret Bondfield and Mrs Bellamy should organise branches, and that the League would approach Labour Party Members of Parliament and candidates for funds in order that a permanent organiser might be appointed at £150 per year. Lisbeth's work 'in her own north-east corner' was indeed commended, but there was no debate about paying her or offering her a full-time job. Instead, Dorothy Lenn (of Central London Women's Labour League, Margaret MacDonald's secretary for the Women's Industrial Council) was described as 'in all ways suitable'.

The General Purposes Committee engaged Dorothy at £2 a week. There had been no previous mention at the executive committee or in the correspondence of dissatisfaction with Lisbeth's work; organising the North-East was in itself a full time task, and travelling difficulties could only have meant disability to spread the organising further afield. Perhaps the executive committee, with London members preponderant, underestimated the need for provincial work. Perhaps there was a desire to establish better administration and direction of the League, but this would have necessitated a more prolonged discussion of ways and means which would have been assisted by Lisbeth's presence.

Lisbeth attended the next executive committee (30 April 1909); Margaret Bondfield was in the chair; Mary MacArthur queried whether the General Purposes Committee had exceeded its authority. Margaret MacDonald was then quite ruthless in pushing through the appointment. She followed the classic mode of gaining consensus, taking the offending issue in two parts, the first being the more generally acceptable. She moved and Katharine Bruce Glasier seconded 'That we confirm the appointment of a permanent organiser. That the salary be two pounds when at work for the League', plus travelling and reasonable expenses. Minnie Nodin, the treasurer, and Mary Macpherson voted in favour; these might be termed the old guard. Mary MacArthur and Lisbeth voted against. It was then proposed that Dorothy Lenn be the organiser. Only Margaret MacDonald, Katharine Bruce Glasier and Minnie Nodin were in favour. None of the others would vote openly against Dorothy Lenn and abstained; Margaret MacDonald had therefore won approval for Dorothy Lenn's appointment by three votes against five abstentions.

It is interesting that Lisbeth feared the appointment of a permanent organiser. The reason may have been personal resentment or principled opposition, but the first seems unlikely when Lisbeth's generous character is taken into account, the second because Lisbeth's husband was a paid full-timer. The grounds for policy difference would appear to be the threat to regional autonomy, distaste for London control of organising time and effort. Mrs James and Marion Curran (both non-Londoners) were present and abstained from the first vote. It might have been thought Margaret MacDonald would be deterred by the committee's scant approval, but Dorothy Lenn was duly appointed. There were plans for Dorothy to undertake an organising tour in Wales and the North; characteristically, Lisbeth invited her home for a week's instruction before she set off.

Lisbeth's husband had already welcomed Margaret Bondfield to his home. 'Man is born to trouble', he wrote to Margaret MacDonald, 'if Mrs Simm and Miss Lenn boss me too much I presume the League won't mind paying my expenses if I have to take lodgings once again . . . Miss Lenn will be properly cared for and instructed and the domestic subjection of the undersigned under the WLL may serve her in another sphere – an awful existence.'[26] Mr M. T. Simm was of the opinion the League was doing invaluable work and was a real political force in the North-East.

Despite her generosity, Lisbeth must have found the choice of the North for Dorothy's work particularly upsetting. In the event, there are records of a spring tour by Dorothy in Wales and the North-West and of a subsequent autumn tour in Wales. She found it difficult to get branches to be involved in winter organising and intended to spend this time at the London Labour Party election rooms. A portion of Dorothy's wages were paid by the Women's Industrial Council, while she helped with research for Clementina Black's book, presumably in the summer. When this support ceased with the research, League funds were low. Dorothy's services were 'discontinued', but not until she had made a substantial contribution to League work in the January 1910 General Election. The East Birmingham branch which she had formed in the process of canvassing was said to be 'quite getting the honours' in the election.

Dorothy reported to Margaret MacDonald (then in India) on her work.[27] The main problem she found in Wales was a lack of leadership, although Mrs Scholefield of Cardiff was 'a great acquisition': Dorothy stayed with her. The first Welsh meeting was formed nearly entirely of men, so Dorothy returned for an afternoon meeting to meet the women. She formed the Swansea branch with Mrs David Williams, wife of the Labour candidate, as secretary. A meeting in the Ogmore Vale colliery district was poorly attended: 'the women are tied to their homes dreadfully'. Moving on to the North-West, Dorothy stayed with Social Democratic Federation members and felt less happy; they were not very enthusiastic about the League and went out every evening, so Dorothy had to find a meeting to attend. Liverpool she found 'hopeless', Clitheroe 'Conservative', but in Leeds the local branch organised her work and paid her 30*s* a week: 'and alas! they demand open air meetings at factory gates etc. How shall I survive it?'

Dorothy's first such meeting was 'hanging over me . . . It's a horrible nightmare – thank heavens a dinner hour meeting can't last longer than half an hour! I must prepare to meet my doom.' In Manchester Dorothy stayed with Annot Robinson, who promised to help 'although she is rather "anti-man"'. Annot said she would join the League, but resign if asked to work for a man of whom she did not approve.

It seems that Margaret MacDonald knew when to acknowledge defeat. When Dorothy's job ended there were no more plans for a permanent, full-time organiser until the death of Mary Middleton. The Lisbeth Simm style of district organisation was seen to be more cost-effective; 'we shall be able to feel our way more surely', wrote Margaret MacDonald, 'if we are not responsible for a full-time salary and big railway expenses'.[28]

Two more part-time organisers were appointed, Bertha Ayles for the South-West and Annot Robinson in Manchester.

Bertha Ayles (née Batt) had moved to Bristol in 1910 with her husband Walter, who worked there as an Independent Labour Party organiser. They were two of a compact Labour community that organised in the docks and factories and in town politics. By 1911 Walter Ayles had published plans for a socialist local council in Bristol, with municipal housing, better control of planning and sanitary regulations and plenteous provision of education.

Mrs Ayles was able to start conferences in the South-West by the summer of 1910, building on Dorothy Lenn's work of the previous year. By January 1911 delegates were attending from Cardiff, Barry, Newport and Bristol. Swansea branch sent a report and Nantyfflon branch sent their greetings. This conference lasted all day and was followed by a more intimate 'round the stove' meeting of the activists (*Labour Leader*, January 1911); in the evening, instead of succumbing to the fatigue one might have expected, the women held a public meeting. Mrs Ayles spoke on the subject of municipal lodging houses for women. Where women worked in industrial areas there was a need for cheap accommodation that would also be the scene for some companionship and provide common cooking and washing facilities. By February 1911 Cardiff branch had requested its local authority to provide such a lodging house. Abertillery, Merthyr and Griffithstown branches were formed that year, and Margaret Bondfield formed Ogmore Vale branch in March 1911. By the April 1911 South-West conference there were thirty-two delegates. Katharine Bruce Glasier spoke at this conference and confirmed Dorothy Lenn's opinion of Mrs Scholefield as 'the all powerful generating centre'.[29] South Wales, as has been seen, was very active in the 1911 industrial agitation. This might have explained why Swansea and Barry branch delegates were unable to afford the fare for the July 1911 South-West conference held in Bristol. It was decided that expenses would thereafter be pooled.

Meanwhile, Mrs Ayles was returning to her home surroundings of Lancashire to organise. The Lancashire and Cheshire area had always been a League stronghold. At its start in 1906 two branches were formed, Preston (secretary, Mrs Rigby, succeeded by Kitty Ralphs and Mrs Duckett) and Wallasey (secretary, Bertha Lancaster, succeeded by Mrs Stallybrass and Mrs Wade). Wallasey remained continuously active, returning Katharine Bruce Glasier to the League executive committee. Katharine, as we know, had worked amongst Lancashire Independent Labour Party women, encouraging them to join the League. In 1907 Nelson (Mrs Acton) and Bootle branches were formed; Preston branch split, its officers leaving to join the Women's Social and Political Union, but the branch continued. In 1909, the year of Dorothy Lenn's organising tour, Blackpool (Mrs Stuttland), Warrington (Miss Robinson) and St Helens (Mrs Bell) gained branches. Four of these eight branches were active in 1910; St Helens branch split in two, with Mrs Burt secretary of the seceding faction and, reflecting the general strength of the League in this year of two elections, three branches in Wigan were added and branches in Blackburn (Mrs Hulme), Burnley (Miss Burley), Hyde (Mrs Bradley), Lancaster (Mrs Fort) and Macclesfield (Mrs Pimblott).

Following the example of the North-East, a Lancashire and Cheshire district conference was held in May 1910. School meals and labour exchanges were discussed. Annot Robinson spoke about divorce laws that would apply equally to both sexes, and divorce at a reduced cost if drunkeness, insanity or criminality could be proved.

There was a solid base from which Mrs Ayles could work to form new branches. She made several tours of the area, speaking and canvassing for support. In April 1911 *Labour Leader* records her tour of Newton Ashton-in-Makerfield (where there was a group of women not affiliated to the League), Oldham and Dunstall Green. The Ashton group joined the League and a new branch was formed in Oldham. Mrs Clynes, wife of one of Labour's leading parliamentarians, became secretary of the Oldham branch.

An unusually full *Labour Leader* report by Mrs Ayles of 2 June 1911 gives an insight into the arrangements for an organising tour:

> On Tuesday I came on to Wigan. I found that it was impossible to fix up a meeting at Lamber Head Green, as I had hoped, the notice being too short, so I went on to Goose Green, another mining village in the Ince Division, where I hoped to work up a meeting for the Wednesday. I visited a number during the evening and made arrangements to get a room for the meeting. The next day I went over again with a League member from Wigan to Worsley Mesnes, an adjoining district.

There Mrs Ayles met a Labour Councillor who gave her a list of the names of about sixty women: 'We just spent a day visiting them, talking about the League and leaving leaflets behind.' As a result of this and succeeding tours, new branches were formed in Goldbourne, Bury, Haydock and Rochdale.

A district conference was held in Wigan in August 1911. Subjects discussed were school meals, women's right to work, the Insurance Bill, municipal workshops, public abattoirs and free lavatories. By October 1911 a further conference was planned in Preston; Preston branch of the League was reformed. The Lancashire and Cheshire district now declared itself a League division and elected its own secretary, Miss Holden. This was not a trouble-free progress; Burnley branch, for instance, seceded to the Social Democratic Federation in 1911. The 'talking about the League' must have been a real exposition of political philosophy and the organising work was, of course, tremendous. Setting up two League districts in as many years took its toil on Mrs Ayles's health; she was found to have heart trouble and forbidden to carry out any more League work for the foreseeable future.

Map 2 shows the branches formed in the Lancashire and Cheshire area and gives some idea of the extent of Mrs Ayles's work. After the Middleton/MacDonald period the district continued to be active. Ada Nield Chew, socialist campaigner and speaker, became secretary of the Rochdale branch in 1912. Ellen Wilkinson, later infamous as 'Red Ellen', the Jarrow Member of Parliament, in 1913 became secretary of the year-old Tyldesley branch. Colne (Alice Burrell) and Leigh (Mrs E. Mottram) branches were formed in 1912. In 1913 Harriet Beanland, suffragist, was secretary of Nelson branch for a year until it dissolved. Eccles branch was formed in

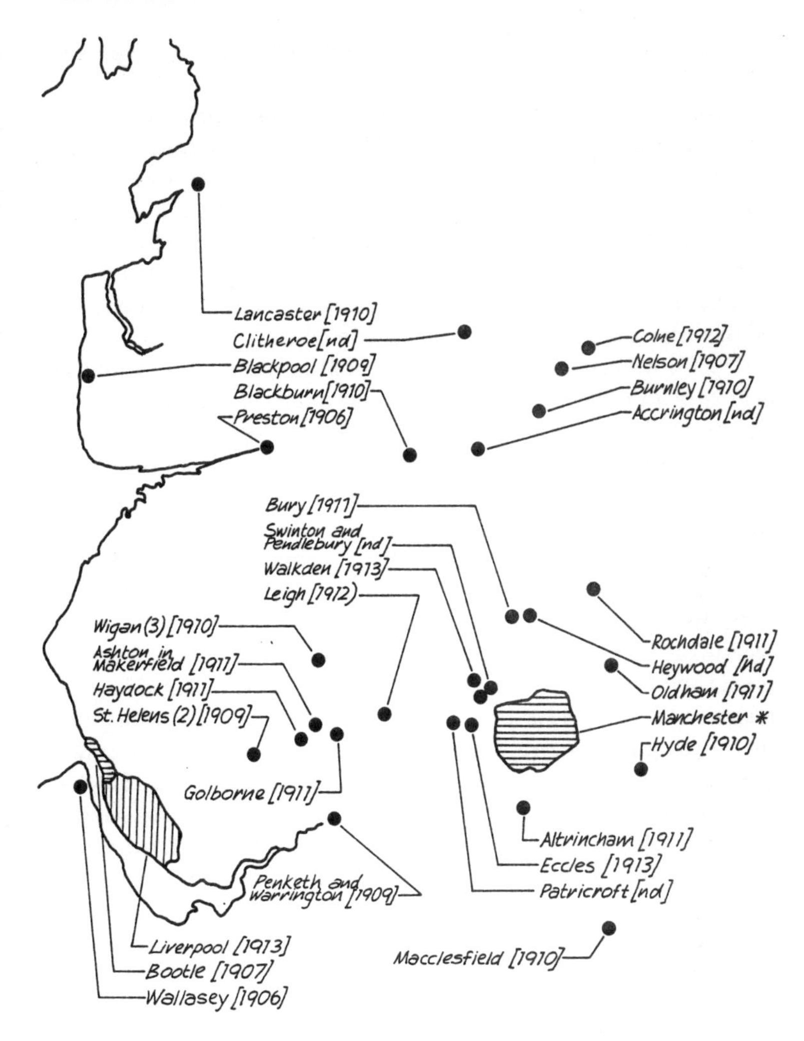

Map 2 Women's Labour League branches in the Lancashire and Cheshire district, showing date of formation
Note Branches in Manchester and environs:
Manchester Middleton [1908]. Gorton [1910]. Manchester Central [1909]. Ardwick [1911]. Manchester North [1910]. Tyldesley [1912]. Manchester East [1910]. Broughton [1917]. Manchester North-East [1910].
Source Women's Labour League Secretarial Correspondence and Related Papers; Women's Labour League *Conference Reports*; League Leaflet (Labour Party Headquarters Archives, London).

1913 and St Helens's two branches merged and then separated again.

A major city in the Lancashire and Cheshire area, Manchester had five branches. Margaret MacDonald's initial idea was that Annot Robinson should confine her organising to the town. Annot was committed to socialism and to women's suffrage. She came from Dundee, where she had worked for the Independent Labour Party. She was a graduate of St Andrews University (Lady Literate in Arts, an external degree). On arrival in Manchester, then Annot Wilkie, she was admitted to Central Manchester ILP branch (June 1907).[30] She befriended Hannah Mitchell and Ellen Wilkinson; she is next mentioned in the ILP branch minutes as the bride of Sam Robinson, the propaganda secretary (December 1907). They quickly had two babies; the second was born in 1911 when Annot was thirty-seven years old and was given a 'socialist christening': 'Baptismal rites and the usual formula were entirely dispensed with'; Keir Hardie came to the ceremony to sponsor the child and pinned the badges of the ILP and Women's Labour League to its clothes.

Annot had not attended Independent Labour Party branch meetings before her marriage, but was very active in the Women's Social and Political Union. Mrs Pankhurst and Christabel had just resigned from her ILP branch as Annot joined. In February 1908 there was a demonstration organised by the WSPU in London; Annot attended and was arrested. Manchester Central ILP sent both Annot and Christabel, also imprisoned, messages of support and sympathy. This gesture of solidarity possibly healed the breach between the ILP and WSPU locally; certainly on her release from prison, Annot became a regular attendee at the ILP meetings.

Manchester Middleton Women's Labour League had been formed in 1908. Manchester Central, however ignored League approaches until 1909. Meanwhile, the ILP branch needed recruits and Annot suggested several methods of attracting members, among them lecture tours and afternoon meetings, which women could have attended. Whether Annot attended the Manchester Central League branch is not known. However, having reconciled her suffragism and socialism locally, she was open to approaches from the League and gave hospitality to Dorothy Lenn. Annot sent Margaret MacDonald a photograph of her first baby and Margaret responded in a 1910 New Year's greeting by asking her to organise for the League.

Annot was concerned about Dorothy Lenn's position. Margaret replied: 'we shall do more wisely if we have some part-time district organisers . . . as we have been doing with Mrs Simm'. A certain ruthlessness in Margaret's character was again revealed: 'Miss Lenn will be able to get work quite easily I think'; 'Don't feel you are ousting Miss Lenn. We needed her until the Election as we wanted to be able to send to every place which had a candidate and we did.' Annot was offered the same terms as Lisbeth Simm: payment for meetings and travelling expenses. As this usually amounted to £2 each month, Margaret suggested that Annot should carry out an appropriate amount of work.

The period of Annot's League work was as brief as Mrs Ayles's but not as productive. Mrs Ayles's work in the Lancashire and Cheshire area illustrates that Annot never developed branches beyond Manchester. She was possibly responsible for the formation in 1910 of the Manchester East, North and North-East branches. There was a Manchester district conference in July 1911, but by then Margaret Bondfield was organising in the area and reformed the Manchester Central League branch which had become defunct.

Annot's time was, of course, in demand to raise her two children. The marriage to Sam was not a success. From a respected Independent Labour Party member, given a testimonial by his branch in 1906, Sam became alcoholic and, when in drink, beat the children. Annot was very reserved about her personal life, but wrote to her sister in 1916 about her 'great emotional disappointment and disillusionment'; 'anything human or kind or civilised in him drink has destroyed'; this may have paralysed her political activity. Politics might just as easily have been the reason for her lack of enthusiasm. The *modus vivendi* achieved locally between suffrage and socialism was less easy to manage at national level. Annot's correspondence reveals some ambivalence about militant suffrage tactics; Dorothy Lenn recorded that 'she seems to have got out of sympathy with the WSPU, but not with the principles of the suffrage movement'; Annot remained a supporter of women's immediate, limited enfranchisement. At the 1911 League conference this argument was lost to the adult suffragists. In that year Annot took up full-time organising for the National Union of Women's Suffrage Societies. She was proud of having always earned her keep and providing for the children; possibly she had need of a full-time wage. Certainly she remained in correspondence with the League during the First World War. Ellen Wilkinson's obituary (*The Women's Leader*, 6 November 1925) shed some illumination: 'proud and reserved as she was in all that pertained to her not very happy personal life . . . she had an exquisite sense of the ridiculous and a sharp tongue that was not infrequently used at the expense of powerful people whom she might perhaps have been wiser to conciliate'.

Some League members in London were possibly amongst the 'powerful people'. Prominence within a London branch meant lobbying at Westminster, meeting the women at the forefront of other Labour movement organisations, acquaintance with the Fabians and the Social Democratic Federationers. Independent Labour Party strength lay more in the provinces, so the ILP flavour to the League was less pronounced in the capital. The Central London League branch had 150 members and worked to return women to Boards of Guardians and Borough Councils. Ada Salter was the first to be returned to a Borough Council (Bermondsey) when women were allowed to stand (1909). There were no paid organisers in London; there were not the distances to travel, nor the women in isolated rural villages to seek out. London was the last area to form itself into a district in Margaret MacDonald's and Mary Middleton's time. The twenty-three London branches organised their first district conference in November 1910. Eleven branches were represented. Discussions began with an exposition of the Osborne Judgement and the difficulties of the Labour Party operating without finance from the political levy. School meals were also debated. Ethel Bentham attended her first League conference as a Fabian delegate. Mrs Pember-Reeves, whose book (*Round About a Pound a Week*, 1914) set out the Fabian women's investigation into living conditions, was the delegate from North Kensington.

At the close of the MacDonald/Middleton period a more systematic and coherent structure had been achieved for the League. There were the three provincial organisers, four districts holding regular conferences and the executive presence in London. Branches were finding their niche in the local Labour movement throughout the country. A system of live and let live had been established at national level with the women's suffrage movement, women's trade unions and socialist party women's sections. The annual conference, in concert with the Labour Party, illustrated that the League had been accepted by 'the Men's Party', yet branches were keenly exploiting their free-lance role. Within the complexities of the Labour movement, women's tradition of separate organisation had established itself, adapting itself to the demands of the parliamentary road whilst not reneging on its forebears' concerns. A type of constitutional socialist feminism could be acted out and thought out in a context alien to neither the turn-of-the century women's movement, nor the quest for working people's democracy. Combining the thrust of both movements into a new philosophy was an attractive challenge which won the League substantial support. Then both Mary Middleton and Margaret MacDonald died in 1911. Mary Middleton had fought bravely against cancer since 1909. Margaret MacDonald's death was thought to be due to poisoning, inexplicable to the medical practice of her time. The greatest epitaph to these women was the survival of the League that they had managed in its free-lance role.

Notes

1 *J.R. MacDonald and M.E. MacDonald papers*, PRO 30/69, (Public Records Office, London), 1375.

2 *MacDonald papers*, PRO 30/69/1376.

3 *MacDonald papers*, PRO 30/69/1373.

4 Sylvia E. Pankhurst, *The Suffragette Movement: An Intimate Account of Persons and Ideals* (London, 1931), cited, p. 181.

5 See C. Collette, 'Socialism and scandal in 1900', *History Workshop Journal*, 23, spring 1987.

6 *Women's Labour League Secretarial Correspondence and Related Papers* (Labour Party Headquarters Archives, London), cited, WLL/30.

7 *League Correspondence*, Lisbeth Simm's letters to Mary Middleton, WLL/81.

8 *League Correspondence*, WLL/3.

9 Manchester Central Independent Labour Party *Minutes* M4211, 1906–1909 (Manchester Central Library).

10 *MacDonald Papers*, 1376, 14.5.1909.

11 *League Correspondence*, Lisbeth Simm's letters, WLL/90.

12 *MacDonald Papers*, 1375, 7.4.1908.

13 *MacDonald Papers*, 1379, n.d. Margaret Llewellyn Davies's and Mrs Bellamy's letters 1373, 20.7.1906, Mrs Gasson's letter.

14 *League Correspondence*, WLL/44, 39, 35, 47.

15 *League Correspondence*, Lisbeth Simm's letters, WLL/135.

16 *The Gertrude Tuckwell Collection 1880–1920*, 353/2–10 (Trades Union Congress Library, London).

17 Lily Gair Wilkinson, 'Women's freedom' in S. Fleming (ed.), *Women in Rebellion*, Square One Pamphlets, no. 6 (Independent Labour Party, 1973).

18 *MacDonald Papers*, PRO 30/69/1376.
19 *League Correspondence*, WLL/89.
20 Manchester Central Independent Labour Party *Minutes*.
21 *MacDonald Papers*, PRO 30/69/1378, Mrs Pethwick-Lawrence's letter, 19.7.1911.
22 *MacDonald Papers*, PRO 30/69/1378, letter about Preston branch, 29.10.1906.
23 *League Correspondence*, Lisbeth Simm's letters, WLL/83.
24 *Annot Robinson Papers* (the property of Mrs H. Wilson, Altrincham), MISC 718 (Manchester Central Library), 28.
25 *MacDonald Papers*, 1373, letter from Lisbeth Simm and *Annot Robinson Papers*, MISC 718/29.
26 *MacDonald Papers*, 1376, letter from M. T. Simm.
27 *MacDonald Papers*, 1376, Dorothy Lenn's reports.
28 *Annot Robinson Papers*, MISC 718/29.
29 *MacDonald Papers*, 1378, Katharine Bruce Glasier's letters.
30 See Manchester Central Independent Labour Party *Minutes* and *Annot Robinson Papers*, MISC 718/32, 33, 81, 94, 98.

3
Activity

'All learn together and none need feel afraid' – Dorothy Lenn, League organiser, 1908

The effect on grass-roots organising of Margaret MacDonald's and Mary Middleton's style of leadership was important in that branches were left much to their own devices. Activity was the result of decisions taken by women locally about how to spend their time. Their choices and priorities reflect for us what concerned ordinary women, their estimation of their own capacity and their place within the Labour community. In Lisbeth Simm's 'corner' there was, indeed, consistent support, replicated to an extent in other districts, but branches generally operated independently. It is remarkable that the pattern of their work varied so little, being devoted to electioneering on their own behalf and on behalf of the Labour Party, campaigning, entertaining to raise the necessary funds, the whole underwritten by a commitment to an educative programme that increased their capacity to contribute.

The first six months' activity of branches as far apart as Leeds, Leicester and Wood Green (London) gave an indication of how this pattern was set. Leeds branch began in June 1906, Margaret MacDonald having spoken at its inaugural meeting. There were fifty members, a monthly general meeting and a fortnightly executive committee meeting. By December 1906 Leeds branch had 'lost' twenty-four of its original members, but gained a fresh twenty-one.[1] It had affiliated to the local Labour Representation Committee and sent two delegates to LRC meetings, confirming its place in the Labour community two years before national recognition was granted to the League. Leeds women had helped in the municipal elections and, having learnt about running a candidacy, the secretary herself was to stand for the Board of Guardians. The branch was to raise £5 0*s* 0*d* for this event and planned a fund-raising concert and social. Recently, local children had been given a tea on behalf of the area's trade unionists. In the summer £6 9*s* 0*d* had been raised to entertain 400 children.

Leicester was Margaret MacDonald's home town (adopted because it was Ramsay MacDonald's constituency). With Mary Middleton, Margaret spoke at the League's inaugural meeting on 1 May 1906, after which there was a social and dinner for 300 people, a grander affair than at Leeds. There were nearly seventy members, but a similar turnover to Leeds meant that there had been three secretaries by the end of the year. Leicester women started with a big success, campaigning outdoors in the Board of Guardians elections, standing on chairs and using a lamp to attract a crowd: they had distributed 4,000 leaflets on *Women as Guardians of the Poor*. The Labour Party ran sixteen candidates in this election, fifteen of whom were successful.

Wood Green was a more modest branch. It was formed in October 1906 after a meeting addressed by Mary Middleton. There were only a few members and they decided to meet monthly, in their own homes because they could not afford to hire a hall, alternating afternoon and evening meetings for the convenience of several members with young children. They supported two Labour candidates in the urban council elections, speaking at meetings; these candidates were not successful. For all three branches, working at elections was the first activity and established their contact with the Labour movement locally.

Election work had been urged upon branches at the League's first conference. League women stood as candidates wherever elections were open to them; at district and parish councils and at the Poor Law Boards of Guardians. The Guardians were local bodies funded mainly through the rates, although there was some attempt at area pooling of resources and some central government provision. In many urban areas private bodies were also active in schemes for poor relief and these had been, in some cases, managed by the Charity Organisation Society. This had pioneered casework with its clients, the obverse side of the face of progress being that the COS still believed poverty to be the result of individual failure.

A Royal Commission had been set up in 1905 to study the Poor Law. the Poor Law Amendment Act of 1834 was still in force; its philosophy was that the recipient of poor relief should be in a worse condition than anyone who could provide for her or himself, and that any relief given outside the workhouse should therefore be kept to a minimum: the 'less eligibility' and 'workhouse' tests. The social surveys of the late nineteenth and early twentieth centuries had illustrated, and the progressive spirit believed, that poverty was due to environment and social conditions rather than individual indolence and degeneracy. Rowntrees' survey of York, in particular, illustrated the poverty cycle; a child born in poverty would achieve relative comfort when first at work without dependants, would be impoverished by low wages coupled with growing responsibilities and thus be unable to save for an old age of miserable dependancy. Measures were growing up outside the poor law system to deal with specific causes of poverty, for instance the old age pensions introduced in 1908.

Nevertheless, the Royal Commission on the Poor Law did not report until 1909, delayed largely by Beatrice Webb's initial insistence on the detailed interviewing that befitted an investigation conducted by such an experienced Fabian. Majority and minority reports were produced, which agreed that the Boards of Guardians should be abolished and there should be better co-ordination of public and private resources, with greater attempts to categorise poor people and provide more specific relief. The argument between the minority (the Webbs and George Lansbury), who wanted the complete abolition of the Poor Law system, and the majority, which would have retained some such comprehensive approach, detracted from the impact of the Report and no measures to amend the Poor Law were introduced. The President of the Poor Law Division of the Local Government Board remained wedded to the principles of 1834 and many local Boards reflected his philosophy. Receiving relief was still a real stigma, naming the recipient 'pauper' and as such, disenfranchised. This, of course, meant that nobody receiving relief could vote in the Guardians' elections.

We do not know the overall total elected to Boards of Guardians. Sister Kerrison had been serving in West Ham since 1897. Mrs Cawthorne, secretary of the Hull branch, was the first to stand as a League candidate in 1906. Hull Trades Council chose her as candidate, donated £5 to her expenses and promised active support. Mrs Cawthorne intended to canvass every household and asked Margaret MacDonald to speak on her behalf: her agent wrote that it would not be possible to pay Margaret's expenses as 'we are only workmen's wives and our incomes are taxed severely for our movement'.[2] Despite strong opposition, Mrs Cawthorne was elected at her first attempt. Lisbeth Simm was elected to the Gosforth Board in 1908; she perceived her election as a 'woman's fight', believing that women could contribute to understanding the poverty which the Guardians had to address. Mrs Gibbin of Benwell branch came top of the poll at her first attempt in 1911 and wrote in *Labour Leader* (3 March 1911) that women should stand as candidates because the Guardians dealt so largely with women and children, the sick and the aged. There had been flooding in Benwell pit and many men had lost work; some had lost their lives. Mrs Gibbin campaigned for out relief to widows, as going into their workhouse added to their misery and prolonged their poverty. The League conference report for 1912 recorded nineteen members elected as Guardians; by 1913 the number had risen to twenty-eight.

Calling on women to act politically according to their traditional gender roles was integral to the Middleton/MacDonald philosophy of gender, and this belief in the value of women's experience was explicitly stated in the *League Leaflet* on Guardians' work (no. 6): 'All sorts of questions arise which a woman knows more about, or can tackle better than a man.' An example was given: 'there are the children, thousands . . . have no other parents than the state, . . . others . . . have to be protected against their own parents. These children want *Mothering*' (original emphasis).

The League believed the skills demanded of a Guardian were particularly applicable to women who managed a household budget. Women who were used to distributing inadequate resources in a caring way, for the good of the whole family, could bring these skills to bear in community work: 'The work of the Poor Law Guardians is like housekeeping for a very big and very difficult family', stated the leaflet; 'we want women's help to run this publicly managed household, just as much as to arrange for their own homes'. Seeing the public economy as an extension of that of the household was another typical strand of Middleton/MacDonald philosophy. Economically, it is probably not a valid metaphor; the possibility of raising loans or receiving grants is alien to the way most households are resourced and the public authority has far more freedom in fixing expenditure. The League, however, was not the last body to use such a simplistic description. It was useful in making the Boards seem accessible to women interested in standing.

The conscious emphasis on women's contribution and skills may have distinguished League women from socialists already serving on the Boards. Alternately, it may have acted as a base for gender solidarity and provided a means of approach to the benevolence of women Liberal and Conservative Guardians. However, many Boards had been male preserves and the particular importance of the League was to provide the organisational and imaginative support that gave women the courage to stand in such areas. Lisbeth, for instance, felt her campaign aroused a new interest in public affairs amongst the working women of the district. As a woman candidate, she also experienced antagonism: 'I was solemnly charged to "stay at home and take care of my husband". Again and again I was told to "realise what a dreadful thing it was for one woman to go and sit there amongst so many men"', reported Lisbeth in the *Northern Democrat* (May 1908). She thanked not only the women who had worked in the campaign, but those whom prejudice had prevented from contributing. Once elected, Lisbeth indeed found that attending the meetings was rather 'a dreadful thing': 'Ours is a "truly rural" Board. A drowsy atmosphere pervades the room, and except for the monotony of the chairman's voice, and an occasional "Agreed" from a few members, we might as well be in Church . . . When all is said and done, the Poor Law is a hopeless machine.' Lisbeth felt the need for a supportive voice at the meetings: 'Our next work must be to continue in preparation and education, for one woman among a crowd of over sixty men sorely needs a companion.' League women's politics, of course, differed from those of non-socialist women Guardians and rather diluted the idea of comparison with the household economy. The League supported the Labour Party's campaign to entirely abolish the whole of the Poor Law System. *League Leaflet* no. 6 made this clear:

Women are working with the Labour Party in order to secure for the disinherited some of those advantages in society to which their labours for the community fully entitle them, and to hasten the day when there will be no more poor in the present sense of the word. There will always be people who need sympathy and help, but there need not always be men and women who toil all the best days of their life, and have nothing for themselves in their old age – widows who have to neglect their children in order to earn a crust of bread for them – children who are starved with cold and hunger.

This was gradualist socialism. The eventual aim was to eliminate poverty; meanwhile, reforms would achieve some benefit for working people. This benefit was their right, not charity, and would entail some redistribution of wealth. Disaffection from the Poor Law was so strong that co-operation, even to win reform, could seem inappropriate. Women had, sometimes, to be persuaded into standing for the Boards (*Labour Leader,* 3 March 1911).

In order to have any hope of its candidates being returned, the League needed to devote a substantial amount of time to making sure working men registered as voters. Apart from the delay in registration caused by the year's residence requirement for non-property owners, there was an inevitable time-lag in drawing up the register after the qualifying period, so that, in practice, those who rented a home might not be able to vote for two years after moving into an area. The contemporary work force being mobile, men might then move before they could use their vote. It was obviously necessary for any group trying for change through constitutional means, Labour or suffrage, to ensure that the people they relied on for support were registered as soon as possible. Work on the electoral register was vital for League women, whatever their views on the respective priorities of women's enfranchisement or returning Labour candidates. Many branches reported that registration work was a large part of their activities; Annie Peters from Barrow was one of the first to report success, in the 1907 municipal elections, after a prolonged period of registration work.

Some of the women who joined the League at its inception were already parish or district councillors: women were eligible to be elected to these from their creation in 1894. Isabella Ford, for instance, was a parish councillor at Adel and Mrs Pease was returned to Godstone Rural District Council in 1914. From 1907 women could be elected to County and Borough Councils in England and Scotland (from 1911 this applied also to Ireland). Sister Kerrison was returned to West Ham Borough Council and Ada Salter to Bermondsey. Marion Phillips and Ethel Bentham were elected to Kensington Borough Council. In Scotland, Clarice

McNab was elected to Leith District Council. Mrs Pease was later returned to Surrey County Council and Ellen Wilkinson to Manchester City Council. Katharine Bruce Glasier wrote to Margaret MacDonald in 1908 that Lancashire District Council elections 'nearly killed me'.[3] Experienced League women such as Katharine were much in demand as speakers at local government elections, but seem to have been selected as candidates less often than for the Boards of Guardians: Labour movement men seem to have shared Lisbeth Simm's perception of the latter as a 'woman's fight'.

Woolwich Labour Representation Committee ran Margaret Bondfield as a candidate for the Borough Council in 1909 and 1911. On the former occasion they had their doubts: 'I can foresee possible objections', wrote the secretary: 'the question is sure to be raised whether Miss Bondfield's health would stand the strain of the whistling sort of election we shall have to put up here. It will be a wicked fight'.[4] There was also the problem of financing her campaign: this must have affected other potential women candidates who were not backed by a trade union. Woolwich LRC decided to commit itself to financing Margaret Bondfield: 'personally I think Miss Bondfield is just the kind of candidate who would call out our best and also strike the imagination of the workers'.

The League would, on occasion, support women candidates who could finance themselves, provided they did not stand against a Labour man. Margaret MacDonald had to explain this position to the Leicester branch.[5] Catherine Gittings stood for Wiggeston Council after the Labour Party had decided not to run a candidate; she had a non-party campaign committee, but as she stated she was a Socialist and would demand local authority provision of free school dinners, Margaret MacDonald had agreed to speak on her behalf. Then Miss Carryer, a radical woman but not a Socialist, decided to contest a ward in Leicester against a Labour man; Margaret decided she could not speak for Miss Gittings without appearing to support Miss Carryer; nor did she want to denounce Miss Carryer; she therefore decided it was best not to speak at all.

League women helped Labour men in elections, including parliamentary elections, from which women were excluded. There was debate about how much priority women should give to this election work, as we saw in Chapter 2. It was policy not to assist in elections where the Labour Party man was opposed to women's suffrage. Unless the candidate proved obdurate in this respect, the League stood to draw benefits from its participation in the campaign. The platform of Labour candidates varied and was open to local influence; the issues to which some candidates gave priority were dear to the hearts of League women. People were more likely to give time to political discussion during an election and League women could be more sure of an audience when involved in an event which focused local political attention.

An example was Pete Curran's candidature on behalf of the Labour Party in the 1907 Jarrow by-election.[6] The issue to which he gave priority was old age pensions, then promoted by Lloyd George, the progressive Liberal Minister at the Board of Trade, and beginning to be more favourably discussed by other Ministers within the Liberal Government. Pete Curran's victory and the socialist victory in Colne Valley the same year, after a campaign in which pensions had again figured prominently, are generally acknowledged to be stimulants contributing to the enactment of the Old Age Pensions Act in 1908. This was a limited measure, granting small, weekly pensions to people from the age of seventy but, nevertheless, saved some from the workhouse and struck a blow against the Poor Law. Jarrow Women's Labour League came into being as Labour women worked together in the campaign and was formally opened immediately thereafter. Jarrow branch could therefore congratulate itself on an extremely successful beginning.

Pete Curran was an Irish working man, secretary of the Gas Workers' Union. He had lost the 1906 election at Jarrow to Charles Mark Palmer, a Liberal and representative of the large shipbuilding firm which had provided Jarrow with local councillors and parliamentary representatives for half a century (Ellen Wilkinson was to call Jarrow in this time 'Palmerstown'). Charles Palmer's death had now caused a by-election. With funds from his union and from the Labour Party Pete Curran was relatively well provided for to be a Labour candidate, but could not hope to match his rivals' resources. Nineteenth-century legislation had outlawed corrupt practices, such as treating voters, and introduced the secret ballot; however, treating could take the form of perfectly legal traditional Christmas gifts and other displays of patronage. The absence of a Palmer candidate perhaps diminished the force of loyalty won in such a way. Jarrow was a labour-intensive town (shipbuilding, engineering, collieries) and every possible help was needed to reach the voters. When the publicity media consisted of written material and word of mouth, it was up to the candidate to reinforce it with leaflets advertising meetings and setting out his opinions and to have these delivered. Pavements had to be chalked and posters displayed. Canvassers were needed to persist in seeing the voters in households often in multi-occupation.

There were two aspects to Pete Curran's campaign; many leaflets and small handbills and frequent public meetings. The handbills were brightly coloured, with succinct messages and smaller than a postcard. They illustrated Pete's international connections, his position in the Labour movement and the necessity for returning working men to parliament. For instance, 'Hands Across the Sea' announced 'Pete's friend from the other side of the earth' (Australia); 'A Word from Dublin' announced support from the Dublin Trades and Labour Council, his Irish connections; 'From the Workhouse to Westminster', the story of Labour Member of Parliament and campaign speaker Will Crooks. Pete Curran seems to have favoured colonial preference, then promoted by Joseph Chamberlain (a Conservative) rather than the more usual Labour platform of free trade, as his Australian friend was to speak on this subject. Most of the handbills were publicising a meeting for the evening they were issued, indicating the necessity for frequent distribution and several advertised 'A Man Wanted – there's a place for you at tonight's meeting'. There were sometimes three or four meetings in one evening; Margaret MacDonald spoke at one. Pete's success, against a Conservative, a Liberal and an Irish home rule candidate, marked the end of an era in Jarrow as it heralded the start of a new age of state welfare provision.

The table at Appendix 2 shows the League branches in whose constituency the Labour Party stood a candidate for parliament. In 1910 there were two parliamentary elections. According to a *South West Daily News* report of the 1910 conference, the League executive had decided to try to form a branch in every constituency where there was a Labour Party candidate. Of the eighty-six League branches active in 1910, twenty-eight were in such constituencies. In fifteen of these a Labour man was returned in either the January or December 1910 election, a forty per cent success rate in constituencies where the Labour candidate was supported by an active League branch. After the Labour Party's 1912 commitment to women's enfranchisement it was presumably easier for a League branch to give unqualified support to a Labour candidate; however, League efficacy is somewhat obscured by the Election Fighting Fund campaign, which targeted candidates to constituencies where there was not necessarily an active League branch. In all, the Labour Party fought fifty-six seats at a time when a League branch is known to have been active and won twenty-six of these. The 1916 Labour Party *Annual Report* records that in ninety-five constituencies there was a local Labour organisation, but no League branch, eighteen of which had a Labour Member of Parliament and fifteen a Labour candidate; eighty-four constituencies with League branches, seventeen of which had a Labour member and sixteen a candidate. There thus seems no conclusive evidence of the benefit of League electoral assistance. The Labour Party, however, certainly valued their contribution and acknowledged it annually at conference.

Elections were, of course, occasional events. Outside them, the League campaigned continuously to involve women in political life and to ensure that public amenities made provision for women. Although they obviously benefited from information gathered by the executive and disseminated in the *League Leaflets,* such campaigns were run by branches on local issues and merely reported afterwards to the leadership. Taking on a public role within one's own community was no light decision. One branch found, by the seats from which they usually listened to the local council debates, a bath and bucket left as an object lesson on the sins of omitted home duties: 'it will take more than bucket, or bath, or man that put them there to keep us away from those monthly council meetings if we are determined to go there'.[7]

One of the ways to interest women who might find it impossible or uncongenial to attend a public meeting was a house-to-house canvass, issuing leaflets and talking to those who would listen. Margaret Bondfield described in *Labour Leader* (21 July 1911) one of these canvasses conducted by Birmingham branch on the National Insurance Bill's inadequate provision for women's sickness and unemployment benefits: 'At 11 a.m. a few members who had risen early and finished their housework and I started to canvass. The shyness soon wore off, and each took a separate section of the streets. Reinforcements arrived in the afternoon. We visited a number of small courts. Oh! the lonely lives of these women, hidden away at the back of a network of small mean streets!.'

Birmingham branch was an example of local determination. One of its first efforts was to gain reforms at Aston Manor baths, swimming baths in a working district where the accommodation for women was scanty. The branch wrote to councillors on the baths committee and sent in resolutions about price reductions and time alterations; they wrote to the local press and won support. The admission price was reduced to 3*d* from 6*d* per hour and one night per week was set aside for women, instead of the Saturday morning previously reserved.[8]

Another example of a local campaign was Glasgow branch's long-running attempt to obtain from the local authority work for unemployed women.[9] This was yet another attack on the Poor Law. Local authorities were able to give relief to able-bodied people in the form of paid work, instead of consigning them via the Guardians to the workhouse. Such municipal schemes as existed, however, were usually of the road-building or digging variety inapplicable to women. On the other hand, the seasonal nature of many of the trades that employed women meant that they were particularly suited to temporary local authority relief work.

In 1909 Glasgow League women lobbied the Lord Provost to demand practical training for unemployed women in domestic work and hygiene and elementary sick nursing. They asked for provision of a Distress Committee workroom. Their case was remitted to a special committee of the Corporation (the Unemployed Workmen's Committee). The Distress Committee ran a labour colony where unemployed men could work on the land and were given basic accommodation and a small wage. It is interesting that in 1909 Mrs Joseph Fells served on the League executive: Joseph Fells had financed a labour colony for London unemployed men. Near Glasgow there were 800 acres on the heights of the moor, land previously not used for farming, where up to 700 men had found employment, thereby avoiding the workhouse. The League visited the colony and thought that women also should be employed, in market-gardening, vegetable-growing and poultry-keeping, and lobbied the Distress Committee to that effect in 1911. At their meeting with the committee, League women drew attention to the estimated 17,000 prostitutes in Glasgow and suggested that the dire need for work could be met by providing needlework and work on the colony. The committee men withdrew to consider and on their return announced that the Unemployed Workmen's Committee would resume meeting and obtain information and statistics 'from the ladies'.

A method of campaigning which Margaret MacDonald wanted to pursue just before her death was holding large demonstrations, the executive committee taking the financial risk and the branch doing the work.[10] This indicates some respect for branch initiative and ability. Such a demonstration had been held in Lees Hall, Leeds, on low wages and national insurance provision for women. Branch members wrote to volunteer for such duties as pavement-chalking and bill distribution at the factory gates. Margaret MacDonald's death seems to have ended this experiment.

Local campaigning and electioneering had to be financed locally. The chosen method was holding teas and social events and organising sales of work. While continually calling on the same people to contribute, these occasions did have an advantage over a fixed fee, in that the wealthier members could be gently pressured to pay more. They also fulfilled several other functions. The labour movement tended to be a world somewhat apart, given to concentrated, serious work; it was a world that benefited from and was to some extent held together by social bonds. The 'new life' ethos that had permeated socialism was based on social experiment within a community. There was joy in Labour's vision of the future, where poverty ceased, and this was celebrated by sharing present enjoyments. Song and dance evenings and drawing-room receptions were a regular feature of Labour movement gatherings. Events held by the League also reached out to women who had previously been wary of joining. Entertainments helped the League to publicise its concerns within the community. By taking children out and giving teas, the League could express, simply, its condemnation of childhood poverty.

Leicester branch reported: 'Socials help to keep us together and bring in new people.' Jarrow's 'first great undertaking' was a tea in celebration of Pete Curran's victory 'with a whist drive for the funds and songs from the labour choir'. In 1911 Bishop Auckland's 'first public effort' was a tea-party and address on children's rights, after which Miss Todd recited Tennyson's 'Lady Claire'. The Central London branch organised a social evening to welcome Margaret and Ramsay MacDonald back from India in 1907, limiting the speeches to these two so as to allow plenty of time for recreation.[11] The professional singer Gretta Park, a League member, gave recitals at some of the more ambitious events. Tongue in cheek, G. Hancock of Shildon captured the flavour of these events in a report on a Shildon Independent Labour Party and League social for the *Northern Democrat* (May 1911):

> . . . songs were rendered by Comrades T. White, G. Corry and Mrs. Hall. Also poems from Burns were recited . . . which contributed largely to the success of the evening's proceedings. Refreshments were then served, after which a lottery quartette competition was held, and then the very sympathetic rendering of the test piece, 'Where is my wandering boy tonight' by the Myers, Smith, Bucks and Corner Quartette held the audience spellbound, and strong men were almost moved to tears. After this unquestionable treat the room was cleared for games and dancing, which concluded our first social in the district.

Some of the wealthier League women enjoyed the hostess role and, more dangerously, accepted the enjoyment of patronage. There were two main areas where one might reasonably feel uncomfortable about League teas and socials; class oppression and gender oppression. The poorer League women may have been subordinated by those who could provide the jumble or work material or bread and butter; the League as a whole may have been relegated to the kitchen while the Labour men took care of the politics. Contemporaries did express doubts. Before the Keir Hardie meeting in Newcastle in 1910, local Labour women had prepared refreshments; Lisbeth Simm feared 'many of them were tired out when the meeting time came' (*Northern Democrat,* June 1910). In the previous month Lisbeth had reported her disturbance at finding 'earnest and devoted' women of Newcastle Independent Labour Party working to finance labour activities by sewing useful and fancy goods:

> It may be that in their ignorance and apathy the men of our movement are countenancing sweating. I have been in other ILP rooms in the district, where the women are sewing to raise funds for the branches, and I have heard most kindly and appreciative references to their work from the men, but I am bound as an onlooker to say that the majority of the men fail to understand the magnitude of the work these women are doing.

Lisbeth summed up her discomfort: 'How can the men continue to receive this money and labour and then still rest content with the women practically outside the movement?'

Nevertheless, when a League branch organised its own entertainments, they were not the residual tasks of a group whose male

Fig. 6 Boldon Colliery Women's Labour League social
Source Labour Party library

Programme of Music.

1. "Meditation" ... *Bach Gounod*
2. "Down South" ... ... *Myddleton*
3. "Anne Boleyn" ... ... *Tolhurst*
4. "Tarantella" ... ... *Diemer*
5. "Memories" ... ... *Taylor*
6. "Petit Duo" ... ... *Tours*
7. "Water Music" ... ... *Handel*
8. "Marche Turque" ... *Beethoven*
9. "Salut d'Amour" ... ...*Elgar*
10. "L'extase" ... ... *Thome*
11. "Canzonetta" ... ...*Ames*
12. "Ziegeunerisch" ... *Sochting*
13. "Marionettes" ... ... *Gurlitt*
14. "Hammock Song" ... *Dunhill*
15. "Serenade" ... ... *Widor*
16. "Serenade" ... ... *Taylor*
17. "Maritana" ... ... *Wallace*
18. "Petite Suite" ... ... *St. George*
19. "Baby's Sweetheart" ...*Corri*
20. "Gipsy Suite" ... ... *German*
21. "Dernier Sommeil" ... *Massenet*

Programme of Songs, &c.

QUARTETTE "Earth was made for Man's Delight" (From "Haddon Hall") *Sullivan*
Miss Allie Booth, Miss Gretta Park, Mr. Arthur Tomlinson and Mr. Frank Plowright.

SONGS · (*a*) "Big Lady Moon" *Coleridge Taylor*
(*b*) "Bonny Blue Kerchief" *Barnicott*
Miss Allie Booth, A.T.C.L. (Silver Medallist).

DUET · "The Gendarmes' Duet" *Offenbach*
Mr. Arthur Tomlinson and Mr. Frank Plowright.

SONGS (*a*) "Little Grey Home in the West" *Lohr*
(*b*) "I Hear You Calling Me" · ·
Mr. Arthur Tomlinson.

DUET · "It was a Lover and his Lass" *Walthew*
Miss Gretta Park and Mr. Frank Plowright.

SONG · · "Chorus, Gentlemen" · · *Lohr*
Mr. Frank Plowright.

DUET · · "Snowdrops" *Liza Lehmann*
Miss Allie Booth and Mr. Arthur Tomlinson.

QUARTETTE · "Sweet and Low" · · *Barnby*
Miss Allie Booth, Miss Gretta Park, Mr. Arthur Tomlinson and Mr. Frank Plowright.

At the Piano · · Miss Jessie Thomson.

Fig. 7 1913 Annual Conference of the League and Labour Party: delegates' reception
Source Labour Party library

members were engaged elsewhere, but a shared part of the total work-load organised by the women of a branch. Mary Macpherson organised a sale of work at her home as an adjunct, not an alternative to her editorial and translation work; Margaret MacDonald a garden-party as an accompaniment to her statistical surveys. Lisbeth was able, on one occasion, to write triumphantly to Margaret: 'You should have seen all the women trooping in and the men in the ante-room preparing for a public tea.'[12]

All branch work, however localised, of whatever variety, was informed by the great League emphasis on education, which went some way to counteract the dangers of subordination to the 'Men's Party'. Education was also the main way that the executive exercised direction and control over branches, suggesting topics, providing information. League leadership in this respect was more akin to nurturing than to regulating. It was the education programme that gave coherence to the League and made more distinct its brand of socialist feminism.

League women learnt together, in a supportive group which allowed both individual experiment and collective achievement. Dorothy Lenn likened the League to a shell, where women 'laugh at one another's mistakes, help one another along – all learn together and none need feel afraid'.[13] She reflected the traditional attitude to women's separate political organisation; that it would be more congenial, less threatening, enabling women to overcome diffidence. The aim was not only to become familiar with theories of class and gender politics, and Labour Party policy on particular issues, but to be able to expound them to others. Given the contemporary methods of agitation, the open-air meetings and gatherings such as Lisbeth Simm addressed, it was very important for League women to be experienced propagandists. As it was necessary to emerge from the shell, so that learning environment had to be the more supportive. A report in *Woman Worker* (1908) made this clear: 'the branches of the League usually hold meetings for educating their members on political subjects and training them to speak and express their thoughts clearly'.

Subjects included women's relationship to the Labour Party, work at home and the franchise. The executive committee considered the 1911 winter programme drawn up by Miss Munro, secretary of Edinburgh Women's Labour League, to be a model syllabus. On 3 October there was to be discusssion of H. G. Well's

New Worlds for Old; on 3 November Olive Schreiner's *Women and Labour* was the topic, and there was to be a lecture on Robert Burns; in December there was to be a discussion on 'Our Noble Families' and a local councillor was to give a talk on town council work. Three meetings in January were devoted to Ramsay MacDonald's *Socialism* and a lecture on ambulance work was to be given; in February the discussion was to be on Kropotkin's *Fields, Factories and Workshops* plus a scientific discussion; George Bernard Shaw's *Mrs Warren's Profession* formed the basis of the March debate, with a lecture on 'the Council and the State'. During the winter socialism had therefore been discussed from constitutional, anarchist and feminist perspectives, interspersed with the more practical lectures. Suggested readings on each book were outlined to expand knowledge between meetings.

Not all branches were so methodical; some relied on visiting lecturers, such as Wallasey, which arranged a lecture by a Liverpool Fabian on 'Women and the French Revolution'. Birmingham started a cookery book and read Fabian tracts and Independent Labour Party pamphlets. Portsmouth read from John Ruskin and from *Labour Leader*. Jarrow had papers once a month on subjects such as League aims, infant mortality, women's suffrage and women at work. Other branches, like Preston, preferred discussion on Labour's policies and campaigns, mixed with musical and literary evenings. Bow and Bromley branch arranged readings during sewing circles, with cheap material on offer, which was found to make the meetings more attractive to prospective members. Dolly Lansbury, daughter of Labour Member of Parliament George Lansbury, and secretary of the Bow and Bromley League branch, asked the executive committee to supply needlework. This approach was in danger of degenerating to the sweated work that Lisbeth Simm condemned; Frances James, secretary of the St Pancras branch wrote that the sewing produced during meetings ('to keep our fingers employed') was traded or sold to raise funds. However, Wallasey branch found that it was not until their sewing circle got under way, with the attraction of cheap clothing and the camaraderie that a shared task brought to women of different backgrounds, that 'we really broke through'.[14]

Because they were well informed and benefited from a shared perspective focused by the education programme, branches could participate in national campaigns on some issues. Over the branches' local initiative was built a second tier, from which the metropolitan leadership could mount an attack on Westminster. The biggest single issue campaign was that on the free provision of school meals, but lesser ones were also mounted, for instance on infant mortality and child health and on sweated work.

Infant mortality had become recognised as a national problem; conferences were held on the subject in 1906 and 1908. The League maintained (*League Leaflet* no. 10, October 1911) that the deaths of working-class babies accounted for sixty per cent of the national average of 128 deaths of children under one year old for each 1000 live births. The *Sheffield Telegraph* related an infant mortality and stillbirth rate of seventy-nine per cent in the Staffordshire Potteries (lead was used in the process of pottery manufacture and acted as an abortafacient) to the personal tragedy of Margaret MacDonald in 1910. Due to attend the League Conference, Margaret mourned her child David, despite her social and financial advantages. Soon after she wrote:

> These statistics of mortality among children have become unbearable to me. I used to be able to read them in a dull scientific way, but now I seem to know the pain behind each one. It is not true that other children can make it up to you, that time heals the pain. It doesn't, it just grows worse and worse. We women must work for a world where little children will not needlessly die.[15]

It was common to blame working mothers for poor child care and inability to breast feed. Women of the working classes were rarely able to stay home from work long after the birth of a child: Clara Collett and the women factory inspectors found resistance even to taking the four weeks' statutory maternity leave that had been introduced following feminist pressure for reform. Much work remained physically heavy and, coupled with poor pay and inadequate nutrition, caused women to lose the ability to breast feed effectively. The pattern followed by women of the working classes was to stay in employment when the children were young and leave the work force when the eldest child was old enough to replace the lost income. The League devoted its *Leaflets* 3 and 4 to working mothers and refuted the idea that they were to blame for under-nourished and sick children: the cause of such misery was laid firmly to the charge of low wages for men and women, bad housing conditions, poor sanitation. These leaflets served both to provide a basis for discussion in branches and to promote measures of child welfare in the community.

The National Insurance Act of 1911 was the work of radicals within the Liberal government and provided a minimum of medical care and protection against poverty. The final measures were the result of prolonged negotiations with interested parties (the medical profession, Friendly Societies who ran sick pay schemes, insurance companies) and within parliament, which had baulked at raising the extra taxation: Lloyd George's budget had provoked the House of Lords into rebellion, causing the Liberal Government to hold the two 1910 general elections and, eventually, to resolve the constitutional crisis by the Parliament Act of 1911 which restricted the power of the Lords. The Labour movement was divided on the wisdom of supporting the Insurance Act, some insisting that wages should be adequate for workers to spend as they chose and opposing the introduction of compulsory state welfare. The Act was in two parts; the first made sick pay and medical treatment available for all workers, contributing weekly to a fund to which their employers and the state also paid a share. The second allowed for fifteen weeks' unemployment pay in specific industries.

Only the very few women engaged in steady trades were eligible for unemployment benefit and this was only achieved after insistent lobbying by women's trade unions and political organisations. Health cover for widows and orphans had been lost in the negotiations and no dependants were covered. It was almost impossible to check whether sweated homeworkers and casual workers were making insurance contributions: the benefits of sick pay and medical treatment were therefore mostly confined to the adult, able-bodied male. For the women the League sought to represent, the 1911 Act had extremely little to offer. There had been demonstrations and deputations by Labour movement women; Margaret MacDonald was accused of 'unscrupulous methods of warfare' by Lloyd George when she publicly revealed on one such occasion a private remark of his to Ramsay, to the effect that married women, if covered by the Act, would be constantly seeking medical attention.[16] The effect of the women's campaign was, perhaps, dimmed by the controversy within the Labour movement: the differences of opinion were illustrated by Members of the Parliamentary Labour Party, voting against each other in divisions during the passage of the Act.

Some families, who could afford the weekly payment, continued to be members of Friendly Societies or insurance schemes outside the Act. Others joined less formal, neighbourhood sickness clubs. For many, a child's sickness remained a catastrophe, while preventative medicine was a luxury far beyond their means. The concern about infant mortality did stimulate private schemes for child health protection. Baby clinics and milk depots, using the newly available powdered milk, were just beginning to be the subject of experiment. Some pioneers hoped to teach mothers to cope better: others realised the hopelessness of poverty and attempted merely to give relief.

In theory, there was provision for the medical inspection of schoolchildren within the terms of the 1907 Education Act (incorporated in the legislation by the Permanent Secretary and largely ignored by parliament). A Department was established by the Board of Education to supervise the new service. Where radicals or Socialists had been elected to local education authorities, for instance in Bradford, school clinics had been provided. These were welcomed by the British Medical Association (*Labour Leader*, January 1911). Margaret MacMillan from Bradford had set up a clinic in Deptford, South London, with her sister Rachel. The League lobbied the London County Council to provide school clinics, was refused, demonstrated and finally, with the Co-operative Women's Guild, met the Care Committee which agreed to reconsider. Margaret MacDonald wrote in *Labour Leader* (17 February 1911): 'the most significant feature of the deputation was, however, the fact that it consisted so largely of mothers of school children . . . who were able to speak from experience'. It was not until 1912 (and the failure of the National Insurance scheme to meet children's needs) that government grants were made available to local authorities to set up school clinics.

When funds were raised to commemorate Margaret MacDonald and Mary Middleton, it seemed natural to branches which had campaigned about child health and whose members knew of the tragedy in the last year of Margaret's life, to suggest spending the money on a baby clinic for pre-school children, for whose health there was no form of state provision.[17] Despite the existence of other, local schemes, the League probably did not exaggerate in claiming that theirs was the first clinic run and fully controlled by a national body of women, open daily to all, requiring of mothers no letter or recommendation of any kind save their presence to receive advice about the child being treated, welcoming children who were well for preventative health care, treating the sick free of charge.

The clinic was run not by the executive, but by a separate committee which included co-opted members. Dr Ethel Bentham was a strong supporter and worked in the clinic, together with Dr Honor and Dr Alexander Hyslop. A resident nurse was appointed. A dentist's surgery was held once a month and there was a dispensing druggist. The position of the clinic in London did mean its immediate work was limited to children of the capital, but the benefits of the achievements and the experience gained in preventative medicine could be spread to the provinces and used to press for local authority provision.

When the memorial funds were exhausted, Dr Ethel Bentham offered to guarantee the expenses. Branches retained the initiative and indicated continuing support by suggesting they would each hold a League Baby Clinic Saturday every year to raise funds. Philip Nodin was the first treasurer of the committee, succeeded by Hugh Franklin (the latter was imprisoned for action in support of women's enfranchisement). The clinic organisation and funding gives an example of branches collectively comprehending a national problem and dealing with it on a two-tier level, branches initiating activity and continuing to present the problem to the local community, yet focusing attention on a London-based experiment.

To swell the funds, the proceeds of the work of a sewing party, initiated by Margaret MacDonald in 1903 and previously used to contribute to the League resources, were diverted to the clinic. This group met every Wednesday in Margaret MacDonald's house. After her death, Ramsay engaged a housekeeper, Marie Bijouvets, who acted as hostess. Not all the sewing party were League members, although Ishbel MacDonald remembered assuming the contrary as a child.[18] Minnie Nodin was a member from the start. Mary Macpherson, Sister Kerrison, Ada Salter, Eveline Lowe and Mrs Shaw were all regular Wednesday attendees. Nance Gossling, who became secretary of Kensington and Paddington branch in 1913, was a staunch supporter of clinic and sewing party. One is tempted to speculate whether the League began as an idea dropped amongst the stitches.

The League commitment to baby clinics continued. In 1913 there was a big campaign to put pressure on local authorities to establish, with the aid of the newly available government grant, clinics for the treatment of babies and children under school age.[19] A model resolution was drawn up 'in view of the high infantile death rate and the large number of children who enter school suffering from physical defects' that such provision be made. A letter-writing campaign was orchestrated amongst the Labour movement, letters of support being sent to the League nationally for use in lobbying. Nineteen League branches supported the campaign, including Tyldesley (Manchester) branch, where Ellen Wilkinson had become secretary. Ethel Denny from Plaistow sent a personal message after a successful, large public women's meeting. Gloucester and York Railway Women's Guild wrote in support. The Women's Industrial Council (perhaps reconciled after Margaret MacDonald's death) also sent in their letter. The Co-operative Women's Guild, Dartford branch, completed the list of women's organisations.

It was heartening that mixed-sex Labour and socialist groups were just as supportive. The Labour Parties in Ealing, Chiswick, Liverpool, Swansea, Glasgow, Westhoughton and Deptford (London) joined in the campaign, together with twenty-four Independent Labour Party branches and fifteen of the British Socialist Party (formerly the Social Democratic Federation). Hastings BSP had first held a public meeting. The Colne Valley Socialist League and four Socialist and Labour Churches also wrote. Of the trade union movement, thirteen trade and labour councils and five trade unions joined in: the latter were the Railway Clerks, Amalgamated Society of Railway Servants (Railway Women's Guild connections), the Postal Clerks and General Textile Workers (both with many women members) and the National Amalgamated Union of Labour (whose secretary was married to Florence Harrison Bell). Dartford Urban District Council lent the weight of the backing of a public authority. Introducing the debate on the Education Bill promised for 1914 and abandoned because of the war, the president of the Board of Education stated that 'schools for mothers' would be the subject of a government grant.

Poverty was perhaps the chief cause of child sickness. A measure of reform supported by some women was payment of a state allowance that would enable mothers to care adequately for their children. The 'endowment of motherhood' was a central issue for the Co-operative Women's Guild and attracted substantial backing, including that of the Social Democratic Federation. The chance of a maternity allowance became a reality in 1911/12 when it was included in the package of measures finally introduced by the Liberal Government on national insurance. There was dispute over whether the money should be paid to the (insured) father or directly to the mother. Labour Members of Parliament differed from one another on whether to give support to the package as a whole and on the provision of a maternity allowance; those who favoured the latter disagreed about the recipient. One of the bargaining counters for unions seeking improvement of men's wages was familial responsibility, dubbed by some women a 'paternal allowance', so there were ample grounds for controversy within the Labour movement.

This was more than tension between class and gender politics, supported respectively by men's and women's organisations. The League had campaigned for the extension of national insurance provision to women (for instance, in the Birmingham canvass of women of the working classes). The final insurance package, meeting only some of the League's demands, met with the same lukewarm response in the League as it did in the Labour Party. The maternity allowance raised further issues. Supporting a payment to the mother begged a question of gender identity; that women, because they were women, had to bear the responsibility for child and home care. It is interesting that the League did not lend its weight to the campaign for the endowment of motherhood. The League had never been willing to restrict women to the home. The issue was not simple and roused much debate, in which the Labour movement divided not by sex but by perceptions of familial stereotypes. Confusingly, those who favoured the 'paternal allowance' tended to end up on the same side as those who wanted to leave women free to work. Maternity allowances were discussed at the special Labour Party Conference on parliamentary performance in 1914; Margaret Bondfield, contributing in the midst of the mêlée, seemed to be of the opinion that legislating to pay the allowance directly to the mother was a patronising interference with working families.

The Co-operative Women's Guild successfully campaigned in 1913 to make the payment the legal property of the mother, but the very small state contribution to the costs of childbearing and child rearing did little to alleviate the misery of poverty. The Guild's campaign to increase the allowance was conducted by collecting and publishing letters from women describing their experiences of deprivation and suffering (*Maternity: letters from working women, 1915*).

The way some women resolved the difficulties of wage-earning and looking after children was to take in sweated work (long hours of work for little reward) that could be carried out either at home or in small local workshops where they could take the children. Such establishments were not subject to regulation by any authority; local councils had power to deal with homework, but it was, of course, extremely difficult to monitor. Very few sweated workers belonged to a trade union. Sweated workers were seasonally employed, especially in the hat, glove and dressmaking trades, and were laid off for long periods; they were therefore forced to suffer long hours in times of employment. The 1905 Unemployed Workmen Act did cover such seasonally employed women, making provision for local authorities to set up workrooms (such as those the Glasgow League branch campaigned for) so that the women would not be dependent on Poor Law relief. The only such workroom recorded was that set up by the Central London Distress Committee. Generally, there was a lack of knowledge about female labour, despite the efforts of investigative pioneers.

The Women's Industrial Council, set up in 1894, had vast experience of studying sweated labour. The Council consisted of two hundred or so women, who collected data and lobbied politicians with the results. Margaret MacDonald collected information on sweating from public authorities in Ireland, Illinois, Massachusetts, Ohio and New York about the regulation of sweated workshops.[20] The reply from Ireland was that most work, for instance on shirts, took place in factories and was finished by homeworkers, making regulation difficult, but the American authorities had a comprehensive system of licensing small workshops. As its legal secretary, Margaret MacDonald gave evidence on behalf of the Women's Industrial Council to the Royal Commission on the Poor Laws regarding women's work and wages. Some idea of her standing as a social investigator can be gained from the letter sent by the Commission's secretary, arranging for the Commissioners to interview her at home (one wonders how they coped with the babies).[21] The Council also participated in the sweated industry exhibition run by the *Daily News* in 1906. This exhibition had an enormous impact on public opinion and led to the founding of the Anti-Sweating League. A Select Committee of the House of Commons was set up (1907) to enquire into sweated work.

Ramsay MacDonald presented a Homeworkers' Bill to the House of Commons, seeking to introduce regulations that would improve conditions.

It was the *Clarion* woman's column editor, Julia Varley, who offered the League what she called a 'golden opportunity to make propaganda over sweating' in February 1907. The *Clarion* was to hold a handicraft exhibition in London, the hall was free, so should the League decide to staff a stall with six workers at £1 per week for six weeks, the cost would be trifling. The executive committee decided to accept the offer; branches collected examples of cloth made up very cheaply by women for local tailors. This involved enquiry into the sweated trades and contact with women home-workers, to the benefit of the branch; holding the exhibition contributed to raising interest at Westminster while Ramsay MacDonald's Bill was on the timetable. A League member from Lowestoft took back items from the exhibition and arranged her own showing at the local adult school.[22]

One dress was shown at the exhibition for which the machinist was paid 1*s* 1*d*, the finisher 2*s* 0*d*; the retailer paid the tailor 12*s* 6*d* and priced the dress at 16*s* 6*d*. The tailor was named Mr Cohen; he had appeared before the House of Commons Home Industry Committee. He offered to pay the League £100 if they could prove their figures and his involvement in fourteen days; he stated that someone had stolen his design and asked the League to pay £25 to the charity of his choosing should they default.[23] The correspondence between the League and Mr Cohen lasted longer than the fourteen days; the League obtained legal advice and offered to produce evidence before arbitrators, asking for the Board of Trade to be represented. Mr Cohen demanded to see the identifying marks on the costume, perhaps in an endeavour to trace and penalise the worker who had given the information. Neither side moved from their position, but the press coverage helped the publicity on sweated work to reach a wide audience. The League gave evidence before the Select Committee about Mr Cohen.

An *ad hoc* committee of the executive, co-opted from the London members, was set up to plan the League's own sweated work exhibition. Reliant on the metropolitan orientation of the leadership for its organisation, such an exhibition would nevertheless have depended upon a great deal of contribution from the branches; there is no record, however, of it ever taking place. The *Daily Mail* campaign on sweated work kept up the pressure for parliamentary action.

The desperation of women sweated workers was illustrated by a letter sent to the League from a woman then in the Royal Infirmary, who wrote that she had reared her children alone with the aid of her sewing machine: 'such a Bill (as Ramsay MacDonald sought to introduce) would have crushed me'.[24] As was the case with women who gave evidence to the Royal Commission of Labour in 1894, many women workers resented any interference with their right to work. Women's trade unions had traditionally preferred to rely on free collective bargaining to improve pay and conditions, but wanted workshops licensed to make sure they were safe and clean. The Women's Industrial Council, on the other hand, had a history of supporting legislation to improve conditions for women workers.

There was now a dispute in the Women's Industrial Council about sweating.[25] Clementina Black favoured the fixing of minimum wage rates and her championing of women chainmakers won huge publicity to her cause: she took pains, however, to word her motion to the Council in support of minimum wages in such a way that no one 'would feel resignation necessary'. Margaret MacDonald supported the trade union position, believing a fixed minimum wage perpetuated low pay, preferring negotiated rates. The proposal, from several sources, to introduce Trades Boards to regulate pay and conditions in specific trades was controversial: the women's trade unions and the Women's Industrial Council had mixed opinions. The League debated trades boards and licensing. Mary MacArthur spoke at the 1907 League conference to the effect that trades boards were necessary to raise wages. She believed licensing to be an inadequate remedy and engaged in an angry correspondence with Margaret MacDonald, who had referred to her American evidence as 'proof' that licensing worked, accusing Mary MacArthur of not being 'up to date'. On 20 November 1907 at the Central London League branch meeting, Mary MacArthur spoke for, Margaret MacDonald against trades boards. The 1908 League conference followed Mary MacArthur and called for a government bill: Margaret MacDonald had sought to amend the proposal on the grounds that it would be futile. At the League executive on 11 February 1908 Margaret spoke against sending a representative to the Anti-Sweating League demonstration because of the difference of opinion within the League, but Mary Macpherson was, nevertheless, chosen and attended as League representative. Bad feeling caused Mary MacArthur to resign from the League executive, but controversy within the League continued.

In 1908 the Central London branch agreed to co-operate with the Women's Industrial Council in an investigation of married women's work. Margaret Bondfield, Sister Kerrison, Edith Macrosty, Mary Macpherson, Minnie Nodin and all League executive committee members were also Women's Industrial Council members, in addition to Margaret MacDonald. Dorothy Lenn was employed to help in the investigation; she worked in Leicester, where Margaret MacDonald raised funds for the investigation, donating some of her own money. Margaret Bondfield carried out an investigation in Yorkshire. In 1910 there was an argument over the handling of the book, later edited by Clementina Black, and over proposed changes in the structure of the Women's Industrial Council (which would have given more power to its leadership). Margaret MacDonald and the League women all resigned from the Council.

The controversy over the remedy for sweated work, its leaders' indulgence in personal animosities and their resignation from the Women's Industrial Council seem to have paralysed branch activity about sweating and perhaps explain why the proposed League exhibition never took place. Trades boards were introduced in some industries (including chainmaking) from 1909 and have remained a source of dispute ever since. Never abandoned by the League, throughout the various arguments, was its commitment to women's right to work.

Where an issue was local, a campaign or an election (even a general election, given the contemporary habit of tailoring manifestos to local need and interest), branch initiative was sufficient to make an impact within the community. Some measure of harmony within the League, however, was necessary for campaigns to develop beyond local boundaries. Dispute (for instance on sweating, on suffrage and on endowment of motherhood) meant that the League lacked a distinctive voice, and that the League women's contribution became diffused in the lively and competitive women's and Labour movements. The League presented itself, as a national body, in voicing those issues not subject to internal controversy: school mortality, baby clinics and above all, school meals. This meant the League drew its identity from domestic, maternal and child welfare concerns in a way disproportionate to the time actually allocated to such topics. The League as the voice of women at work was lost.

It was the prolonged attempt to enforce the adoption by local authorities of the permissory Education (Provision of Meals) Act of 1906 which was the biggest single League campaign. The Inter-Departmental Committee on Physical Deterioration (1904), set up after the South African wars because of the concern at the ineffectiveness of the undernourished and unfit British infantrymen, included in its recommendations feeding schoolchildren and recovering the cost from parents wherever possible. Having interviewed generals, surgeons and physicians, the Committee concluded that Britain's 'racial stock' was not deteriorating; however, by seriously considering and publicising such fears, the effect of the Committee's deliberations was to add to the disquiet of the ruling elite of an aggessively imperialist nation such as Britain. Parliament discussed the recommendations at some length. In 1905 the Board of Guardians were empowered to give relief to children without insisting their fathers entered the workhouse, provided steps were taken to recover the cost. Few Boards availed themselves of the opportunity.

If the problem was to be met, there obviously had to be some commitment to public provision. The passage of the Education (Provision of Meals) Act was typical of the way the Liberal Government edged up to such a commitment and halted just short, dipping its toe into the pool of state resources, but not caring too much to make an imprint in the sands of private wealth surrounding the waters. In the words of a contemporary, feeding schoolchildren illustrated 'that process of tentative transformation from a private charity to a public service by which we are accustomed to disguise the assumption of new reponsibilities by the state'.[26]

Mr Tyson Wilson, the Labour Member from Westhoughton, was allowed time to introduce a Private Member's Bill which gave local authorities discretionary powers to feed schoolchildren, who were unable to benefit from education because of hunger, either by co-operating with voluntary agencies or by spending the product of up to a halfpenny rate. The president of the Board of Education backed the Bill and it was referred to a Select Committee. Arthur Henderson, Labour Member, gave his opinion that the powers should not be discretionary. In the event, the limited Bill had to be fought clause by clause against a small core of Conservative resistance. Boards of Guardians lobbied against the Bill, passing a model resolution: 'That the Guardians view with alarm the Education (Provision of Meals) Bill now before Parliament, first as the state would be taking over in part the primary duty of parents and second as an enormous expense would be put upon the ratepayers of the Kingdom'.[27] The House of Lords amended the Bill to exclude Scotland from its provisions (a new Bill was introduced in 1908 to remedy this). The Lords also attempted, unsuccessfully, to return the powers of feeding schoolchildren to the Guardians and to disenfranchise the fathers of recipients, on the grounds that they had betrayed their parental responsibilities.

The Parliamentary Labour Party accepted the limited Act, which gave them nearly everything Wilson had originally requested. The League did not find the discretionary measure acceptable. Initially, its impact on local education authorities was negligible and children continued to go hungry. The League therefore campaigned for the Act to become mandatory, so that locally there could be no evasion and as a corollary, to make state funds available to underwrite local expenditure. The League campaign was an interesting exposition of its brand of socialist feminism; responsibility for feeding children was to be cast directly on to the community: the mother was not to be the isolated source of care. Reflecting its concern with children, the League campaign took questions of child care which had originated with domestic need into the sphere of municipal politics, to be resolved by corporate action.

League concern with feeding schoolchildren also reflected the women's belief in the importance of education. In her paper on 'The Effect on the Nation of Forty Years of Universal Education' given to the National Union of Women Workers Congress (reported in the *Northern Democrat,* February 1911), Lisbeth Simm wrote about the increase in the ability to communicate which education made possible, how reading and writing had helped working people to articulate their needs to each other and to a wider audience. Participation in civic affairs was the outcome and the consequent extension of municipal interests. There was also the hope of being able to escape poverty through better paid employment. 'To rise to toil,' wrote Lisbeth, 'to be absorbed in the routine work of cooking, cleaning, nursing and such like . . . made a very narrow outlook for some of our mothers.' Lisbeth questioned whether the gifts of education were being fully used: 'the growth of picture halls, music halls, skating rinks, picture papers, the growing sensationalism of the daily Press, the weekly supply of Sunday newspapers devoted mainly to athletics, picturesque details of murders and murderers, the life stories of prize fighters, divorce cases and such like' – the list of things which caused Lisbeth to doubt sound uncomfortably familiar. She concluded that whether or not education benefited an individual depended on the circumstances of study; whether there was leisure to devote, whether the buildings were adequate. The fact of a child being undernourished was entirely germane to its ability to learn. Earlier, Lisbeth had stimulated working parents to interest themselves in the circumstances of their children's education (*Northern Democrat,* October 1907): 'Is it always to be that the workers' child shall be pushed on one side and neglected while the workers make profits for capitalists?' She wrote again (*Northern Democrat,* March 1912) of a woman's despair at passing a school in a 'poverty stricken' town: 'It is heartbreaking to see the poor little things crying quietly outside, when they ought to be eating a nice warm dinner.'

It was Liskeard branch which first (1907) raised the issue of school meals within the League.[28] Birmingham branch reported that the City Council had adopted the Education (Provision of Meals) Act. Hull branch urged its adoption on the local education committee and lobbied its Members of Parliament. Portsmouth branch urged the Act's adoption, then Leeds. Jarrow League members, including Marion Curran, sat in the gallery of the Council meeting to witness the progress of their memorandum about feeding schoolchildren from public funds. With a fine disregard for timing, Jarrow Council adjourned its meeting for the mayoral banquet. When it reconvened, there were League and Independent Labour Party or Labour Party visitors in every seat of the gallery; the motion to adopt the Act was ruled out of order, because the necessary powers lay with the education committee, and was therefore referred to that committee. The education committee had no Labour representatives and referred the motion to the school attendance sub-committee. As the latter's members were not aware of any child suffering through lack of food, they decided against adoption of the Act.

The London County Council remained equally obdurate. It did, however, have a special committee on physical deterioration. The St Pancras League branch collected evidence for this committee, two of its members being school managers.[29] St Pancras League women suggested a petition to the London County Council, asking it to reconsider and allow local education authorities to make a rate to carry out the Act. Branch members on the care committee of a local group of schools were able to persuade the authorities to begin school dinners in their area. Central London branch began collecting evidence on which districts of London contained needy children, how many there were and of what age in each district and where the parents worked. A resolution was then sent to the London County Council asking for the adoption of the Act; it was refused: Central London branch collected 1,000 signatures and petitioned the Council to receive a delegation; they were denied. However, a central Council care committee was set up, on which Dr Salter (Ada Salter's husband) served; at a League meeting he spoke of the 60,000 London children who needed opthalmic treatment, the 10,000 needing orthodontic treatment, the thousands suffering from tuberculosis. Eventually, in 1908, the London County Council agreed to raise £10,000 from the rates to feed schoolchildren.[30]

Leicester branch perhaps displayed the most remarkable feat of organising. The education committee had adjourned its debate on the Act, so the League branch organised a huge demonstration in the market-place. J. R. Clynes (one of Labour's most prominent Members of Parliament and once a textile worker) and Margaret MacDonald spoke; a petition was sent to the Council, where 'our Labour men worked harder than ever because they felt the force behind them'.[31] However, the Council decided to leave feeding schoolchildren to charity. Leicester branch then organised a repeat meeting in the market-place, at which local women spoke and collected signatures to a further petition. They were opposed locally by the Charity Organisation Society, on the grounds that parental responsibility would be diminished. After repeated lobbying, a conference was held, attended by representatives of the Charity Organisation Society and the National Society for the Prevention of Cruelty to Children, and a voluntary scheme was proposed. Leicester Town Council decided to co-operate and formed the Children's Aid Association which provided school meals.

Lisbeth Simm chaired a meeting in Gateshead 'for the purpose of calling attention to the condition of many of Gateshead's schoolchildren' (*Northern Democrat*, March 1908). Gateshead Council's trust in voluntary charities' ability to feed children was misplaced: 'about sixty of the worst cases have been supplied with breakfasts; the others . . . do without'. Margaret MacMillan, an Independent Labour Party member whose chief concern was the welfare of schoolchildren came to speak: 'she showed that among the children of the better class artisan, 8 per cent were at the age of 12 deformed – that is, had crooked backs or rickets; 28 per cent suffered from adenoids, a throat and nose disease which would never cure of itself; 25 per cent were anaemic – blood in a poor and unhealthy condition'. Margaret MacMillan had carefully investigated: 'the quantity of real food required by a school child . . . To provide this, 2*s* per week was required for food for each child, so that a man and his wife with a family of five would need to spend 17*s* to 18*s* a week on food alone. With the average wage of about a pound a week, for many working men such a proceeding was impossible!' A resolution was taken at the meeting, with only one dissentient, urging Gateshead Council to adopt the Act and a petition was organised.

Margaret MacMillan's logic had proved irrefutable in her own town of Bradford. This was the only town in which the Guardians had provided out relief under the 1905 provision for any length of time. After eight years' experimentation and investigation, schoolchildren were being provided with a variety of seventeen different dinners at a cost of 3*s* 4*d* to 1*s* 1½*d* per meal. The district auditor regularly made a surcharge because the meals were provided in school holidays as well as term-time, and the product of a halfpenny rate was exceeded. Lisbeth Simm reported her joy at witnessing this operation (*Northern Democrat,* March 1912): 'It was just dinner time and the smell of savoury meat and potato pies greeted us at the door.' Three teachers and six of the older girls served the dinners. Every child either bought, or was given, a dinner ticket 'so that they were all on the same footing at the feeding centre'. There was full use of new technology; a central kitchen prepared the dinners, which were sent out on vans: 'I . . . admired the wonderful appliances for lightening labour . . . "Here we wash all the plates with hot water, slide them down that board into the cold water and then put them in this rack, and turn on a hot air tap to dry them."' Margaret MacMillan remembered how influential the Bradford experiment had been in proving to local authorities that community feeding minimised labour and the cost of each portion of food; socialism made sense: 'Bradford grasped the nettle . . . Its splendid

Central School kitchen with its scientific equipment, its worked-out menus, its fine transport, its expert direction and trained staff helped lift the whole question into a new atmosphere.'[32]

Humanitarian but half-heartedly funded, experimental, introduced in an *ad hoc* way rather than as part of a structured programme of reform, it was not surprising that, Bradford apart, the provision of school meals was clumsy and chaotic. Sometimes the local authority took control, at others, as in Leicester, charitable agencies were responsible. The original wording of the Act had been taken to mean meals could not be provided outside school terms, because no educational benefit accrued. The original stimulant had been to ensure physical fitness; however, health was rarely used as a criterion for deciding provision. Poverty was the factor most frequently used and was variously defined. Selection was usually made by teachers; where it was left to parents to refer their children it was found that very few meals were provided. The stigma of pauperism and the punitive Poor Law were still feared and there was antipathy to contact with any form of state bureaucracy.

League branches were amongst those organisations that had to make sense of piecemeal reform on the ground. They needed a universal measure, that did not stigmatise the parents or the child, that was simple and involved no complicated system of referral to an alien authority. League branches wanted children well-fed and mothers freed from the kitchen. They therefore initiated collective League action, asking the executive committee to co-ordinate their campaigns. It was an issue that the leadership had studied in depth; Margaret MacDonald had collected evidence from women's groups in France, Belgium, Switzerland and Austria.[33] The system operating in Paris was similar to Bradford's; children were equipped with tokens, bought by their parents or provided by the local authority, that they then exchanged for dinner in the school canteen, no-one knowing which child was receiving the subsidy. Surprisingly, it took a while for the executive to decide on action: it seemed content to leave the branches to cope; the pressure for a national petition, however, became irresistible. The latter came into use by 1909 and read: 'We the undersigned women of . . . petition our local authority to put into force the Act for the providing of meals for necessitous schoolchildren and consider that the expenses should be defrayed entirely out of public funds without any appeal to charity.'

As well as local campaigns, now making use of this national petition, the League applied pressure at Westminster, producing pamphlets and calling on Labour Members of Parliament to introduce amending legislation. This was, in turn, reinforced by branches urging their own local Members of Parliament to act. By 1911–12, of 322 authorities, 131 made some provision for feeding schoolchildren.[34] The League campaign appeared to have some effect. Pressure was not relaxed; at the 1914 Labour Party conference, D. McCarthy criticised Labour Members for not pursuing the issue with enough 'holy zeal'; Marion Phillips again moved a League resolution demanding compulsory provision of school meals and also asked that catering be carried out by local authority employees, not left to contract labour. In that year it seemed success was in sight, when the government announced that the exchequer would grant half the cost of school meal provision and that proposals to legalise feeding schoolchildren during the holidays would be included in next session's Education Bill. The First World War destroyed this immediate chance of progress.

By such actions, the League was in the vanguard of the progressive movement, seeking out the best methods to turn good intentions into practicalities, arguing for collective action for state provision. League women witnessed the effects of reform on the ground, dealt with the anomalies of a Poor Law that was beginning to disintegrate, knew what it meant for women to be unemployed, what suffering there was when a baby died. In their work, gender politics were as important as those of class; it was to spare women domestic chores that League members campaigned for school meals, it was because they understood the double burden that they were concerned with sweated work. League women operated as an integral part of a local community, conducting their campaigns not in isolation but in response to local events. They were constitutionalists; they saw that in towns with socialist councillors, such as Bradford, achievements could be won. League branch autonomy did seem to explain some of the League's vitality and persistence. League strength perhaps lay in its diversity. Yet through its education programme and its commitment to entertainment, the League did provide women wth a comprehensive response to capitalist society. Within her branch, the socialist woman could live a rounded life in the Labour movement, overcoming class barriers in her relationship with women from different backgrounds, joining in a common cause. The work was demanding, but the individual contribution was recognised and nurtured.

Notes

1 *Women's Labour League Secretarial Correspondence and Related Papers* (Labour Party Headquarters Archives, London), WLL/45.

2 *J. R. MacDonald and M. E. MacDonald Papers,* PRO 30/69 (Public Records Office, London), 1373, 13 July 1906, 15 July 1906.

3 *MacDonald Papers,* 1375, 7 April 1908.

4 *MacDonald Papers,* 1376, 10 March 1909.

5 *MacDonald Papers,* 1374, 8 October 1907.

6 *James and Lucy Middleton Papers:* The Ruskin Collection (Ruskin College, Oxford); Pete Curran's by-election papers, 1907, MID/138; see also Ellen Wilkinson, *The Town that was Murdered* (Gollancz, 1939).

7 *League Correspondence,* WLL/98.

8 *League Correspondence,* WLL/3.

9 *Glasgow Record,* 19 November 1909 and *Labour Leader,* 1 September 1911.

10 *Labour Leader,* 29 September 1911.

11 *League Correspondence,* WLL/64; *Labour Leader,* 11 August 1911; Central London Branch *Minutes,* 1907.

12 *MacDonald Papers,* 1376, 31 March 1909.

13 *Labour Leader,* 28 March 1905.

14 *League Correspondence,* WLL/11, 35, 39, 42, 66, 119.

15 Labour Party *Subject Files* (Labour Party Headquarters Archives, London), LP/INF/13/BAB.

16 *MacDonald Papers,* 1378, 1911.

17 Labour Party *Subject Files,* LP/INF/13/BAB.

18 *Idem:* Letter from Ishbel Peterkin (Margaret MacDonald's daughter) to Lucy Middleton, 16 October 1976: 'wherever we went, Lincoln's Inn Fields, Hampstead, Downing Street – the sewing party followed us'. It continued until 1937. During the 1929–31 Labour government radio appeals were broadcast on its behalf. In 1930 Sybil Thorndike organised an All-Star Matinée at the Palladium to raise funds. After Minnie Nodin's death (1936), James Middleton's third wife, Lucy Cox joined the sewing party and the baby clinic committee. James had been protective about Lucy meeting Minnie Nodin, who remembered Mary Middleton, to whom the clinic was jointly dedicated. The clinic was taken over by Kensington Borough Council in 1937. The MacDonald and Middleton families made no stipulations about its renaming. As late as 1941 Nance Gossling was telling James Middleton 'I keep in touch with clinic friends' *(James and Lucy Middleton Papers,* MID 66). In 1919 the baby clinic group also set up a baby hospital. This was run by the local authority in the war years and was taken over by the National Health Service in 1948.

19 Labour Party *Subject Files,* LP/INF/13/1–104.
20 *MacDonald Papers,* 1373, 1906.
21 *MacDonald Papers,* 1373, 30 July 1906.
22 *MacDonald Papers,* 1374, 13 November 1907.
23 Correspondence to and from Mr Cohen is divided between the *League Correspondence,* WLL/S1-56 and *MacDonald Papers,* 1366 and 1375.
24 *League Correspondence,* WLL/98.
25 *MacDonald Papers,* 1374, 11 May 1907 and 1375, 7 April 1908. For an account of the Women's Industrial Council and its approach to Trade Boards see Ellen Mappen, introduction to Clementina Black, *Married Women's Work,* (Virago, 1984) and Ellen Mappen, 'Strategies for change: social feminist approaches to the problem of women's work' in Angela John (ed.), *Unequal Opportunities: Women's Employment in England 1800–1914,* (Blackwell, 1986).
26 M. E. Buckley, *The Feeding of Schoolchildren* (London, 1914) p. xi, introduction of R. H. Tawney.
27 *MacDonald Papers,* 1373, see also Hansard's *Parliamentary Debates,* 4th Series (1906), vols. 152, 166, 167.
28 *League Correspondence,* WLL/64.
29 *League Correspondence,* WLL/42, 65.
30 *The Gertrude Tuckwell Collection, 1890–1920* (Trades Union Congress Library, London), 45/1.
31 *League Correspondence,* WLL/66.
32 Margaret MacMillan, 'Citizens of Tomorrow', in Labour Party Publishing Co., *The Book of the Labour Party: Its History, Growth, Policy and Leaders,* vol. ii (London, 1925).
33 *MacDonald Papers,* 1373.
34 M. E. Buckley, *The Feeding of Schoolchildren,* p. xii.

4

Transition

'Alas these changes' – Ramsay MacDonald of the League, 1912

When it lost its leadership in 1911, the League, as do many organisations in similar circumstances, gave priority to continuing its work with as little disruption as possible and looked for familiar and congenial souls to take over. The search at first seemed successful but the transition was not easy for the League. As it had been impossible, perhaps inappropriate, to be inflexible in the resolution of many issues (relationship with the Labour Party, for instance, or with the suffrage movement) the League might have expected that new women would introduce fresh ideas and make their own stamp on League philosophy. Disruption, not avoided, was uncomfortable: the League traversed a bridge from 1911 to 1914, going from the relative relaxation of the free lances to experience some anxiety about its future situation. That this period was, nevertheless, characterised by political vigour was illustrated by the fact that branches nominated eighteen women for twelve executive committee places in 1912, causing Ramsay MacDonald to lament: 'Alas these changes'.[1]

On Mary Middleton's death in April 1911, the League executive committee decided to create a new role of organising secretary; a paid officer (£2 per week, with six weeks' paid holiday) who would support Margaret MacDonald by helping with the secretarial work and also assist the Labour Party at by-elections. The 'moving spirit in the little group of women in London – Mary MacArthur, Margaret MacDonald, Gertrude Tuckwell, Julia Dawson and others – who were the life and soul of the Labour movement in all its relations with their own sex' was, according to her biographer,

Margaret Bondfield, 'to whom the equal place of full recognition to women by Labour is largely due'.[2] A known quantity, Margaret Bondfield at first slid into the place of organising secretary; after Margaret MacDonald's death, Marion Phillips became temporary general secretary.

Margaret Bondfield's biographer was justified in placing her amongst the leaders of women in the Labour movement, although anyone acquainted with the League would want to credit the movement's recognition of women as much to the efforts of the rank and file activists as to any one leader. Margaret's successful career illustrated the respect in which she was held, until her association, as the first woman Cabinet Minister (1929), with the grudging public assistance available during the depression tarnished her memory. Familiar photographs of the older, much harassed Minister obscure the confident thirty-eight-year-old appointed by the League. Margaret's speaking voice was renowned for its clarity and melody. According to Sylvia Pankhurst (a hostile witness, because Margaret opposed limited women's suffrage) Margaret pulled no punches in debate: 'attired in pink, dark and dark-eyed, with a deep throaty voice many found beautiful. She was very charming and vivacious and eager to score all the points that her youth and prettiness would win for her'.[3]

Margaret Bondfield's career had already been rather spectacular when she was engaged by the League. She was not from a comfortable middle-class background, but had worked as a shop assistant; coming to London, she joined the Social Democratic Federation and became assistant secretary of the Shop Assistants' Union. Her place among the leadership of labour women had been won by proven organising and rhetorical skills. After illness in 1908, Margaret worked as a propagandist for the Labour Party and for the Independent Labour Party; having become disillusioned with the Social Democratic Federation she joined the ILP. Margaret stood for a London County Council seat (Woolwich).

Margaret worked with Clementina Black on the report on married women's work for the Women's Industrial Council and with the Women's Co-operative Guild on maternity and child welfare. She was therefore identified with the campaigns for a minimum wage and for maternity allowances, both of which the League opposed. Moreover, she was a great admirer of Mary MacArthur, who had become disenchanted with the League. A professional woman, Margaret believed women's separate organisation to be a preliminary step to their integration into the full, mixed body; such an opinion, inevitably implying some inferiority of the primary, protective women's organisation, might have been a point of dispute with some League women.

Nevertheless, since its inception, Margaret Bondfield had been interested in the League and carried out propaganda work on its behalf after 1908. She was elected to the League executive committee in 1909. On her appointment as organising secretary, Margaret worked fairly happily with Margaret MacDonald, although she had disliked her when they first met. Both were experienced and practised speakers, rather than committee women. Margaret Bondfield, who had already undertaken informal organising trips for the League, set off confidently on a series of tours, giving heart to the branches in Wales and the North West, where she picked up Mrs Ayles's and Annot Robinson's work. During this period, Lisbeth Simm was organising the North-East while Dorothy Lenn was secretary of the Central London League.

Mary Middleton's death from cancer had been expected; Margaret MacDonald's subsequent illness was not. Recovery was fully expected and Margaret Bondfield took over some responsibilities, such as writing an account of League activities for *Labour Leader*. Then in November 1911 came the sudden, inexplicable death of Margaret MacDonald leaving bereft a young family and numbers of women who mourned her personally. It was the beginning of a period of unhappiness and uncertainty for the League.

The general secretaryship was offered, temporarily while Margaret Bonfield recovered, to Marion Phillips. Until December 1911 Marion was organising secretary of the Women's Trade Union League. She was a very different type of leader than Margaret MacDonald or Margaret Bondfield, a trained and experienced administrator. Marion Phillips's education was more extensive than that of other League leaders; she had graduated from Melbourne University and won a research scholarship at the London School of Economics, gaining a DSC in Economics. She worked for the Royal Commission on the Poor Laws until 1910 as an investigator. When A. J. Braithwaite (the civil servant who conducted negotiations with women's organisations as part of his duties in working out the details of the new national insurance scheme) met Marion Phillips (then representing the Women's Trade Union League), he considered her to have 'the best brains of the whole lot' of the women representatives.[4] Marion was paid £1 per week for half-time work and 7*s* per day expenses for work outside London; she was to attend the office every morning, from 10.30 a.m. until 1.00 p.m. These were not particularly generous terms.

The difficulties the League experienced at this time were expressed as rivalry between pairs of adversaries: Margaret Bondfield and her friend Maud Ward versus Marion Phillips and Ethel Bentham. Maud Ward and Ethel Clarke lived with Margaret Bondfield in 1911; Marion Phillips and Mary Longman were accommodated in Ethel Bentham's house. Marion Phillips founded North Kensington Women's Labour League in 1910, the year Ethel Bentham was elected to the executive committee; Marion Phillips was elected to the executive in 1911. Apparently Margaret Bondfield had originally agreed to stand as organising secretary only because she feared a split in the League. The reasons are not clear, but may have included suffrage policy and the continuing disagreement between Mary MacArthur. Later, Margaret believed her first fears of a split had been exaggerated, but that division would ensue were she to stay in office: 'I have decided not to hold office in the League', wrote Margaret Bondfield: 'I shall be a member of the Executive Committee only. For the first time I have met with people with whom I *cannot* work . . . At present my attitude divides the Executive Committee and is frightfully bad for the League.'[5] After Margaret MacDonald's death Margaret Bondfield had taken over the whole of the secretarial work, while Minnie Nodin acted as treasurer, so her departure would have been a great loss; in the event she fell ill while on a League tour of Lancashire, so events hung fire.

Anyone who had survived the Social Democratic Federation, a job as union secretary and various by-elections was not easily intimidated. Margaret had, of course, been ill and had the responsibility of an elderly mother, but even if she were worn down by illness, it would be surprising if Margaret Bondfield was unable to deal with confrontation to the extent of resigning from her job. Unfortunately the records are silent on political reasons that may have accounted for personal animosities. Both Margaret Bondfield and Marion Phillips were keenly interested in working women. On suffrage, of course, there were differences; Margaret Bondfield was an extreme opponent of limited women's suffrage; however, while Marion Phillips had been secretary to the National Union of

Women's Suffrage Societies, she also had come round to opposition to the propertied women's vote. The real problem appears to have been organisational; Margaret Bondfield evidently felt she had insufficient say in policy-making; she was the travelling organiser whilst Marion Phillips was ensconsed in the office, at the nub of the League. Margaret continued: 'I do not choose to be the nominal head without any real power.' The real power after 1912 resided with Marion Phillips.

Ramsay MacDonald was regaled with Katherine Bruce Glasier's version of events: even allowing for Katharine's usual purple prose and her quickness to spot a plot (of which ample evidence is given in the troubles over the editorship of the *Labour Leader*), the personal acrimony within the League executive committee does appear to have been excessive. Katharine wrote:

> I wish I had Margaret Bondfield's confidence or quite understood her: but her friendship with Miss Ward which your dear wife dreaded got right between us. These violent attachments don't seem to help, or to be good servants of the commonwealth. They have in them all the disproportionate heats and chills – and passionate impulsive actions against outsiders who touch one of the beloved one's supposed interests or dignities that belong to lovers.[6]

Katharine Bruce Glasier, however, while admiring Marion Phillips's intelligence, heartily disliked her: 'the personality of Dr Phillips is a real difficulty. If only your dear wife had lived to train her', wrote Katharine to Ramsay MacDonald, 'hold her, *compel* her to less egotism she might have grown great as well as clever to a degree, and capable . . . she is as hard and cold as glass. Brilliant as diamonds are *none* of us can love her except Dr Ethel Bentham.'[7]

It is hard to know how much to read into Katharine's various letters. The protagonists lived in two single-sex feminist households. Ideas such as Ramsay MacDonald's of the female household partner taking a secondary role were obviously untenable. Nevertheless, it can be assumed that relationships within the household provided personal support, its members sharing commitment and encouraging each other; as no household member was expected, because of her gender, to be the subsidiary partner, the championship of the other's cause may have been the more formidable. Whether the women's relationships were also sexual is not known and does not matter; they were separatist, and as such, maybe antagonised heterosexual League women such as Katharine sufficiently to add to the difficulties of the transition period. As her conduct to Dora Montefiore in 1899 had shown, Margaret MacDonald could be prudish and her influence had maybe been prejudicial to Marion Phillips's reception; certainly the latter always evaded opportunities to commemorate the League's founding figures.

Margaret Bondfield resigned as organising secretary in January 1912. The executive committee obviously valued her contribution; she had made her flat available to store League literature and the woman with whom she lived, Ethel Clarke, worked on the literature sales and accounts. The League continuously sought Margaret Bondfield's return and paid half her wages until June 1912; she returned the salary with equal persistence. It was not until September 1912 that the executive committee accepted Margaret Bondfield's resignation. During the whole of this period Marion Phillips's title remained carefully distinguished to allow for Margaret Bondfield's possible return. Marion Phillips's position was not ratified and made permanent until the 1913 League conference.

These difficulties seem to have dissipated somewhat by this conference. Margaret Bondfield was asked yet again to be full-time organising secretary. Maud Ward had by now left the executive, so perhaps an accommodation was easier, or better health may have made Margaret Bondfield more amenable. She and Marion Phillips together put a resolution to the general purposes committee about the organising work. The outcome was, once again, that Margaret Bondfield decided not to commit herself to full-time League work and Marion Phillips's conditions of service were improved so that she was paid £100 per year as general secretary, a position she held *de facto* for the rest of the League's existence, apart from a few months in 1915 when Mary Longman acted as secretary. The League stalwarts were reconciled; Katharine Bruce Glasier wrote: 'she (Marion Phillips) identified the Women's Labour League with herself and toils for it untiringly . . . we have accepted Dr Phillips' amazing energy and powerful lead as the only thing to do in very difficult circumstances'.[8]

During these changes, Ramsay MacDonald continued to provide rooms at his house for League meetings and the League offices. These were found to be insufficient so the League eventually rented two rooms and a storeroom at Ramsay MacDonald's house. Ethel Bentham guaranteed the rent of £25 per year. The League was allowed the use of the telephone and had its own extension fitted. Apart from Ethel Clarke, who helped until 1913, Miss Schloesser worked voluntarily in the office for three days a week. In 1913 the League stole Agnes Brown (who became Mrs George Dallas) from the National Federation of Women Workers (not unnaturally causing a further breach with Mary MacArthur); Agnes Brown worked full-time as an organiser and undertook some district visiting, but soon left to get married. Now with a pemanent staff, the League equipped the office with typewriter, map and clock. It also met a request frequently made by branches and designed a League badge (the letters WLL in red on white background, the two halves of the W incorporating one L each). The office had become a fixed focus for League work in an entirely different style to its occupancy under Margaret MacDonald's hasty and erratic distribution of attention, time and house space.

Its leadership, accommodated, now turned its attention to shaping the League into a more professional organisation. This was, perhaps, inevitable now that the leaders were themselves the product of a more rigorous education and training in administration than the Middleton/MacDonald partnership had undergone. District committees, including district conferences, on the model of Lisbeth Simm's north-eastern district were encouraged; the Lancashire and Cheshire district was extended to cover the West Riding of Yorkshire, the South-West and London districts were to continue and a new one was formed in the Midlands. Leeds by now had several League Guilds and a League central committee. These districts were to establish their own constitution and methods of operating, but had no say in central League policy-making.

This had been challenged by calls for district representation on the executive committee. However, as no conference resolutions were submitted to that effect, the executive felt free in their 1914 *Annual Report* to 'believe branches agree with their recommendation against the proposed innovation'. Districts therefore acted rather to contain branch activities than to transmit them to the leadership. The executive committee minutes made no mention of district existence. Decisions at district conferences were not passed on to the leadership. Their success depended entirely on local women. In Lisbeth Simm's area it was great and in the Lancashire area, also very effective, as the Lancashire League map (p. 87) illustrates. When Annot Robinson, Mrs Ayles and Margaret

Bondfield were all lost to the League there was more of a vacuum in their areas. (Mrs Ayles partly recovered and was elected to the executive committee, but left in 1913 when she was expecting a baby.)

Meanwhile, a number of procedures were established which allowed the leadership to control conference more tightly. The executive committee always reported to conference; from 1911 a description of sub-committee work was added. From 1913 the report was expanded to include discussion of a paper in the morning session: the branches were originally intended to suggest subjects for discussion, but in the event, the choice was made by the executive committee. In the same year the practice of taking branch reports first was dropped. Taken together, these changes meant the executive committee monopolised a large part of the agenda, especially as conference also discussed motions from the executive before reaching opinions put forward by the branches. Marion Phillips gave the paper in 1913; it was a complicated, skilled and detailed account of 'how to raise money for public services without increasing the burdens of poverty'; taxation on consumption, property and capital and local taxation were considered, and the recommendation made that taxes should be levied on luxury consumption and a graduated tax set on income from property and profits. In 1914 Lisbeth Simm gave a much more general paper on 'the working woman in politics'.

Resolutions in the League's name were put to the Labour Party conference and a delegate nominated; initially, these resolutions were first discussed by the League conference, but from 1912 they were despatched directly from the executive committee. The League could make nominations for the Labour Party executive trades council section; these nominations were also sent by the executive committee.

Nominations for the League executive committee were invited before conference and distributed for branches' information. In October 1911 it was decided branches should give brief particulars of local women, as a guide to the conference delegates who would vote in the new executive. Further requirements were then added, a statement of length of membership, office position in the League, membership of other bodies and attendance at League executive committee meetings, if appropriate. These measures might have seemed to favour existing office holders but, in fact, new members were brought into the leadership. Table 2, page 54 (Women's Labour League executive committee) illustrates that 1912 was a watershed. Of thirty-three women who served on the executive committee, eighteen were elected up to and including 1912, but not thereafter; seven were elected in and after 1912 but not before, eight were elected in both periods. Of these eight, only four were elected before 1910 (Katharine Bruce Glasier, Sister Kerrison, Minnie Nodin and Lisbeth Simm). The change in League leadership thereafter extended beyond the secretarial positions to involve the whole hierarchy.

Of the newcomers, Jennie Baker, Florence Harrison Bell, Ada Salter and Mrs Scholefield were League activists. Eveline Lowe was a member of the sewing party and baby clinic committee. Mary Longman was an investigator for the Poor Law commission. Clarice NcNab had been recruited by Lisbeth Simm on the latter's Scottish tour; she was a local councillor in Leith and secretary of the Socialist Sunday Schools. This was an organisation for socialists' children, a religious body but one which taught, as its objects stated: 'human, historical and idealist aspects of socialism'; Lizzie Glasier, Katharine's daughter, edited the Socialist Sunday Schools' magazine *Young Socialist*. Louise Donaldson was involved in the Leicester commemorative day nursery and was married to Frederick Lewis Donaldson, the Christian Socialist who became Canon of Westminster.

Of the four most consistently elected League members, two were from the provinces, Lisbeth Simm (North-East) and Katharine Bruce Glasier (Lancashire). Before 1912 other known non-Londoners elected had been Bertha Ayles (Bristol), Miss Bell (Leicester), Marion Curran (Jarrow), Mrs Gawthorpe (Leeds), Mrs James (Stanley), Mary Muir (Bradford) and Mrs Rigby (Preston). After 1912 the metropolitan orientation of the League was much increased: apart from the two long servers and Mrs Ayles, who retired part-way through 1913, only four non-Londoners were elected: Florence Harrison Bell (Newcastle, elected once in 1913), Louise Donaldson (Leicester, 1913–17, Clarice NcNab (1916–18) and Mrs Scholefield (Cardiff, 1913–18).

The metropolitan trend was exaggerated by the 1913 decision that standing members of the executive would comprise the London members. No reasons were given. It was obviously cheaper for Marion Phillips to convene the London women in the newly refurbished League office, not having to pay travelling expenses. Provincial women would, of course, have been in a minority when the subject was raised. Marion Phillips undertook few of the speaking tours for the League at which Margaret MacDonald had excelled, and it would have been wasteful to spend her time in travel to Newcastle or Cardiff if the committees and their meeting places had been more broadly based.

The number of executive sub-committee meetings (general purposes and literature/publicity) had risen after 1911; moreover the general purposes committee increasingly took upon itself the role of an inner cabinet, debating matters that were to come before the full executive and making recommendations. Power was effectively concentrated in the hands of the relative London newcomers, Lisbeth Simm and Katharine Bruce Glasier being excluded from the inner circle. Sister Kerrison was by now quite elderly and Minnie Nodin an invalid (although, according to Ishbel MacDonald, Minnie's housekeeper and husband were very active in 'the work arising out of her enthusiasm from the sofa'.[9] This was important in later discussions on the League's future, in that the voice of the early League, of the 'free lances', was cut off from an audience.

It was not surprising that the style of the League organ also changed to reflect the new professionalism. From 1911 it had been decided to produce a regular magazine rather than pamphlets on specific issues; in view of the diversity and size of the League, a central publication to keep members informed was a necessity. It would also be useful in attracting recruits. As the League office staff were appointed, it became possible to prepare a more professional magazine. In the first of the regular leaflets, the League set out to publicise itself as a respectable body of political activists by printing laudatory statements from Beatrice Webb, Margaret Llewellyn-Davies (Co-operative Women's Guild), George Barnes (Parliamentary Labour Party Chair), W. G. Anderson (Independent Labour Party Chair) and Ramsay MacDonald. The Women's Trade Union League and National Federation of Women Workers were allocated a page. Mary Macpherson undertook international correspondence. The *League Leaflet* was sold through local newsagents.

In the executive committee traumas of 1911/12 the *Leaflet* became an issue of dispute. Margaret Bondfield tried and failed to get editorial control, but the literature committee was renamed the publication committee and decided to retain the editorship and also to expand the *Leaflet*. By May 1912 it had been decided to have a double-page leaflet, wired, two pages allocated to the Women's Trade Union League, one to the Co-operative Women's Guild and one to the Shop Assistants' Union. Advertising was sought to help defray expenses. By September 1912 the *Leaflet* had grown to twelve pages with a distinctive two-colour cover (red on white). In April 1913 the leaflet became a full-size magazine, *Labour Woman,* which had 181 subscribers by the next month. Copies were sent to the British Museum, *Daily Herald, Daily News* and *Morning Leader, Common Cause Manchester Guardian* and the British Museum of Social Science.

Labour Woman did not differ remarkably in tone or content from the original *League Leaflets*. There was the same mix of advice on work on public bodies, assistance to trade unions, information on social reform. There were also recipes and notes on homemaking and short stories. For a while a children's section was run, the 'Green Sprig Party'. One very useful column was 'Facts and Figures' which gave succinct information on issues with which the branches dealt. For instance, figures on the school medical service were given (May 1913); 317 school medical officers had been appointed by local authorities, 314 of them men; on housing (July 1913) occupancy was given as 5·20 people per house in 1901, 5·05 in 1911; on infant mortality (August 1913) the figures were 130 deaths per thousand births in 1911, the highest figures being Bradford, 163 and Shoreditch, 160.

One innovation was discussion of birth control. Florence Harrison Bell wrote on this subject in August 1913, advocating limited families for working people who were thrown into poverty by coping with large numbers of children. Emily C. Fortey, the next month, castigated birth control as evil, although she would not blame working people who were faced with poverty for following a custom already set amongst the upper classes. This raised a lively correspondence, most writers agreeing with Florence Harrison Bell's line, although Jennie Baker wrote to express her disappointment that ways and means were not explained for working women to follow. Marion Phillips closed the correspondence in December 1912, without comment. As editor, she was proud of *Labour Leader* and told the 1914 conference it 'holds the field as the only journal giving a thoroughly reliable record of working women's views'.

The self-supporting fund raising that financed the League branches was obviously insufficient to pay the expenses of the bureaucracy that had established itself centrally. In addition, the chief private contributions to the funds had ceased with Margaret MacDonald's death. On 6 November 1911 the executive committee recommended a 6*d* entrance fee to meet growing financial difficulties, but fees, purposely set low, were never going to provide sufficient income.

The League therefore made the decision, crucial to its future, to accept a Labour Party grant and, furthermore, came to rely on this source of income. Such a grant had been requested by the League as soon as affiliation was achieved; in 1909 the Labour Party had been unable to provide a grant, stating that there was no provision within its constitution. However, 1910 was the year of two general elections. By meeting some of the need for election workers, the League caused the Party to look more kindly upon its endeavours: 'I have to express the Party's obligation and gratitude', Ramsay MacDonald told the Party conference, 'for the splendid election work done on behalf of the candidates by the various branches of the League during the recent election.' In 1911 £50 was granted to the League from the Party's general fund and £50 from its special fund.

The Labour Party grant was tangible recognition of the League's efficiency and the esteem in which it was held. It also meant that the links with 'the Men's Party' grew stronger. As the League grew more metropolitan and its hierarchy more formal, these links were strengthened by contact between the officers of the League and the Party and by the League leadership lobbying parliamentarians in Westminister. It was at this time that Braithwaite described the League and other women's organisations as 'very much organised by the bourgeoisie and the intellectuals . . . progressive women'.[10]

One has a sense of diminution of some of the warmth and energy that had characterised the League under its amateur direction. The changes were subtle, of tone rather than policy. One should be scrupulous in discovering a trend when the effect is partly created by the accident of the records that have survived. Mary Middleton's and Margaret MacDonald's personal correspondence with branches is obviously not available for this period. Nevertheless, what the new leadership chose to save is an indication of what they valued and the record of the executive meetings is good. There is no evidence that causes the League had traditionally championed were abandoned; on the contrary, 1913 witnessed the great letter-writing campaign about infant mortality and the school meals and school clinics campaigns certainly continued, so that success looked near. There were eighty-six League branches active in 1914. On the other hand, there were no new branch initiatives and the provincial districts saw less of the League leaders. Their efforts seem to be channelled into getting the organisation right, making this transition period an inward-looking one for the League, obsessed with personality. The charismatic leaders, holding the League together carelessly, with illuminating oratorical sentiment, were gone; to replace them professional, but pedestrian organisational directives were issued. There was, perhaps, an acceptance of standards laid down by the masculine-oriented Labour Party, a concentration on membership figures and finances.

At the same time, the mother and baby imagery in League speeches and writing diminished, more emphasis being placed on women at work. Margaret Bondfield and Marion Phillips were unmarried, working women; it was inevitable, perhaps, that their rhetoric was more about women's capacity or inclusion in the mainstream than about their 'special powers'. One has to be careful with the terminology; 'working women' then was taken to mean women of the working classes; 'industrial women' meant women in wage labour; this language tends to exaggerate the change. The industrial unrest of 1911, however, continued and League women, of course, were involved. They took care of striker's children during the London dock strike; the 1912 executive resolution to conference congratulated women who stood 'shoulder to shoulder' with men in the disputes. A second executive committee resolution demanded that there be no interference with trade union rights. At the 1914 conference delegates were reminded that 'the wives of strikers had participated in the rough and tumble of the movement outside their home. In some cases, they had taken their turn when picketting was to be done.' Fifteen League branches had strike funds by 1914. Class politics were being more firmly stated; 'the League has always felt very strongly that in organising women politicians we must not separate them from the labour movement of both men and women.'

The very first issue of *Labour Woman* contained an article by J. J. Mallon in praise of the new Trades Boards. These had proved bitterly controversial within the League. Now branches were urged to help unions operate the Trades Boards Acts in their area; twenty were reported as so doing. Ironically, J. J. Mallon started his article with an account of wages set much too low for Leeds tailoring workers. Male and female employees had campaigned, successfully, to have the rate set higher and in the process formed the Amalgamated Union of Clothiers' Operatives. Wages for women were less than the men's. One can assume branch initiatives in Trades Boards work. They were also instructed to seek representation on local bodies administering the national insurance scheme. Both Margaret Bondfield and Marion Phillips spent much energy on insurance work. However, this took the form not of local agitation, market-place meetings, petitioning, as with the school meals campaign, but in the setting up of special bodies on which the leaders sat. The Industrial Women's Insurance Advisory Board was created in 1912 with representatives of the League, the Women's Co-operative Guild and the National Federation of Women Workers. It met in the League office. This was a further statement of the League commitment to industrial women.

It was quite true that the League had always perceived itself as an integral part of the Labour movement. Yet it had also claimed therein a special place for women, emphasised the importance of those with experience putting the case. Lisbeth Simm expressed this in 1912, writing in the *Aberdeen Daily Journal* (13 December 1912): 'Women were realising that they could not even do their duty in the home unless they took some interest in public and outside affairs. The League was educating women to formulate their demands for better opportunities of life and leisure, more education and better means of enjoying the arts of life than existed today.' The concentration on women as wage labourers allowed less space for this type of feminism to develop. There were, indeed, calls for the men to stay home and mind the baby while women attended League meetings (for instance at the 1914 conference). More frequently, the problem of the double burden was not addressed.

There was another, ominous change in League priorities. One of the executive resolutions to the 1912 conference condemned secret diplomacy and the Foreign Office for acting as if war was inevitable. At the 1913 conference Katharine Bruce Glasier moved the first resolution, protesting against militarism and fearing an expansion of the war in the Balkans. Lisbeth Simm spoke to the effect that war was a hindrance to social reform. She wrote in *Labour Woman* on 'War against War' (June 1913) that 'the Labour Party had always stood for international friendship and peace'. She found army training and discipline degrading, turning men into alien beings; she remembered seeing a camp as a child: 'it seemed to us as if these soldiers were not men, but something that was drilled while sober, and drunk and helpless when off duty'. Lisbeth wrote that the price of production of life for mothers was too heavy for it to be wasted. War demoralised a nation. 'Facts and Figures' in November 1913 amplified Lisbeth's statement about social reform; Britain spent £18,729,000 each year on education, £27,860,000 on the army and £44,085,000 on the navy; spending on the armed forces amounted to 12*s* 4*d* per head. The 1914 conference voted against arms expenditure, against conscription and in favour of the joint action of workers internationally against war.

Labour Woman always carried international news. Jennie Baker took over this column from Mary Macpherson in April 1914 and headed it 'Our Sisters Abroad'. She reported activities of European and American women socialists and their greetings. Mary Longman, in July 1914, was recorded as having participated in a peace demonstration, speaking to the crowd in German. Sympathy was sent to Rosa Luxemburg on her arrest in April 1914. The Women's Council of the Labour and Socialist International was given space. Mrs Murby, of the Fabian Society, had taken over the secretaryship of this after Margaret MacDonald's death and Mary Longman took over from her within the year. The International was due to meet in Vienna in 1914.

The League identification with class politics was becoming stronger by its emphasis on industrial women and on internationalism and because of the League perception that these issues should not be addressed 'separate . . . from the Labour movement.' Women's views on these issues were expressed and the change in philosophy from the free-lance League should not be exaggerated; nevertheless, there was a new orientation. It was at this time that the League again approached the Labour Party for more money, thereby further consolidating the links between League and Party.

Greater contributions from the Labour Party to the League funds were partly made possible by a profound constitutional change in 1913, the Liberal Government's enactment of legislation to pay Members of Parliament in order to redress the punitive effect of the Osborne Judgement on the Labour Party. The Osborne Judgement had made it impossible for the trade unions to provide political funds; the new legislation meant that Labour Members were free of their sponsors and opened the House of Commons to working men (and later women). Immediately, the Labour Party, released from the need to fund its parliamentary members, could afford to be more generous to its affiliates. The League grant was doubled.

The bureaucracy, however, demanded servicing: increased expenditure on publications and the office soon disposed of the League funds and a joint committee was set up in 1914 from the Party and the League executive committees to decide how the Party would finance the League. Almost immediately, this led the League into a danger that seems to have gone unremarked: discussion of the League's autonomy.[11] The League was given fair warning: 'There was a feeling (on the Party executive) that branch organisation of the League, so far as it has come to the notice of members of our committee, was not as efficient or as strongly developed as it could be', wrote Arthur Henderson, Party secretary, to Marion Phillips. The League promised to see what savings it could make; Marion Phillips agreed to forego her salary, the hours and pay of the office clerk were cut and the pages of *Labour Woman* reduced. Arthur Henderson was not challenged, nor was he asked to specify his complaints.

Paradoxically, it was in this period, when its identification of women's separate culture was weakest, that the League involvement in the women's suffrage campaign grew. Partly, this was because the Labour Party policy changed; partly, it was due to Marion Phillips's appointment. Although she was now in favour of full adult suffrage, Marion Phillips gave much more time to the women's suffrage campaign than had other leaders. Her style of leadership was less antithetical to Mrs Pankhurst's reign over the Women's Social and Political Union and she had the background of work for the National Union of Women's Suffrage Societies.

Branches were asked by the executive committee to pass resolutions in favour of the Local Authority (Qualification of Women) Bill, a positive step that had not been taken previously. The League next became one of the organising societies of a conference of the Women's Suffrage Joint Committee and the Adult Suffrage Society called specifically to discuss the vote and working women which Mary MacArthur was to chair. Following this, the London-based general purposes and publicity committees decided to support the

Joint Campaign Committee in urging the immediate introduction of a Reform Bill. The executive committee decided (31 May 1912) not to take official part in a Women's Social and Political Union demonstration in Hyde Park, even were they to have their own platform, but to urge branches to pass resolutions demanding the introduction of a Reform Bill and requesting the Prime Minister to receive a deputation.

The catalyst that may have stimulated the League to greater activity, as it stimulated so many women to militancy, was the Liberal Prime Minister (Asquith)'s 1911 introduction into the House of Commons of a Franchise Bill which did not include women. The Independent Labour Party campaigned against this action and the Labour Party conference finally took the decision that no franchise reform was acceptable unless women were included. With the Labour Party now committed to support, a restraint on League activity was removed.

Liberal women also were appalled at their Prime Minister's action and were drawn towards co-operation with Labour, as the only party resolute on their behalf. The National Union of Women's Suffrage Societies contained many Liberal women, who started to look to Labour. H. N. Brailsford, a radical Liberal academic and journalist, approached the Labour Party on the Society's behalf and with great patience, cajoled both groups into an alliance. The leadership of each organisation was reluctant, the Society articulating a desire to remain non-party-political. It might have been expected that the League women would be called into negotiations, but there is no record of any approach from the Party on the issue. Catherine Marshall, of the Society, dealt directly with the Labour Party men. Eventually, an Election Fighting Fund was set up to combat constituencies where there was no Member of Parliament committed to women's suffrage, and to fight these on behalf of the Labour Party. The Labour Party, extraordinarily, asked for the words 'in the Labour interest' to be removed from the fund appeal letter, which in the circumstances, would have been a misrepresentation of the purpose of the fund, besides making it redundant. The NUWSS perpetually attempted to raise money and it was the exceptional goal of fighting elections on behalf of Labour which gave fresh impetus to the latest appeal.

In the constituencies chosen for combat, the Society women and Labour Party men appear to have worked well together and to have been reasonably successful. There were thirty-two by-elections from June 1912 until August 1914, five of them in mining constituencies; as mining was labour-intensive, it was particularly important to win support from the mineworkers, who because of their numbers, could dominate politics within their constituency. The NUWSS and Labour Party alliance fought eight seats, including mining constituencies; although the Labour candidate was not returned in any of these eight constituencies, the Liberal vote was reduced in each. Had there been a general election in 1914, the alliance of Labour and women may have been able to capitalise on its work. The Election Fighting Fund did contain women who were, or had been, League members (Isabella Ford and Ethel Snowden) and many NUWSS members were League women (all the north-eastern district committee, for instance), but the League otherwise appears not to have attempted to recruit for Labour any of the NUWSS women involved in the alliance, an omission for which there is no explanation in the records.

By October 1912, the League was sufficiently active on women's enfranchisement to allow the Women's Freedom League (which had seceded from the Women's Social and Political Union in 1907) to inscribe the League name on a scroll recording societies which supported women's suffrage, with the wording 'Unity in Adversity' as its logo. The League executive committee joined the Women's Freedom League at its international fair and took part in the Women's Freedom League national conference in December 1912. A special suffrage edition of the *League Leaflet* was issued late in 1912 (no. 23), a statement of the Labour Party position on suffrage and that the League was working for its achievement.

This was signed by Marion Phillips and started in a stateswomanlike way, regretting that the Women's Social and Political Union had seen fit to campaign against Philip Snowden (Independent Labour Party and Labour Party) in his constituency and giving the history of the Pethwick-Lawrences' recent split from the WSPU. It was reported that the Labour Party, in line with conference resolutions, was trying to persuade the House of Commons to adopt an amendment to the Reform Bill then before it, to include women's enfranchisement. The Woman's Social and Political Union's position was that the amendment was inadequate and therefore the whole Bill should be rejected; the *League Leaflet* reiterated that such a course would be a betrayal of Labour women in constituencies which had returned Labour Members of Parliament.

Philip Snowden wrote that the feeling of the House of Commons was moving in favour of women; what was needed was constituency pressure and the support of the Irish Members of Parliament. (The latter were seeking home rule and supported the Liberal Government in so far as it seemed inclined to grant their claims.) What course the Labour Party should take if the Bill were to reach its third reading in parliament and still not refer to women was hotly debated, Marion Phillips's advice being to wait and see:

> Let us, who represent the working women in politics, be forward in the fight, pressing our supporters in the House of Commons onward to the victory which justice demands. And let us do this from within our own ranks, under our own banner of freedom and hope, not scattered through our societies, but solidly organised as Labour women demanding economic and political equality for working women and working men.

So that, in the event of women not being included in the Reform Bill, the Labour Party would be equipped with the right response, the League executive committee, however, decided on the safeguard of a further resolution to the Labour Party conference. They also decided to take part in a national suffrage conference. These actions were supported by the 1913 League conference, the year Florence Harrison Bell, an ardent suffragist, was elected to the executive committee. The executive began to take its own direct action on women's suffrage, deciding on 31 March 1913 to send resolutions to the Prime Minister, Lloyd George (Chancellor of the Exchequer), the People's Suffrage Federation and the Labour Party, demanding the immediate introduction of a government measure to enfranchise women. Having been offered the chance to discuss this action with a League delegation, the Parliamentary Labour Party offended by replying that Members would meet League women together with delegates from the National Union of Women's Suffrage Societies and the Women's Co-operative Guild. From tentative support, the League had moved to claiming the right for its own voice to be distinctly heard on the issue of women's suffrage. It claimed, 'as an organisation of the Party', the right to a private deputation and discussion.

Some executive committee members, such as Katharine Bruce Glasier, felt that concentrating on suffrage in this way reduced the League to a 'stage army'. In contrast with controversial provincial initiatives, under Mary Middleton and Margaret MacDonald's leadership, support for suffrage under Marion Phillips was conducted by the London leadership and set in Westminster, an issue of high politics. However, the coercive measures against the militant suffragettes won them support generally and in the League. A resolution calling on the House of Commons to redress the grievances of women who resented coercion was sent to the Prime Minister, the Labour Party and the press, and the secretary was empowered to urge Labour Members of Parliament to abstain or vote against the Bill, which was intended to abolish plural voting, unless it also enfranchised women. Plural voting, the right to vote in more than one constituency where ownership of property or residence qualified the elector, was obviously reactionary and discriminated against men of the working classes. Asking the Labour Party to forgo the passage of legislation removing the plural vote was therefore a serious matter, which illustrated how committed the League had become to the suffrage cause.

As militancy grew, so did the League support. Delegates were sent to the conference held to protest against the Cat and Mouse Act (which enabled women prisoners on hunger strike to be released until they had recovered sufficiently to complete their sentence). The poster produced to publicise the horrors of the Cat and Mouse Act was exhibited and the League called for a Labour Amendment to the Address following the King's Speech (setting out the government's legislative programme). Marion Phillips wrote an obituary for Emily Wilding Davison in *Labour Woman* (July 1913), applauding her courage (she was killed, having thrown herself under the King's horse at the Derby. Emily Wilding Davison 'stood rather apart from the organised disorder of the militant movement' in Marion Phillips's opinion, braving the consequences of her own actions. A sizeable number of Women's Social and Political Union members retained their League membership. The executive decided they must choose between the two bodies, but after a debate that would have seemed impossible even two years earlier, when Marion Phillips was writing her leaflet.

Katharine Bruce Glasier, no suffragette, wrote to Ramsay MacDonald to complain about his use of the epithet 'man hungry' to describe the militants: 'a suggestion for which even I feel ready to strike to defend my sex's honour . . . for that reason I grieved a little over your "suffragette" diagnosis, "physiological"

. . . (you wouldn't like me to define *your* duties in certain education in terms that would apply to mere malehood)'. The text of Ramsay MacDonald's letter has unfortunately not survived, but he would seem to have fallen into vulgar error in supposing disenfranchised women to be compensating for their celibacy in their quest for citizenship. Katharine Bruce Glasier might not like the style or the extent of the League suffrage campaign, but she would never have felt the need to apologise for women's political activity.

By 1914, the League had found its balance on its bridge and was deciding to step out into new territory, a closer relationship with a Labour Party that had provided the bulk of its funds. The acrimonious personal disputes were over and the League had settled down under Marion Phillips; Margaret Bondfield had left the executive committee. Cohesion had been achieved, even on the suffrage issue, so potentially divisive. A press report, praising the political knowledge and skills presented at the League 1914 conference, proudly printed in *Labour Woman* (March 1914), illustrated the respect the League had won: 'The probabilities are that the six hundred delegates (to the subsequent Labour Party conference) will say in long winded and halting fashion what the women said in tabloid speeches and resolutions.' All this was at the cost of branch initiative. However, the campaigns already under way had been thoroughly pursued and it looked as if the Liberal Government was about to act on school meals and school clinics. The League was more firmly identified as an organisation supporting the waged woman, in addition to woman in the home. League members on the joint committee with the Labour Party had a fair bargaining position. Then came the next tragedy, so long foreshadowed, this time not personal to the League, but shattering all the known landmarks of the ground it was about to tread; the declaration of war.

Notes

1 *J. R. MacDonald and M. E. MacDonald Papers*, PRO/30/69 (Public Records Office, London), 1157: letter from Ramsay MacDonald to Katharine Bruce Glasier.

2 Mary Agnes Hamilton, *Margaret Bondfield* (London, 1924), p. 110.

3 Sylvia E. Pankhurst, *The Suffragette Movement: An Intimate Account of Persons and Ideals* (London, 1931), pp. 177–8.

4 Sir H. N. Bunbury (ed.), *Lloyd George's Ambulance Wagon: the Memoirs of A. J. Braithwaite* (Methuen, 1957), p. 235.

5 *MacDonald Papers,* 1156: letter from Margaret Bondfield.

6 *MacDonald Papers,* 1157: letter from Katharine Bruce Glasier to Ramsay MacDonald.

7 *MacDonald Papers,* 1157.

8 *MacDonald Papers,* 1158: letter from Katharine Bruce Glasier to Ramsay MacDonald.

9 Labour Party *Subject Files,* LP/INF/13/BAB (Labour Party Headquarters Archives, London), letter from Ishbel Peterkin to Lucy Middleton, 16 October 1976.

10 Sir H. N. Bunbury, *Lloyd George's Ambulance Wagon,* p. 235.

11 The records of the League negotiations with the Party are in the Labour Party *Subject Files,* LP/WLL/08/31–66 and the Women's Labour Executive Committee *Minutes 1914–1918* (Labour Party Headquarters Archives, London).

5

Shoulder to shoulder

'The revolution would be here' – Ada Salter, League conference, 1914

'In one short week the whole fabric of civilisation has been shaken', wrote Marion Phillips in the September 1914 *Labour Woman*. She hoped the suffering would end in a greater humanity, the furtherance of the interests of the working classes. Lisbeth Simm reported from the North-East on the drilling, training and recruiting along the sea coast. The war was a catharsis for the Labour movement, a time of political and industrial upheaval. Against this background, pressure for change within the League built on several fronts. First was the closer relationship with the Labour Party brought about by the League's financial needs. Second was franchise reform. Third, the outbreak of war altered the nature of League activity while stimulating new connections of class and gender politics, a process heightened by the Russian revolution of 1917. It was Marion Phillips's duty to guide the League through the interaction of these disturbing, exciting, distressing and awful events.

One of the more mundane, yet far-reaching effects of the war was added expense for branches taking on new work, yet finding the traditional means of fund-raising through entertainments inappropriate. Perhaps it was to save money, but the decision at this time not to print a calendar illustrated with photographs of Margaret MacDonald marked the end of the influence of the original founders along with the end of traditional methods. It was now that the Labour Party lost Keir Hardie, sickened by the war; one is glad to record that the League sent a telegram of sympathy to Lillie, his widow. The League and Labour Party joint committee still demanded savings; the general purposes committee had empowered

Marion Phillips to engage anyone she found useful in the office; she found Miriam Norman, who worked for a miserly 10*s* a week. Miriam Norman was succeeded in turn by Marion Cooper and Edith Bryant. In May 1915 this cost-consciousness was approved by the Labour Party; a deputation met the League executive committee. This consisted of W. C. Anderson, Mary MacArthur's husband, and Mr P. Egerton Wake, who now had the task of representing the League on the Party executive, together with his reponsibilities for trades councils and local Labour parties. A supplementary grant of £150 was made to the League, these gentlemen being sufficiently impressed with League organisation.

Meanwhile, Marion Phillips's vistas had opened with the entry of women to the industrial work force. She resigned as League secretary, the executive committee (19 February 1915) accepting 'with sorrow' but acknowledging their inability to tie her down to routine office work. Mary Longman took over. Marion Phillips lived with Mary Longman and remained on the executive, also retaining the editorship of *Labour Woman,* so her influence remained great, despite her resignation as secretary. Mary Longman's appointment was for six months only in the first instance, because she had no experience of organising the branches; it was made permanent in October 1915.

Negotiations with the League and Party were now left to the officers; James Middleton, Labour Party assistant secretary since its inception, and the relatively inexperienced Mary Longman. In negotiations, she changed the emphasis of the traditional League position:

> the executive would like to be regarded not merely as one among a number of societies affiliated to the local Labour Parties, but as something much more closely connected, as part of the Labour Party itself – meanwhile the League asks the Labour Party Executive Committee if they will help, firstly by pressing on the local Labour Parties the view that the League is an organic part of the Labour Party – its women's section – and as such has a special claim on it for support and help.[1]

Each request for money, each new articulation of the relationship included a threat to League autonomy. The dangers of disappearing within the Party structure were clear enough and were illustrated by Mr Higginbotham, Labour Party organiser, when he spoke to the Wolverhampton Labour Party. He set the value of a small, but active, League branch low, to the anger of the League delegate to the meeting. Mary reported:

> in the first place, he said he did not know how many members the League had in Wolverhampton, but he ventured to say we were not growing and he advocated the starting of a Women's Labour Association for social functions, say to meet the prospective candidate and his wife, and to have a cup of tea provided and light refreshments, etc., he thought we might get recruits for the League when their ideas were more advanced.

James Middleton, to whom Mary Longman complained, wrote that there must have been a misunderstanding; he further stated that he wanted to keep the League intact.

Negotiations continued. James Middleton (then and throughout his career) seems to have been one of those fortunate people with whom anyone could work, however sensitive the matter in hand. Mary Longman sent him privately drafts of her suggestons for co-operation between League and Party. These appear to have won favours as they differed only in layout from the proposals presented in October 1915 by a League committee elected for that purpose (Mary Longman, Ada Salter, Marion Phillips, with Minnie Nodin as sole representative of the League founders, elected by the general purposes committee).

After a preamble stating there were ninety-five constituencies where there was a local Labour organisation but no League, eighteen of which had a Labour Member of Parliament and fifteen a Labour candidate, these proposals were limited to seeking publicity for the League. Local Labour parties were asked to assist the League with rooms, publicity and opportunities for organising; Labour organisers were to be instructed to call a women's meeting with a League speaker when they visited branches or when new branches were formed; *Labour Woman* was to be distributed to branches when the organisers visited. Further suggestions were that, at the annual Labour Party conference that year, representatives of existing or potential League branches should meet with the Party executive committee and organisers. Mary Longman ended by asking that the organisers follow the League's outline of work for any new branches founded.

These proposals became the working document for the Party organising sub-committee during 1916. They still enshrined a very clear idea of the League as a separate organisation. It had, however, become a very fragile one. On 29 September 1916

Marion Phillips proposed to the executive committee that a private and confidential letter be sent to branches calling attention to the 'serious condition' of the League and offering personal letters to members whom it was feared would lapse, or to prospective members.

During 1916 three decisions were taken which perhaps betray fear for the future as well as lack of concern for the past. Together, these decisions very nearly ensured that no memory survived of the League and its work. First, Hodder & Stoughton offered 1,000 copies of Margaret MacDonald's biography, which were declined. Second, after receiving letters from Lisbeth Simm, Katharine Bruce Glasier, Mrs Donaldson and Miss MacNab, the League hurriedly moved out of its offices at Ramsay MacDonald's house from which he also intended to remove. The content of the letters was not specified, but appeared to cause the executive committee some alarm and to indicate some distaste for their accommodation. The League moved to the Labour Party offices at 1 Victoria Street. Ramsay MacDonald had Margaret MacDonald's papers, most of which he burnt. Third, because of the removal, Marion Phillips was instructed to destroy correspondence before 1912 and 'unimportant letters' after that. The minute books luckily survived the flames, as did a collection of papers presumably saved by Mary Middleton (these were kept by James Middleton and finally rescued by his third wife, Lucy Cox).

One bright hope during 1916 was a legacy left to the League by Miss Hollins, with which it was hoped to pay a full-time organiser. Mary Longman resigned because she was to marry (she had not married in 1919, when she was contributing to *Labour Woman;* perhaps her relationship was a casualty of the war). Lisbeth Simm was offered and refused the secretary's job (at £150 per year). Miss Coates was then appointed office secretary (at £2 per week) after exhaustive interviews; while the appointment was for a six months' trial, the prospect was held out of succeeding to the general secretary's job. Marion Phillips acted as honorary secretary while Miss Coates learnt her job. These actions were legitimised after the event by rule changes at the January 1917 conference.[2] The number of women on the executive committee was increased; these, an unpaid general secretary and treasurer, were to be elected at conference. All other officers were to be appointed and dismissed by the executive committee.

Marion Phillips was thus back at the reins and her position differentiated from that of the other paid officers; the power of the executive committee, of which she remained the most influential member, was increased. Other changes were put in hand without conference approval; sub-committees of the executive were to be set up on specific items and the branches were to elect correspondents for each matter; which strengthened executive direction of branch action; moreover, the general purposes committee was to meet monthly and have full control between the thrice-monthly meetings of the executive committee, thus devolving effective administration of the League to the London cohort. The only matters which lay outside the prerogative of the general purposes committee were those dealt with by the joint organising committee with the Labour Party.

The new efficiency of the leadership under Marion Phillips, the greater importance of the London women in positions of power and the relative diminution of branch initiative had paved the way for these changes. The effect, at a time when the League 'courtship' of the Party was finally being resolved by a rather grudging acceptance of a dowerless bride, was probably not envisaged by the negotiators; the influence the rank and file League women had lost was matched by that gained by Labour Party men. Partly, it was a question of organisational changes imposing their own philosophy, gathering their own momentum. The League, having been unique, had no role model of a merger between a gender and a class-oriented group to follow, in order to salvage the best terms. Also, the League appears to have had none of the fear that, in the circumstances, would have been healthy. It would be anachronistic to credit it with the suspicion women in like circumstances later learnt. Finally, nearly all the League founders, who had delighted in the exploration of the free-lance role, were gone.

The joint sub-committee with the Labour Party was now to consist of four Labour men and four League women. It was intended to involve trade union secretaries and to address the question of appointing women's organisers in each of the League districts, agents common to Party and League, and financial help to the League. The four women were as those originally appointed, except that Jennie Baker replaced Mary Longman. A conference was to be held in Leicester on the best way to bring women into the Labour Party and among those attending were to be Party agents and candidates. It was thought that appointing organisers in League districts would cost £1,000 each year; Miss Hollin's legacy was to provide half and the Labour Party would fund the rest.

For the time being, the Labour Party made a grant of £150 to League funds: it was also asked to pay for two organisers. Mary Longman's offer of closer co-operation with the Party, based on the perception of the League as its local women's sections, was taken a stage further; the executive committee was informed (28 September 1917): 'Dr Phillips has consulted with the Labour Party sub-committees and they agreed with the suggestion she put forward for making the League an integral part of the Party, while still preserving independent expression of opinion for women.'

At this time (summer 1917) there was rather an unsavoury episode, unfortunately quite in keeping with the normal League style of treating its employees. Miss Coates's first six months in office had expired. She was called to a League executive committee meeting, kept waiting and then dismissed, on the grounds that the League needed a more efficient typist and shorthand writer. Naturally, there was some resentment; Central London branch championed Miss Coates. Marion Phillips offered her resignation and when this was refused, left it in the hands of the executive until the situation should be more stable. Several women were interviewed for the post of office secretary (including Rose Rosenberg – later Ramsay MacDonald's private secretary – thought to be too inexperienced); Miss Stevens was finally appointed. Branches were informed that Miss Coates's departure was 'foreshadowing changes in staff and organisation'.

Until 1908 the Labour Party had left the League alone to succeed or fail as it might; having accepted League affiliation in that year, the Party had accepted help in election work and from 1911 gave financial assistance in return. It was not until 1914 that the Party seriously addressed the problem of women's participation and representation within its own structure. Motives were mixed: partly, the League had become a familiar body, with a recognisable bureaucracy and a standard of professional work that matched the Party's own. The Party had also, through the Election Fighting Fund, had a lesson in the benefits of women's co-operation. Yet women's trade unions were, in general, not affiliates of the Party and the problems of attracting female membership remained.

What made a compact with the League of immediate interest were the Party's proposed new constitution and franchise reform. Arthur Henderson and the Webbs were engaged in drafting, together with policy documents that balanced constitutionalism with the chiliasm needed to present Labour's plans for an egalitarian post-war world, a clear structure for the Party. This would allow individual membership, in branches affiliated, as would be trade unions, to local constituency bodies. These fulfilled much the same function as had local representation committees, but were very different constitutionally; the LRCs had mirrored the national Party as agencies, peopled by representatives of local Labour movement bodies, including the League. New were the geographically devised branches containing the individual members, women and men, forming the absolute grass-roots structure; each member had a say, through a representative, to the second tier constituency body, whether or not she or he belonged to a trade union or a socialist society. The functional and organisational problems that had so hindered women's membership of the 'men's party' were alike resolved by the new constitution; the party's political function had been clarified while individual membership became the basis of participation. With its house in order, the Labour Party could be generous in giving the League a room, especially as the space the League claimed was modest and ill-defined, 'integration' and 'local recognition'.

As the new constitutional proposals demanded negotiations be conducted with some urgency, so did franchise reform. The arguments for women's enfranchisement had been made by 1914 and would have been a major issue at the abandoned 1915 General Election. A Liberal government seeking re-election would have found it extremely difficult to resist rank and file pressure for the inclusion of women's suffrage in their appeal to the electorate. Without such a catalyst, it was far from easy to get enfranchisement accepted by a House of Commons which still contained stonewallers suggesting that registration amendments would suffice to rectify the deficiencies of the electoral system. Chief amongst these faults was that mobility disqualified the voter who owned no property; absence from home on war service obviously magnified the problem. No government could welcome its heroes home from the trenches with the news that they had lost their right to vote. A Speaker's Committee was set up to address the problem. Labour

Members of Parliament, committed to the suffrage cause, had joined the wartime coalition government. Arthur Henderson had accepted a Cabinet position. One of the Labour Members assigned to the Speaker's Committee was Mr Wardle; he had addressed the Railway Women's Guild back in 1904 on the need for women's politicisation and inspired Mary Macpherson to set about the creation of the Women's Labour League. One may assume that Mr Wardle argued strongly in favour of women's enfranchisement.

The eventual proposals emanating from the Speaker's Committee almost ignored votes for women yet again; however, a timely amendment included the necessary recommendation. The Reform Act of 1918 enfranchised women over thirty years of age. It would have an enormous effect on the electoral register. With the women voters definitely there to be won at the next election, the value of a women's organisation within the Labour Party was enhanced, providing a point of identity and means of persuasion of the new voters. The Labour Party wanted to begin organising the women's vote long before the election; the new constitution therefore had to be structured accordingly. A League sub-committee on 'The Organisation of Women as Voters' held whilst the Speaker's Committee was still deliberating (13 April 1917) was perhaps indicative of the feeling within the Labour movement:

> organisation was urgently necessary so that the new voters shall come into the labour movement by joining our organisation and not be caught by any of the separate women's organisations which are bound to be set on foot. It is most important that, as workers, they should join with men and not form a special women's party.

It was ironical that the success of the suffrage campaign, while making the League attractive to the Party, caused the League to renege on separatism. Although the League had always been ambiguous about retaining a separate organisation, seeking affiliation and then financial help and identifying itself strongly with the Labour Party, it had also appreciated the value of women's autonomy. Now, winning the vote, League women had become 'workers' first and 'women' second. One must look further than the sheer momentum of the organisational changes to find out why the League was so anxious to 'join with men'. The answer lies in the complex effect of war on gender politics.

War disrupted all political activity and the League did not escape its consequences. In 1915 it was agreed that conferences be postponed, with only two branches in oppostion. Conferences were held in 1916 (Bristol) and 1917 (Manchester), but the problems of organisation were immense. In 1916, Bristol branch had to be cajoled into giving any sort of entertainment; in 1917 there was no social activity at conference. The difficulties in calling conference indicate first, that branches were likely to lose more ground to the Westminster leadership and second, that there were problems of isolation, which would be deeply felt by League women outside London, whose usual round of political activity and social support disappeared because of the war. 'Some of us are feeling very timid and useless', wrote Lisbeth Simm.[3] At every executive committee the list of branches which had 'died' or 'collapsed' was ominously long. Appendix 2 (Table of League branches) shows thirty branches closed during the war years and only sixteen opened.

To help combat isolation, district conferences were strongly encouraged. There were by now six League districts: London and the South-East (Eveline Lowe); the South-West and Wales (Mrs Scholefield); the Midlands and 'if possible' the Eastern Counties (Mrs Donaldson); Lancashire, Cheshire and the West Riding of Yorkshire (Katharine Bruce Glasier); the North-East and Durham (Lisbeth Simm); and Scotland (Clarice McNab). Although one woman was identified with each district, there was still no place for district representatives in the League hierarchy. These were to meet with the executive committee once or twice a year, but otherwise had no say in League decision-making. Two women were appointed as paid district organisers, receiving £2 a month each (as usual, a rather miserly wage); Mrs Scholefield and Lisbeth Simm. Lisbeth had thought she would have to retire following an accident in 1914, but was persuaded to accept the 'new' position of Northern Organiser and Correspondent to the Scottish branches (a job she had been doing since 1908). Characteristically, although she could not afford to attend conference in 1916 until she was bullied into treating the expenses as organising costs, Lisbeth offered to forgo her salary in 1917 and to submit expenses when necessary; an offer the League, inevitably, accepted.

An organiser's job, however, meant just that and did not carry any special weight in influencing League policy, as Margaret Bondfield had discovered in 1912. Other district women lacked the respectability even of the organiser's title. The powerful general purposes committee remained firmly in control. Each district was to pursue its own course. In effect, this meant that district organisation represented a disintegration of the League rather than a contribution to its strength. This is not to say districts were ineffective in their own area, some well-established by now; Mrs Scholefield was able to build quite successfully on Mrs Ayles's work in Wales, and in the Lancashire area enough cohesion was gained for the district to make occasional demands of the executive, for the leadership to tour the area. Clarice McNab was perhaps most successful because, representing the League, she had a seat on the executive of the Scottish Advisory Committee of the Labour Party, so that the League was directly represented by a woman, unlike the position in England and Wales, where the League had to be content with the attention of Mr P. Egerton Wake. Clarice McNab later completed this coup by marrying Ben Shaw, secretary of the Scottish Labour Party.

Branches received direct instructions from the executive committee, rather than their district organisation. They were urged to carry out local distress work, making sure women received pensions, agitating on behalf of those who were ineligible (such as the dependants of merchant seamen). League women were instructed by Marion Phillips to ensure they were elected to local citizens' committees. Some women would have been nominated by their trade unions, but were nevertheless to insist on a League delegate, as women's organisations were entitled to be represented. *Labour Woman* in September 1914 also instructed branches to raise the issues of workrooms for the unemployed, free meals for schoolchildren and pre-school children, free milk and meals for nursing mothers and their children and adequate housing for dislocated workers. In October 1914 Lisbeth Simm wrote also of the need for 'cheery letters' to be written to keep up members' spirits and action to comfort those whose menfolk had gone away; she wrote of forcing one grieving woman out to work at a League meeting and thereby providing the solace of employment. There were Belgian refugees to be supported and work to be done in preventing the smashing of aliens' property and the prejudice which led to such violence. *Labour Woman* again began printing branch reports to keep members in touch; one woman wrote: 'we have had to come out of our comfortable Branch rooms and practice what we have been talking about'.

The Central London branch *Annual Report* for the year ended 31 March 1915 illustrated the effects of war:

The depression and misery all over the world were necessarily reflected in Central London branches of the Women's Labour League and made it hard to carry out its work. When the war broke out, members felt that it was impossible to keep to the usual lines of work, and especially to hold the same social gatherings as have been held in past years.

The Central London branch had been able to hold regular monthly business meetings and there was, in fact, a slight increase in members. Deportees from South Africa had been welcomed. Educational meetings had been arranged on 'Small Nations and the War', 'The Terms of Peace', 'Drink in War Time', 'Maternity Clinics' and 'The Work of the French Women's Socialist Group'. Delegates had attended the London County Council election conference, the League for Striking Children annual meeting and meetings on war work, pay and prices, convened by the Workers' National Committee. Activity had included work on the allowances paid to soldiers' and sailors' wives and the supervision of these women by the police; a circular had been issued requiring wives to register at the local police station and giving the police the right to enquire into their behaviour, make reports, visit the women at home and *admonish* them (League emphasis). There had also been agitation on building state cottages for disabled soldiers; the employment of schoolchildren in agriculture; the 'possibility' of Great Britain and France bringing their influence as allies to bear to induce Russia to change her policy towards her subjects. Members and supporters were sewing children's clothes and maternity outfits at home. This was the traditional round of League activity, education and agitation, given a new focus by the war. Lacking was the entertainment that had fulfilled so many functions, including women's companionship. This was an important diminution of the League's day-to-day work because, as women lost the chance to share experiences and ideas informally together, they were less able to act collectively in presenting women's opinions.

The Central London branch experience seems to have been fairly common within the League. Some of the campaigns of the war years reflected traditional League activity. Chief amongst these was the campaign on housing; the sensible construction of the home, eliminating unnecessary labour in climbing stairs, heating water, carrying coal, had long been a League ambition. Ada Nield Chew, in 1913, had advocated building houses without kitchens, transferring the chore of cooking from the home to a communal kitchen that would be labour-saving and provide cheap, nutritious food.[4] A housing committee was now set up (Jennie Baker, Ada Salter, Marion Phillips, its secretary a non-executive member, Averil Sanderson Furniss). Each branch was to elect a correspondent and report to the housing committee. Fifty thousand copies were sold of a leaflet which enquired: 'what are the chief defects of your home?'; 'where do you think the larder should be?'; 'where do you want cupboards?'; 'what floor is the scullery?' Many of these questions were the subject of a debate at women's meetings, some of them arranged by the Co-operative Women's Guild, and replies were sent after thorough discussion. While middle-class women were consulted by the architects who designed their homes, working women were ignored by jerry-builders who put prices first, wrote Averil Sanderson Furniss, articulating the League opinion that the women who experienced a problem should have first say in its remedy: 'The various housing resolutions, which from time to time have been passed by conferences of working women of the Labour Party, have reiterated the demand that in all housing schemes the opinions of women for whom the houses were being constructed should be taken.'[5]

Some branches had begun work on housing; Glasgow, for instance, had set up a Women's Housing Association in 1915 and Annot Robinson was a member of such a group in Manchester. An experimental model public kitchen, on the lines suggested by Ada Nield Chew, was set up in Westminster Bridge Road and supported by the League. National kitchens, with restaurants attached, were run by the Ministry of Food and local authorities to help overcome war shortages and dislocation. Averil Sanderson Furniss, however, discovered that 'working women who have had experience of the common wash house or common kitchen have come to the very definite conclusion that if co-operation is to work well the whole work must be done by highly skilled people and not by providing appliances which each in turn may use'. A restaurant was appreciated, but women wanted their own home to be self-sufficient. The League influence on housing was lasting; Marion Phillips sat on the Women's Advisory Committee of the Ministry of Reconstruction and League work, based on its enquiry leaflets, contributed to that committee's two reports. Averil Sanderson Furniss served on the Ministry of Health Housing Department advisory council after the war and pressed for women to sit on local authority housing committees.

Similarly, the great League campaign of the pre-war years on school meals was continued into 1914–18 and given impetus by the obvious need to provide meals for children whose mothers worked in the munitions factories. Immediately on the outbreak of war, Katharine Bruce Glasier recommended in *Labour Woman* (September 1914) that branches lobby local authorities to follow the example of Hull, which had begun to feed schoolchildren three times a day, seven days a week. Portsmouth branch succeeded in achieving daily meals for children. The long-term interest in food prices was reflected by Marion Phillips's membership of the Consumer Council, as one of a number of investigators. (Mary MacArthur had been approached by the Ministry of Food for this work; she declined and Marion Phillips was nominated.) Taking July 1914 as the index of 100, in the first year of the war prices rose to 117 (December 1914) and then 137 (September 1915).[6] The concern of women about food prices was so overriding that the women's council of the British Socialist Party left that party to work solely on the issue. There were strikes and agitation in the Labour movement in general on rising prices and rent increases: 'Shall we pay more rent?' asked the November 1915 *Labour Woman*, and gave its answer: 'No.'

None of these concerns was pursued with the same single-mindedness as the pre-war campaigns because the great interest of these later years was, of course, the war. Desiring peace, the League was not pacifist; it believed the invasion of Belgium must be redressed: in its annual report for 1914 (not delivered until the 1916 conference) the executive committee stated: 'The League has accepted the position that there is no ground on which we can adopt a policy of opposition to the war.' This position was amplified in a League manifesto printed in the October 1914 *Labour Woman*: 'the League interests lay in peace', 'every soldier slain left a woman desolate'; governments made war, with their secret diplomacy, armaments, aggressive foreign policies; people allowed this to happen through their apathy or self-interest. The Labour and Socialist movement in Europe should 'stay aloof from the rancour' and seek after the war ended 'a United States of Europe, a free Belgium, free Finland, free Poland, free womanhood and free working classes'.

This manifesto marked a change in League philosophy. League socialist feminism, constitutional, reformist, had hitherto avoided such clear articulation of class politics. Previously, especially before 1912, the special contribution women could make to social reform, from their own experience, had been emphasised. Then, from 1912 to 1914, the identification of working women with men of their class had been more pronounced. This trend was taken further by the manifesto; gender was not ignored ('free womanhood') but was included in the list of socialist gains, a benefit from the operation of a socialist vanguard. The suffering of the wife and mother who survived a soldier's death was used to show an identity of interest between men and women on the battlefield. Two systems of government were juxtaposed in the manifesto, as aggressor and peacemaker; the aggressive capitalist was contrasted to the socialist which would set free nations, men and women. The references to apathy and to the need for the continued existence of international socialism again implied support for a vanguard socialist consciousness, rousing people to a positive sense of humanity. It may have been that war radicalised some League women who had previously experienced the effects of capitalism more by observation than by personal impact; now, the war seemed a dreadful fulfilment of socialist prophecies of the evil of capitalism. The response was to stand shoulder to shoulder together with the proletariat, whatever one's social class or gender. Henceforward, this greater emphasis on socialism, as opposed to gender politics, became natural to the League.

Other women's groups were affected by the inescapable priorities forced on them by the war. The British Socialist Party women's council, as we have seen, took the opposite course from the League and severed its connections with the mixed party. The women's suffrage movement was sundered; the Women's Social and Political Union, characteristically bellicose, dissolved itself in favour of recruitment. The National Union of Women's Suffrage Societies formed militarist and pacifist wings; the latter developed into the Women's International League for Peace and Freedom. There was not, then, one feminist response to war; these embraced greater unity with the male party (the League); separatism (the Women's Council) and pacifist–separatism (WILPF). The League response was an evolution of its own brand of socialist feminism, rather than a transformation.

As the League perceived war as a class issue and had not opposed the declaration of war, it was obviously inappropriate for it to affiliate itself to a pacifist–separatist organisation. There was disagreement in the League over recruitment; some League women differed from the manifesto, which opposed the use of women to persuade men to volunteer; as women did not themselves fight, the manifesto thought it shame for them to call men cowards. The League was opposed to enforced enlistment of any kind, by government conscription or because of poverty at home. Some women did attempt to embrace a purely pacifist line and others to promote the active solidarity of the workers across the battle lines; Ada Salter proposed sending a resolution to the 1916 League conference that would have called on soldiers to lay down arms, but it was amended in executive committee meetings until it more closely resembled the manifesto statement. The majority of League women, at least in the leadership, remained committed to the manifesto opinion.

Accordingly, the League was one of the earliest bodies to affiliate to the Union of Democratic Control (14 January 1915). This was founded, partly by Ramsay MacDonald, to press for the democratic conduct of foreign affairs. The Union of Democratic Control was not a purely pacifist organisation; it resisted war, but once hostilities were declared, believed they should be pursued with regard to the persistence of the civil liberties and democratic rights of combatants and civilians. Immediately, the UDC sought a negotiated peace. It believed diplomacy should be open and foreign affairs subject to public debate. Jennie Baker, nominated by the League, was elected to the UDC council (as member for Finchley); Jennie Baker, Ethel Bentham, Sister Kerrison and Marion Phillips attended a UDC women's conference, so the expression of women's point of view was not entirely lost.

Combat and conscription were of the utmost importance to the League women whose menfolk were subject to service in the forces. Recruitment was voluntary until 1916; conscription was controversial. Its introduction split the Liberal Government and Lloyd George thereafter headed a coalition of Liberals and Conservatives. Those Labour Members of Parliament (the majority) who had not resigned on the outbreak of war, also countenanced conscription and coalition. The Labour movement, however, was divided: the Union of Democratic Control was very much opposed to conscription. There was war resistance, supported by international anarchists and syndicalists who could provide escape routes (such as the International Workers of the World). The trade unions largely supported the war effort and there were bellicose patriots (such as Harry Hyndman of the British Socialist Party and George Belt, then leading the Herald League).

The League, however, had no doubts about conscription; it remained entirely opposed. This was perhaps a healing of the rift with those women who had supported voluntary recruitment. The League motion ot the 1916 Labour Party conference was: 'That this conference declares its opposition to the Military Service (No. 2) Bill and in the event of it becoming law, decides to agitate for its repeal.' Mr Bellamy, president of the National Union of Railwaymen (husband of the League's Mrs Bellamy?) seconded the motion. Arthur Henderson opposed. The miners and the engineers were in favour of the first part of the motion, but had no instructions about the second, which implied industrial disputes for their members. J. H. Thomas was in favour, Will Thorne against the second part, G. Roberts against the whole. The final voting was 1,718,000 in favour of the first part, 360,000 against, a splendid victory for the League, and 614,000 in favour of the second part, 649,000 against; the miners abstained.

Mrs Ayles's husband, Walter, was one of the founders of the No Conscription Fellowship which represented the pacifist, often religious faith that was an integral part of much socialist feeling. Walter Ayles's experience illustrates the suffering of conscientious objectors to the war effort and that of their families.[7] Bertha Ayles, we know, had a heart disease and by 1916 was the mother of a young child. Walter Ayles was arrested for demonstrating against the introduction of conscription (15 July 1916) and sentenced to sixty-one days' imprisonment. He was relieved of combat duties, the court accepting that he had a genuine religious conviction, but not exempted from government duties. These Walter refused, as they amounted to assisting the war effort. A military tribunal thereupon charged him with desertion and Walter was sentenced to 112 days' hard labour (21 November 1916). Immediately on his release Walter was again arrested and sentenced to six months' hard labour (3 March 1917). Again, as that sentence expired, Walter received another two years of hard labour (9 August 1917). Apart from one month, Bertha Ayles brought up her child and bore the misery of the war alone, from the time conscription was introduced until a year after the end of the war.

The effect of the separation of parents, because of the war, on babies and young children was of much concern to the League, carrying over its traditional championship of child welfare into the new wartime conditions. One small success, reported in *Labour Leader* (3 September 1914), was achieved when Norwich League raised the problem of women at home not being able to afford the delivery charge for unstamped soldiers' letters. This was taken up by the Postmaster General, who agreed such post would be delivered free of charge. Soldiers were not always able, or willing, to keep in touch and sometimes never knew of the birth of a baby whose mother they might not have had the time or inclination to marry. Since the law had no regard for children born out of wedlock, their upkeep was fraught with difficulty. No allowance was due from the Services and there was only the Poor Law to fall back upon. The League campaigned for changes, that children born to parents who married after their birth would be declared legitimate and that a woman should be able to get an affiliation order before the birth of her child. Some mothers were forced to board out their babies, perhaps giving them up for life; the London County Council was attempting to get powers of inspection in all cases where babies were received for profit and the League pressed the Labour Party to lend its support. Jennie Baker continued work in this field, becoming secretary of the Council for the Unmarried Mother and her Child after the war.

Related to this was a fear articulated by some League women that men who had served in the forces would learn to think of male sexuality as an impulse to be accommodated irrespective of the wishes of the female partner and without regard to family life. Accordingly, the League affiliated to the Association of Moral and Social Hygiene and campaigned against licensed brothels in France. Branches arranged lectures on venereal disease. The correspondence about birth control in *Labour Woman* was revived in 1916, the same arguments being put about contraception to escape poverty/the evil of family limitation, but with a new input, that women should use contraception or celibacy as a strike weapon, refusing to produce male children who were killed by a careless government. Marion Phillips again ended the discussion without comment. One has to remember, in considering this debate, that the contemporary treatment of venereal disease was extremely hazardous, abortion was illegal, women were hung for infanticide and there were no public funds to support unwanted children. However, Marion Phillips's abrupt cessation of the correspondence indicates some distaste and it is interesting to note Ishbel MacDonald's explanation of Ethel Bentham's reluctance to give advice about birth control when this was sought at the baby clinic: 'she told me privately that one reason she was against it was that, if he knew the risk of his actions were less likely to lead to pregnancy, a husband felt at liberty to overtax or molest his wife unreasonably'.[8]

One major change in League work during the war years was caused by women's employment in the trades traditionally restricted to men, then serving in the forces. It was not the case that women, *en masse*, worked for the first time; in fact the war initially caused 'enormous' unemployment; 75,000 women lost work in December 1914 alone and many more were put on short time. Many domestic servants lost their jobs as their employers grandly decided to donate their wages to the war effort; the net result was extra work for the remaining servants. By August 1915 the situation was improving and, moreover, women were changing jobs to labour-intensive sites where they were visible (as opposed to the self-effacing servant) and could be organised into trade unions. Table 1 (p. 28) compares women's trade union membership in 1914 and 1918, illustrating that women entered previously male-dominated trade unions, sometimes for the first time, in substantial numbers. This, in itself, had an effect on Labour Party membership, as affiliated unions now had a greater proportion of female members.

Mary MacArthur became secretary of the Central Committee for Women's Employment, formed on 20 August 1914 to help deploy women workers and safeguard their interests; its chair was Lady Crewe and it aroused some suspicion in the Labour movement. The movement had formed its own body to represent workers, the War Emergency: Workers National Committee; this body nominated four Labour women to the Central Committee for Women's Employment: Susan Lawrence, Mrs Gasson, Margaret Bondfield and Marion Phillips. Their first job was to prevent lady volunteers putting the seamstresses and tailoresses out of work by excessive and misguided zeal (the same spirit of delegated sacrifice that led to the dismissal of servants). Work was accepted only if the women in the appropriate trade were fully employed; in such cases, government contracts (for instance the making of grey army shirts) were taken and put out to skilled women.

The demands the Labour movement women made on behalf of the industrial women, accepted by the central committee, sounded feminist: equal pay for equal work, a living wage and work after the war, jobs being sacrificed solely to men who had served in the forces. However, the demand for equal pay arose partly as a safeguard for the men who had resigned their jobs and were expected to return. The League representative felt she had four interests to consider; the employer; the male worker; his dependants; the woman worker. Writing in *Labour Woman* in June 1916, Marion Phillips explained that the problem of women workers after the war could not be left to the trade unions, nor to women's organisations, because both would forget one or other interests; she felt this problem must be discussed thoroughly before any action was taken. The League position was moderate in its ambiguity, although there was justice in the concern for dependants. To be fair to the League, it did try to ensure the problem was discussed; in May 1916 it arranged a meeting on 'Industrialised women after the war': 125 trade unions and societies sent delegates, as did nine national trade unions, twenty-three branches of the Co-operative Women's Guild, twenty-three Independent Labour Party branches, twelve Trades and Labour Councils, the London Labour Party, eleven League branches, three from the British Socialist Party and three from Adult Schools. However long the discussion, the interests were, of course, irreconcilable so it was not surprising that League policy never became coherent enough to give a lead.

The small number of League branches attending the meeting was also indicative of a problem; the issue was being addressed not on the shop floor, by the branches, but at leadership level in London committees. Disputes at the workplace were therefore outside the League's area of experience. Although they had become more involved during the period of industrial unrest before the war and had joined the insurance bodies, branches always had been careful of trespassing on union ground. Their diffidence, however, meant that the League addressed the problem of industrial women from a distance. Militancy in industry was not diminished by the war, but found new channels of expression: while union leaders supported the war effort, shop stewards were appointed to represent the dislocated workers. Skilled and unskilled workers sometimes found common cause, for instance, over the war service exemption certificates in the gift of employers. More often, craftsmen fought to preserve their skills against undercutting by the new workers, including women; interfactional disputes were therefore rife and the subject of dilution (of craft skills and jobs) controversial. These tensions of class and gender were not addressed by the League.

Perhaps an unmet need was perceived because, representing the League, with Mary Longman, Marion Phillips was one of the founders of the Standing Joint Industrial Women's Committee. The occasion was a conference called by Mary MacArthur on 11 February 1916. The Co-operative Women's Guild, Railway Women's Guild, Women's Trade Union League and National Federation of Women Workers were also represented. Mary MacArthur was elected chair, Margaret Llewellyn Davies vice-chair and Mary Longman became secretary. The organisers wanted all women's organisations to join which were 'national in character, consist of women only and have at least 1,000 members'. Each member organisation instructed its branches to work together locally, especially on pensions committees. The SJIWC corresponded with local councils informing them of the name of the women's representative in their area. Beatrice Webb was a member of the committee and helped prepare memoranda. National representation of working women was also demanded; Margaret Bondfield, now a member of the Trades Union Congress parliamentary sub-committee dealing with negotiations for war workers, could help to lobby the trade unions and the Government about this claim for recognition.

From 6 March 1917 Miss Coates, then acting Women's Labour League secretary, represented the League on the Standing Joint Industrial Women's Committee and also served the latter body as secretary. After she was dismissed from the League office, Miss Coates, not unnaturally, failed to undertake these additional, unpaid duties. Marion Phillips reported that correspondence had not succeeded in changing Miss Coates's mind. Marion Phillips was elected secretary to the SJIWC in Miss Coates's place. It would appear that Miss Coates's fortuitous deposition from the League secretaryship was not entirely disinterested.

Marion Phillips had managed to create and partly control a body that was to some degree a replacement for the League, less democratic, with no grass-roots organisation save that imposed from above, dealing in the main with women at work, her own prime interest. As spokeswoman for the Standing Joint Industrial Women's Committee, Marion Phillips extended her role so that she was acting as the main representative for most of the pre-war Labour movement, single-sex organisations; the Co-operators, the unions and the political party. Such a feat in conjoining the three wings of the Labour movement – consumer, industrial and political – was remarkable, a coup of organising ability. The Labour women's movement had, perhaps, never been so united as it now was under the SJIWC.

The relative influence of the League was weak. Locally, League branches joined in the mixed pensions and citizen's committees; nationally, the League was relegated to the lowly place of a small component of a broad-based group, which contained the far larger Co-operative Women's Guild and the women's trade unions, more intimately involved in workplace negotiation. A distinctive League voice, articulating a specific socialist–feminist philosophy, was unlikely to be heard in the crowd. Considering their size and good bargaining position, as women were so necessary to the war effort, neither were the grand national committees particularly good at voicing gender interests. Unity did not necessarily mean greater efficacy in this respect. Lacking was the energy stimulated by the medley of single-sex organisations that had characterised the turn-of-the-century women's movement; the particles of this had either congealed into the moribund mammoths or disintegrated, swept up in the mixed campaigns with male pacifists, prisoners, war resisters, internationalists, workplace agitators, consumer protectors, campaigners against promiscuity.

The effect of the war on the future of the League was crucial. The League never consciously abandoned its past brand of socialist feminism: reformist and constitutional, bringing forward issues that affected women and demanding they play an active part in moulding their world. The wartime campaigns on housing, on school meals, about illegitimate and abandoned babies, about male sexuality, illustrated that these traditional concerns remained integral to the League. Yet in every instance when the League engaged in national, war-related campaigns, it was to the detriment of the development of a distinct gender philosophy. In joining the Union of Democratic Control, in campaigning about women war workers without regard to workplace tensions, the League relegated gender to a subordinate position. Added to the impossibility of sisterhood in a social setting and to the loss of vigour in branch life, this amounted to a profound change in League identity.

To many League women, it may have seemed that the time for integration with the Labour Party was ripe; that Labour women had benefited from a preliminary, single-sex organisation and had now won inclusion in newly sensitive class organisations. Far from being a weakness, the diminution of their separate input may have seemed a victory, proof of gains made in affecting the Labour movement philosophy of gender as a whole. Ada Salter had foreshadowed this when she spoke at the 1914 League conference on the potency of a socialism that included women:

> They noted all over the world signs of the change that was coming, and women of the working classes have taken the foremost place in it. A tremendous transformation was going to take place on this earth; and the injustices of the ages, the misery of the oppressed classes, and the sorrow of the poor, and the tyranny of the wealthy were going to be swept away for ever. Nothing could stop the movement. When the trades movement fully realised that all workers, men and women, youths and maidens, were members one of another, then they would hear more than the rumble of revolution in the distance; the revolution would be here. [10]

The engines of war carried the protagonists towards revolution. As the Labour movement became more class-conscious, so socialist women may have felt its new nature deserved a new response. The Labour Party itself was profoundly affected; on the one hand it was imbued with the general militancy of the working classes: the workplace agitation, the strikes against rising prices. Reflecting this, in 1917, a United Socialist Council was formed in Britain: it was hoped the British Socialist Party (formerly Social Democratic Federation) and the Independent Labour Party would merge with the Labour Party. The pacifist nature of the ILP and the militarism of the BSP prevented any immediate action. On the other hand, Labour's claim to respectability grew; local Labour parties were enhanced by administration of the allowances that working people did not trust to charity or government agencies; the conscription issue had split the Liberal Party in the constituencies and at Westminster, diminishing the strength of its competition as the people's champion. Labour, in the form of Arthur Henderson, participated in the coalition Cabinet.

Britain was not alone in experiencing this arousal of class-consciousness, nor had war wiped out the internationalism of the Labour movement. Belief in the common interests of the proletariat survived the workers' participation in their various countries' war efforts. Thus, in the early stages of the war, at least, the League hoped combat would be conducted with chivalry and warned against ready acceptance of the horror stories about the enemy that would inevitably be published. The second International had, indeed, been broken up, but there were always hopes of revival. The British Socialist Women's Council of the International, of which Margaret MacDonald had been secretary, was now named the Women's International Council and still gave its address as 3 Lincoln's Inn Fields. The League sent delegates (Mary Longman, Marion Phillips, Ada Salter and Margaret Bondfield) to the 1915 Labour and Socialist Women's International, at which women from Germany, France, Belgium, Russia, Poland, Italy, Holland and Switzerland declared war against war:[11]

> War against War! We demand a peace that will recognise the rights of peoples and nations, both large and small, to independence and self government, will enforce no limits and unsupportable conditions against any country, and will require expiation of the wrong done to Belgium, thus clearing the way for the peaceful and friendly co-operation of the nations.

Throughout the war, *Labour Woman* continued to print reports on 'our sisters from abroad'. Rosa Luxemburg's one-year prison sentence was reported and Alexandra Kollontai's expulsion from Sweden (January 1915); so was Clara Zetkin's arrest in November 1915. Reports were made on German socialist women's work, much the same as the League's; relief work, help for children, work on separation allowances and unemployment pay. In January 1915 Clara Zetkin's reply to the League manifesto was printed, containing her thanks and support and her belief that the war was exploitation of Labour by Property.

The Russian revolution of February 1917 stimulated this internationalism and imbued the constitutionalist, as much as the militant in the Labour movement, with zeal for the cause of the proletariat. The Russian dictatorship had long been a *bête noire* of the Labour movement; the Central London League branch, for instance, had hoped the Allies would counter Russian despotism; in April 1915 Mary Longman denounced in *Labour Woman* the Allies' agreement to unite their financial resources; far from countering tyranny, this, she wrote, was tantamount to supporting the destruction of Finland, the arrest of the socialists in the Duma and the persecution of the Jewish people. The revolution was much welcomed. *Labour Woman* printed an appeal to common sisterhood from Russian women, calling for peace and the withdrawal of the working classes from the war. The Petrograd Council of Workers' and Soldiers' Delegates sent a telegram to the League: 'Workmen's Council would be extremely glad to see amongst Labour (talent) (sic) delegates coming to Russia representing Women's Labour League and Women's International Council.' The League had already asked the Labour Party to fund a delegate and decided on 18 June 1917 that Mary Longman should go. She applied for a passport, but this was refused, so Mary continued to help out in the League office. The League also supported the attempts to revive the Second International of Labour and Socialist Parties; Marion Phillips was to be the delegate, funds being raised through advertisements in *Labour Woman*. British delegates were prevented from attending by the refusal of passports; Arthur Henderson, who had witnessed events in Russia and retained a lifelong commitment to the internationalist ideal, resigned from the War Cabinet in protest.

The United Socialist Council, hitherto quiescent because of the difficulties of accommodating both pacifists and members of the war cabinet, was revitalised by the Russian revolution. A conference was organised 'to hail the Russian revolution' on 3 June 1917 at Leeds. The League was invited to send delegates; Marion Phillips and Lisbeth Simm were chosen (in the event, Lisbeth was unable to attend). Branches were informed and their delegates invited to meet the executive committee representatives beforehand. The League was bolder than the Standing Joint Industrial Women's Committee in respect of the Leeds conference; the SJIWC decided to decline the invitation, the trade union women being in favour, but the Co-operative and Railway women against. Some Co-operative women did attend the Leeds conference; together with the Women's Labour League and Women's International Council they accounted for fifty-four of the 1,200 or so delegates. The 290 Labour Party and Trades Council delegates outnumbered those of the British Socialist Party with eighty-eight. The Independent Labour Party sent 294. The crowd and the hoteliers gave the delegates a hostile reception, but it was with acclamation that the first resolution to welcome the Russian revolution was received (moved and seconded by an unholy alliance of Ramsay MacDonald and Dora Montefiore, who had once successfully sued Margaret MacDonald for libel).

The League supported the first resolution, as it did the second, calling for peace without annexations and indemnities and the third, on civil liberties. The fourth, controversial resolution was too much for League moderates, calling for the immediate creation of Workmen's and Soldiers' Councils in Britain. The fourth resolution won widespread support and was considered by the League executive committee and by district conferences in Scotland and London. The London meeting came to no decision; at the Scottish conference one branch was in support, four against and three undecided. At this point the League executive, perhaps troubled by the progress of events in Russia, thought of shelving discussion. Mrs Scholefield and Lisbeth Simm, however, reported that the matter was under active discussion in their areas.

Class politics had been transformed by the war and the revolution beyond the claim for industrial action and citizenship to redress grievances. The mood of chiliasm affected Labour's plans for post-war reconstruction and shaped its constitution beyond reorganisation and into a more socialist statement of its philosophy: 'To secure for the workers by hand or by brain the full fruits of their industry and the most equitable distribution thereof that may be possible upon the basis of the common ownership of the means of production, distribution and exchange, and the best obtainable system of popular administration and control of each industry and service.' *Labour Woman* (November 1917) called the new constitution 'a transformation', 'almost a revolution in itself'. Some of the active League women may have been swept on by revolutionary impetus past Labour's reach; others were maybe willing to submerge past feminist ideals in their new perception of class unity. Arthur Henderson seems to have had a relatively easy task when he came to the League executive committee meeting on 12 October 1917 to explain what the new constitution proposals were for women's organisation.

Ready for debate at Labour's conference in the beginning of 1918, the new constitution proposed women's sections in the local Labour parties be created and the reservation of four National Executive Council seats for women members. The executive committee minutes for the meeting with Arthur Henderson record: 'in the discussion it was felt very strongly that special provision should be made for women to have opportunities of discussing special women's questions or problems from the women's standpoint'. Yet no such claim was made for 'special provision' for the League within the Party structure. Any chance of amending the constitution was thrown away when Marion Phillips's proposal was endorsed, that discussion be postponed until *after* 'the Labour Party was more settled'. Later, in October 1917, the general purposes committee empowered itself to meet the Labour Party organising sub-committee to continue discussions on organising women within the Party. In November there was still no agreement, the particular difficulties being the holding of an annual conference of women's sections and the constitution of the Women's Advisory Committee. Some minor drafting amendments were made to the Labour Party constitution.

It was decided, at this late stage, to hold a meeting to discuss with branch delegates the effect of the reorganisation on their work and to hold a conference in January 1918 to discuss the new arrangements. Detailed records of this crucial conference do not survive (the only extant copy of the League conference reports is Minnie Nodin's own; perhaps she did not attend). There are, therefore, only the short and bland executive reports in the *Minutes* and in *Labour Woman* by which to judge branch reception of the results of the executive's negotiations. These report agreement to the proposals with just two dissenting branches. Branches had, of course, been presented with a *fait accompli*; the time for negotiation with the Party was past because its new constitution had been agreed; women's representation in the new structure was voted upon not by the League, but by the delegates (still overwhelmingly male) at the Labour Party conference.

One matter on which branches did insist was that some sort of national women's forum should continue; this would have a great effect on how the new arrangements were perceived. With a national conference of women, the women's sections and four national executive places made political sense: the executive women would have support and guidance from the grass roots and could speak with some authority at national meetings. Locally, women would know there was an opportunity to express opinion and share experiences at national level. Without such a vehicle for conveying women's opinion, the local sections would have less esteem in their constituencies and might dwindle into talking shops. The League leadership did accept the depth of feeling about a national women's forum and convey it to the Party; however, the crucial question about the weight the Party gave to nationally expressed women's opinion, the mechanisms that would ensure that the voice of women was considered and acted upon were not raised because the League was a stage behind, still arguing the need for a national committee, instead of that committee's role.

An indication that League women would resist any attempt to subordinate them in the new structure was the objection they made to the proposed Party subscription fees: 1*s* for men and 6*d* for women. Otherwise, the League almost nodded the proposals through. The Lancashire and Cheshire district secretary wrote deploring the arrangements: the response was merely an extract, sent by the executive, of Katharine Bruce Glasier's speech to the Lancashire and Cheshire conference, welcoming the new organisation. The League leadership seemed to have closed its ears to any dissent; any alternative opinion, dismissed at the time, has therefore not survived for us to evaluate. The evidence is that the executive believed its proposals were good and felt confident of support. There is no sense of excitement or of foreboding in the official records: little that the decisions being taken were of any particular importance.

The last League executive committee, as originally constituted, benevolently, if not typically, raised the clerk's salary to 15*s* per week. Some of the League stalwarts now appear to have realised, too late, the implications of the new constitution. Minnie Nodin, at the first 1918 executive committee meeting (22 January) reiterated that the League 'should push for an annual conference'. In February 1918 the general purposes committee was informed that the Labour Party had accepted responsibility for all monies spent after January 1918. Miss Chettle and Miss Clarke, who had been carrying out League organising work, were recommended to the Labour Party. A leaflet was to be prepared for branches on the work and organisation of Party women's sections. *Labour Woman* was still to be produced monthly.

In March 1918 the executive committee discussed critical letters received from two branches about the transition (unfortunately, the text of the letters and the arguments used do not survive), and Central London branch asked again for an annual women's conference: 'Dr Phillips explained the position, showing that an elected Advisory Committee would be a practical impossibility and recommending that we should wait a little while with regard to the question of the Annual Conference. There might be a large Conference of women arranged in June.' Marion Phillips now revealed her tactical prowess; she suggested that the Standing Joint Industrial Women's Committee (of which she was, of course, secretary, following Miss Coates's dismissal from the League): 'on a slightly different basis would act as an advisory committee to the Party, preserving the right of independent action and continuing its independent work'. There were to be eight League delegates and four from each of the other groups (women's trade unions, Railway Guild and Co-operators). Marion Phillips would then have been head, at the same time, of the women in the Party and Labour women outside the Party.

The other implications for the League were that, losing its separate identity, it would lose the right to affiliate to its cherished sister groups. This was now considered for the first time. Minnie Nodin asked what would happen to the four delegates who represented the League on the committee of the baby clinic, the memorial to its first leaders. It was decided it would not be possible to transfer this responsiblility to the Labour Party, and that the delegates would have to withdraw. All other affiliations were also withdrawn. Railway Women's Guild members were urged to join the Labour Party in a circular signed both by Marion Phillips and the Railway Women's Guild president. In April 1918 the executive committee decided unanimously that the Standing Joint Industrial Women's Committee should become the Labour Party's Women's Advisory Committee. On 14 June 1918 the Women's Labour League money, office furniture and fittings and literature were handed over to the Labour Party.

It was Margaret Bondfield who addressed the Albert Hall meeting that year to announce the new party constitution, at once Labour's political programme and its party structure, an evolution of 'the men's party'. Women were no longer distinct because of their separate organisation. Partly, they had achieved what they set out to accomplish, participation by women in the Labour Party. Women's sections in every branch and constituency may have seemed a good bargain in return for dismantling the League. *Labour Woman* reported in May 1918 that there was 'no need to exist as a separate organisation'. Some League women had always thought that the existence of a women's group was recognition of a weakness to be overcome; now, they had the confidence to merge with the men. Partly, the League had been outmanoeuvred by the adept Arthur Henderson, not presenting its claims until too late; its own leader, 'brilliant as diamonds', was, perhaps, insufficiently sensitive to the riches of sisterhood that had been experienced by the local branch activists with the support of a national, autonomous, female leadership.

The League had been one shape in the great patchwork of the Labour and women's movements. Mostly, it changed because the whole changed, torn apart by the war, by the Russian revolution, the zeal for class politics, by the very success of the suffrage movement; these made stale the images of the separate sex politics and of the confident ruling class of the pre-war world. The female flying cloaks were folded, the morning coats packed away. It was Marion Phillips's strength that she had found a place for the League in the post-war world.

The last meeting of the Central London branch of the League provides a fitting epitaph.[12] It called for either a federated Council of London Women's sections, or a London aggregate meeting open to all members of London women's sections: 'It was felt that the new constitution did not admit of the existence of the branch in its present form and that the first duty of all members who had local Labour Parties in their own area was to devote their energy to them. At the same time, the value of central meetings (for women) was emphasised by all.'

. . . For Labour, and for women . . .

Notes

1 Labour Party *Subject Files,* LP/WLL (Labour Party Headquarters Archives, London), LP/WLL/108/44.

2 *Women's Labour League Secretarial Correspondence and Related Papers,* WLL/68 (Labour Party Headquarters Archives, London).

3 *Labour Woman,* August 1914.

4 *The Gertrude Tuckwell Collection 1880–1920* (Trades Union Congress Library, London), 345/76.

5 Averil Sanderson-Furniss, 'Citizenship of women', *The Book of the Labour Party, its History, Growth, Policy and Leaders* (London, 1925), p. 254.
See also A. D. Sanderson-Furniss and Marion Phillips, *The Working Woman's House* (London, 1920), cited, pp. 10, 49.

6 *The Labour Party Year Book, 1916* (Co-operative Press, 1916, cited pp. 40 (prices), 363 (Women's Council).

7 *James and Lucy Middleton Papers: The Ruskin Collection* (Ruskin College Library, Oxford), MID 139, Walter Ayles's Papers.

8 Labour Party *Subject Files*, LP/INF/13/BAB.
9 *The Labour Year Book, 1916*, p. 23 ff.
10 *The Gertrude Tuckwell Collection*, 345/79. This is a *Daily Despatch* report; the report of the speech in the League's annual report is much less racy, so presumably Ada Salter improved on its presentation.
11 *The Gertrude Tuckwell Collection*, 353/6.
12 *League Correspondence*, WLL/177.

Conclusion

In 1918 the Women's Labour League carried into the new Labour Party the long experience of the women's movement; the 'men's party' of a decade before had enshrined into its first real constitution women's organisation at every level. It was the beginning and the end of an experience in socialist feminism; at once the League's zenith and nadir. The League contained no great theorists to deliberate which; it consisted of practical, busy women, working out their politics as they canvassed from door to door in the courtyard slums, reaching women shut away from the world. The League had been typical of its time, reflecting the prevailing ideologies of class and gender; when times changed it succumbed to the general mood. It left its life to be assessed, its brand of socialist feminism, its relationship to the Labour Party and contribution to the Labour and political movements of its time, to the women's movement and to those living out personal relationships in the labour world. It also left notes for survival for future women who engaged in class politics.

Its disappearance, as times changed, does not mean separatism had been a failure. The League had overcome the enormous institutional difficulties of women's membership of the Labour Party. Women joined the League in substantial numbers; were active in various parts of Britain; developed their own understandings of Labour politics; were involved in decision-making in local government and within the Labour Party (having, then, the right to send their resolutions to Party conference); added their own priorities to the political agenda. There were weaknesses; sometimes a poverty of sisterhood: Margaret Bondfield never felt comfortable; the argument between Margaret MacDonald and

Mary MacArthur paralysed League work on sweating; the angry exchanges between Margaret Bondfield, Maud Waud, Marion Phillips and Ethel Bentham were nearly fatal to the League's continuance. Some disputes were positive, such as the long debate on suffrage which ended in the League taking a confident and considered position in favour of working women and adult suffrage (though this may have ended Annot Robinson's association with the League). The treatment of staff was deplorable; Lisbeth Simm, Dorothy Lenn, Annot Robinson and Bertha Ayles worked very hard for little pay, some to the detriment of their health, some being abandoned without compunction. Office secretaries were hired and fired at will and paid minimum wages.

And yet there was an endeavour and an energy about the League that enabled it to triumph over its shortcomings and draw the best from its much tried organisers. Lisbeth Simm was able to rejoice in her work and the achievements of the League; she rejoiced in

> 'The New Spirit' . . . spreading amongst the women and the men in both town and village . . . I rejoice to see that many men in the ILP are now quite cognisant of the situation and are doing their level best to interest and to bring in the women . . . 'At one time' said (a comrade) 'we used to put (women) on committees for social and domestic work, then we got them on to the general committees; and we found that women as well as men have brains for successfully carrying out all kinds of work.'[1]

The note of surprise in the comrade's remarks indicates how hard League women must have worked to overcome prejudice and their own irritation at its expression. They were not restricted in their work, because they made this struggle; nevertheless, the most indelible impression of the League is that of the social reformers of its first phase, the concern with health care, a mother-and-baby image, which, together with League gradualism, might lead some to think League politics were women's concerns, a 'soft option'. We still tend to leave the bath and bucket beside the committed woman. In fact the struggle against infant mortality and child poverty was far from easy, and brought League women into conflict with public authorities locally and nationally, taking them from Jarrow council chamber, to Leicester market-place, to demonstrations in Leeds, chalking the streets, standing on chairs under a lamp. In Margaret MacDonald's day child welfare was, indeed, a priority; the baby clinic and hospital were the lasting League memorials and the campaign for school meals was the League's biggest.

The mother-and-baby image, however, does not suffice to portray the League. It wanted to shift these concerns from the individual woman to the community; it wanted ratepayers to finance the care of the sick child. Moreover, the League wanted women to present and act on these demands; it exhorted women to do so in its *Leaflets*. The League claimed the public sphere for women, for instance, when Lisbeth Simm wrote: 'women were realising they could not even do their duty in the home unless they took some interest in public and outside affairs. The League was educating women to formulate their demands . . . .'[2] In this light, the change under Marion Phillips to giving greater priority to the needs of industrial women and to gaining the vote was one of emphasis. *League Leaflets* had stressed women's right to work; Margaret Bondfield had drafted the laundry workers' charter; the League had engaged in the 1911 industrial unrest in the Welsh coalfields and Hull docks. The focusing of the suffrage campaign on to working women gave cohesion to this second phase.

It was one of the League's weaknesses that there was no attempt to evolve methods of working which encouraged responsibility amongst the rank and file; neither was there any experiment with non-hierarchical organisation amongst the leadership. The executive committee was usually chaired by the same woman (Ethel Bentham), took minutes, made formal resolutions; conference was in the traditional format. At branch level this pattern was not so rigid and there were more or less imaginative attempts to involve all the members – sewing circles, educative talks, entertainments. However, the metropolitan pull reduced branch initiative. Marion Phillips paid less attention to the grass roots than previous leaders; branch reports were left out of the conference agenda, conference was provided with discussion papers of the executive's choosing, the districts were refused admission to League policy-making. The diminution of branch participation was extremely important in its effects on League politics and therefore its future. Socialist feminism usually flourishes at grass-roots level, where the connections and challenges are easier to make because less is invested in reputations to maintain and received truths that must hold sway, where bureaucratic inertia lies less heavy.

The effect of Marion Phillips's leadership was an illustration of how one untiring heroine can change the group about her. Marion Phillips seized opportunities brought by the war to make grow national bodies, connected to the government and to the hierarchy of Labour, a remarkable achievement. She was a swell amongst swells. She was unable to overcome branch isolation in the new conditions, the disruption of the social round, the collapse of some of the rank and file who felt 'timid and useless'. With the war came also a new phase in League socialist feminism; class politics gained in importance as League women stood shoulder to shoulder with Labour men, for peace with honour and better workplace conditions.

Throughout the League experience, internationalism was a part of its philosophy. Margaret MacDonald was first secretary of the women's Labour and Socialist International British Section, a responsibility held by the League throughout its existence. Mary Longman spoke in German to the demonstrators for peace in that country before the war; Jennie Baker continued the notes on 'our sisters from abroad' throughout the period 1914–28. The League received its invitation to the Petrograd Soviet and sent delegates to the conference hailing the Russian revolution. It baulked, however, at British Soviets and retained its constitutionalism.

The League relationship with the Labour Party was always at the forefront of its political mind, because of this constitutionalism, because the League was committed to direct labour representation. The relationship evolved as League philosophy changed. At the outset, the 'men's party' ignored the League; the League became an autonomous body. Always ambiguous about the extent of its separatism, the League sought affiliation; this was achieved and the League embarked on the adventure of its free-lance role, separate from, but living out, a connection with the Party. Then came assistance from Party funds, Party control over some of Margaret Bondfield's time and a closer identification of interests. By the 1914 conference this 'separate organisation in one movement' seemed fruitful, to outsiders as well as League members; the press reported:

> It is a well desired arrangement to hold the annual conference of the Women's Labour League in association with the Labour Party conference. The importance of women's views on political issues is no longer derided, but they are often expressed in places remote from the machinery which moves affairs. These two conferences, coming together, show men and women in separate organisations, but in one movement, seriously attacking social and economic problems and making it above all things plain that, being bound up in the same society and with the same share of livelihood and happiness in the hazards of life, they should be able to carry on their work with equal liberties and equal rights.[3]

The League had always a duality; that of its organisation was a reflection of its dual duty, for Labour and for women; then, in its third phase, it reneged on separatism. The change in its own philosophy made this possible as the need for Party funds made it practical. Separatism was a position renounced. It was not a pass sold to the enemy, not a prize snatched from women's hands; separatism became an untenable position for the League when its politics changed in freshly class-conscious, wartime Britain, when women won the right to vote and inclusion in the male hierarchy. The League merged with the Labour Party because it seemed the right thing to do, because women's sections had been won at every branch, in every constituency.

Despite Marion Phillips's concern with industrial women, it was the caring, social welfare image of its earlier years that was the League's biggest contribution to the Labour movement. There has been debate about how far the early Labour Party was concerned with measures of state welfare. In parliament, honours had been taken by the Liberals. It is not clear that the Labour Party wanted to compete with them; Labour wanted to dismantle the Poor Law, not amend its provisions; it wanted freedom of industrial agitation and association, collective bargaining for a living wage that would enable working people to buy the necessities of life, not beg for them. Annually, the Party introduced the Right to Work Bill. Labour was also concerned with foreign affairs, imperialism and trade. The Party, before the First World War, was not the obvious precursor of the 1945 administration.

It was partly the League that helped to change Labour's outlook. One might perceive the fell hand of the stereotypical middle-class woman reformer, delaying the revolution by ameliorating living conditions. League women, however, dealt daily with misery. Their babies died. Their neighbours were left widows when the pits flooded. They saw hungry children. The League never relaxed its pressure on behalf of the poor, the sick and the aged and much of the weight was directed at the Labour Party, an insistent calling for action. The Party would have accepted the limited measure of free school meals; the League did not. The Party would not have fought for women's inclusion in the national insurance provisions, nor for the financing of school medical inspections; the Party did not found a baby clinic; the Party did not experiment with houses to suit working women. Margaret Bondfield, in retrospect, believed the

League affected Labour's policy and programme.[4] The evidence was printed in Labour's manifesto for the 1918 General Election, *Labour and the new Social Order,* which laid down a programme of reformist socialism.

The Labour Party was not the sole recipient of the League contribution in this field. Because the League worked out reforms in practice and had first-hand experience of what they meant to people affected, it became one of the interpreters of the working classes. Before 1914 workers were being classified and stratified by politicans and philosophers and social scientists. The reforms the progressives achieved were *ad hoc* measures, slid past the government, like the provision for school medical inspections, or championed by irresistible individuals, like old age pensions. Compromises amongst various interests, for instance, in sickness insurance, meant that the final measures approximated to intentions. For administrators, such as Poor Law Guardians trying to decide if an individual merited relief outside the workhouse, the result was often chaos. The League provided hard evidence for administrators and reformers; League women gave Glasgow District Committee statistics about unemployed women and supplied London County Council with information about the location of the most destitute children. They added to the data on sweating and on infant mortality. There were biological metaphors of society as an organism with many constituent cells; the League illustrated which were cancerous.

The League succeeded substantially in its own stated objects. The first was furthering labour representation. The Labour Party had obviously valued League election work to the point of paying the League to organise and eventually buying it out. The importance of women appealing to the electorate, of canvassing, was made clear. The lesson on the use of networks to reach out into new areas was underwritten by the courage of League women who travelled throughout Britain with their message, braving the lunchtime meetings, the chance of hospitable accommodation, the open-air speaking season, the weather and the loneliness. There was, in fact, no evidence that League work increased Labour Members of Parliament before the First World War (there were twelve fewer in December 1910 than in 1906), but the inheritance of League attention to the electoral registers and amongst women must have assisted Labour to increase its vote by 400,000 (to 2,374,000) in the

1918 election. A respectable sixty Members were returned, despite the first-past-the-post system and the attractions of the coalition platform put forward by Lloyd George, hero of the hour. Labour was able to claim its place as the official opposition to the coalition and in 1922 returned 142 Members. In 1924 the Labour Party formed a minority government.

The second League objective was the direct representation of women in parliament and on all local bodies. Its success in this field was a contribution to the women's movement. League women lived out their citizenship, standing and campaigning in elections, raising women's political expectations. The League returned women to many local bodies, a tradition of public service that continues. Women councillors portrayed their political acumen; suffrage demonstrators advertised discrimination and prejudice. Lisbeth Simm was told to stay at home when she first stood in the Guardians' election; she stayed to face out the men on her drowsy, rural Board. Ada Salter eventually became Mayor of Bermondsey. The League claimed a place for women in domestic wartime administration, nationally and locally. Marion Phillips demanded that branches be represented on their Citizen Committees. She helped promote the Consumers' Council and reminded women of their powers as purchasers.

It has also been argued, in Chapter 5, that the League engagement in local politics and electioneering generally contributed to women's enfranchisement; the League helped win the Labour Party to the cause and the Party's presence in the wartime coalition (not least, the position of League supporter Mr Wardle on the Speaker's Committee dealing with franchise) gave the suffragists a political ally with power to enforce enfranchisement. League women were among the first female Members of Parliament (Margaret Bondfield, Marion Phillips, Ellen Wilkinson), although the direct representation of women in parliament remained (and remains) extremely low.

Four Labour women stood unsuccessfully for parliament in 1918. Two of these had League connections, Mary MacArthur and Mrs Despard. More candidacies might have been expected; Lisbeth Simm in the North-East, Katharine Bruce Glasier or one of the Lancashire League women (Lisbeth's husband was a Labour candidate in 1916; Lisbeth is never referred to after 1918. In September that year, her daughter (Edna) died, while Lisbeth was away from home nursing her son. This tragedy may have worn out her selfless spirit). Annot Robinson did think about standing should she be nominated, but would have been handicapped by her anti-war stance. Even Labour's past parliamentary leaders, Ramsay MacDonald and Philip Snowden, failed to be elected, having opposed the war. Conscientious objectors had lost the right to vote because of their prison sentences. Bertha Ayles and Jennie Baker would have suffered from this prejudice. Minnie Nodin was ill, Ethel Bentham committed to medicine, Marion Phillips to Labour Party administration. Few women suffragists stood for election.

There are two feminist reasons why women might have been loath to stand for parliament: first, they had worked in single sex groups, enjoying women's companionship and identifying with women's interests; entrance into the Westiminster male club may have seemed neither congenial nor particularly pertinent: 'one woman among a crowd of men sorely needs a companion'. Second, some of the less prominent women may have been adverse to the role of heroine and the personal promotion that their candidacy would inevitably entail.

It was, however, within the Labour Party itself that one might expect League influence to continue after 1918: it was here that League women continued to organise, amongst the rank and file. In 1925 Averil Sanderson Furniss wrote about 'The Citizenship of Women' for the Labour Party; her comments on the League may also serve as an indication of contemporary women activists' opinion:

> The League not only wanted to further the cause of its own particular party, but it wanted also a share in it as electors on equal terms with men. The members contributed invaluable service to the party not only in consolidating the efforts of women as immediate and practical ends, but also in clarifying and presenting their point of view.[5]

Of Margaret MacDonald and Mary Middleton she wrote: 'Their spirit lives on in a network of women's sections now covering nearly every constituency in the country.' These sections were notes for survival; they were successful in gaining members and raised funds for the Party. Moreover, membership of a women's section carried with it the right to individual membership of the local Labour Party and representation on the local executive.

There was, as had been promised, a national women's conference in autumn 1918. Ethel Bentham chaired; apart from the League stalwarts, Beatrice Webb and Margaret Llewellyn Davies attended. For the Party conference in 1918 there was a League slate for the four women's places on the National Executive Committee: Ethel Bentham, Florence Harrison Bell, Eveline Lowe and Minnie Nodin. The first two were elected. Marion Phillips had also been nominated but declined, perhaps because as National Women's Officer she had no need to use a place. Susan Lawrence of the Fabian Society and Ethel Snowden were the other successful candidates. Mary MacArthur failed to win a place, so did Lydia Aspinall of the United Textile Factory Workers. In 1919 Ethel Bentham, Ethel Snowden and Susan Lawrence were elected, and Mary MacArthur took Florence Harrison Bell's place. The ex-League members were, therefore, able to influence Labour in the creation of the new women's sections. That year, a National Conference of Labour Women was held, but no motions were tabled and discussion was informal. Florence Harrison Bell was reported in *Labour Woman* (July 1919) as insisting that work must be found for women to do, although 'she would not despise tea parties, for much useful discussion often took place over the tea cups'.

Marion Phillips, of course, devoted much of her time to organising women's membership. In 1920 she was able to announce the first properly constituted National Conference of Labour Women held separately from the Party conference and attracting over four hundred delegates. The conference was held under the joint auspices of the Standing Joint Industrial Women's Committee and the Labour Party. It was a big success, many of its delegates being young women, who were presumably present because the Labour Party seemed to have something to offer, rather than from past loyalties. There was much press attention. The League can certainly take its share of credit for laying the foundations, although it might also be criticised for not foreseeing some of the problems: at the 1921 conference, women were already demanding that the women's conference should elect the nominees for the four women's places on the National Executive Committee.

The League had helped its bets on winning either women's parliamentary presence or direct influence within the Labour Party. Foremost amongst its notes for survival was the foundation of the Standing Joint Industrial Women's Committee. This was a caveat that enabled women, even after submerging the Women's Labour

League in the Labour Party, to retain a separate organisation of their own. Although the Standing Joint Committee still exists, conditions were never right for it to develop its autonomy in the 1920s and 1930s, with their militant industrial organisation, the growth of trade union mammoths, the short-lived experiments of Labour government and the rise of fascism.

In this period, the Women's Trade Union League and the National Federation of Women Workers followed the Women's Labour League in abandoning separate organisation. The Social Democratic Federation merged into the new Communist Party of Great Britain (Dora Montefiore was one of the founder members) and did continue women's congresses, although the class struggle remained the priority. The Independent Labour Party itself disaffiliated from the Labour Party in 1932 on the issue of creating a united front against fascism, and did not build a separate women's organisation to compare with the League. Here also, the League, notes were overlooked; by the Second World War the concept of a separate women's organisation within the Labour movement and socialist societies seemed anachronistic.

As women's separatism was submerged within class politics, the women's movement scattered. Women put their energies into the birth control movement and equal standards of sexual morality for both sexes, into peace and internationalism and into the continued claim for full enfranchisement for female adults. They were divided about family endowment and how to find a balance between the right to work, to leisure and to rear their children. The Co-operative Women's Guild failed to overcome a drop in membership which caused a generation gap between the stalwarts and new recruits, thereafter making organisation difficult. Of the suffrage organisations, the Women's Social and Political Union had disbanded during the war, when Joan of Arc went to the trenches, and the National Union of Women's Suffrage Societies diversified into the National Union of Societies for Equal Citizenship and the Women's International League for Peace and Freedom. There was not, therefore, outside pressure to stimulate Labour women to make greater claims for recognition.

Continuing to face challenges within the Labour movement, women's need for personal support was not diminished. The final League contribution is the most difficult to assess because it was the least public, that of personal politics. Rather than the negative, sterile reflection of the man's point of view which Theresa Billington Grieg once accused it of portraying, the League offered heterosexual women an example of the positive, opinionated, equal woman partner. A partnership of two dedicated people presents innumerable problems of sharing burdens, domestic and at work. Lisbeth Simm, Katharine Bruce Glasier, Margaret MacDonald, Mary Middleton, Marion Curran, all attacked these problems, not as superwomen who coped with everything, but as people sometimes sad, sometimes ill, who nevertheless created a lifestyle to their own satisfaction. Some exhausted themselves, such as Margaret MacDonald, Mary Middleton, Bertha Ayles. Some failed, such as Annot Robinson. Many, as the biographical appendix illustrates, found satisfaction in 'separate organisations within one movement', in the League, their women's party, their work equal to that of the spouse in the 'men's party'.

For women in single-sex households, possibly lesbian, certainly separatist, the League became the focus of political work. It enabled class politics to be pursued in a way that included issues of gender, where discussion of the women's point of view was inherent in the organisation. League social events were a celebration of its autonomous existence, a proclamation of the success of a women's group.

The paradox that ends the discussion of the League is that in its mother-and-baby phase it was most defiantly free-lance; when it was led by single, professional women it renounced separatism. The lesson would appear to be that organisation is as important as philosophy in giving a group its identity and that we can create politically only the organisation that is appropriate to our time and place. Run by Labour Party male leaders' spouses, its rhetoric of women at home, the free-lance League encouraged branch initiative and was characteristic of its period, a separate women's organisation. Run by separatist women, its rhetoric of women's right to work and vote, the League hierarchy became swollen and allowed itself to be assimilated, almost without making any demands. The constraints of historical consciousness would seem to have overwhelmed the League, so that it lost the idea of itself as a separate entity. Yet it was leaving the notes for future rebels to reclaim some of the League territory. The claims today for greater power for the women's conference and advisory committee are examples. This operation of praxis is perhaps our final understanding of the notes of survival left by the Women's Labour League.

Notes

1 *Northern Democrat*, October 1907.
2 *The Gertrude Tuckwell Collection* 1880–1920 (Trades Union Congress Library, London), 345/79, a *Daily Despatch* report.
3 *Aberdeen Daily Journal*, 13 September 1912.
4 Margaret Bondfield, *A Life's Work* (London, 1949), p. 124.
5 Averil Sanderson-Furniss, 'Citizenship of women', in Labour Party Publishing Co., *The Book of the Labour Party* (London, 1925), pp. 248–54.

Appendix 1

Biographies of League women

Abbreviations

Cllr	Councillor
Conf.	Conference
EC	Executive Committee
ILP	Independent Labour Party
NUWSS	National Union of Women's Suffrage Societies
Pres.	President
Treas.	Treasurer
UDC	Union of Democratic Control
WLL	Women's Labour League
WSPU	Women's Social and Political Union

An entry in J. Bellamy and J. Saville (eds.), *Dictionary of Labour Biography* is indicated in capitals.

Sources

Women's Labour League Secretarial Correspondence and Related Papers; League Leaflet; Women's Labour League *Conference Reports; Labour Leader; Labour's Who's Who* (1924–27).

Acton, Mrs
1910, Nelson WLL branch sec.
Ainslie, Mrs
1910, Benwell WLL branch sec.
Annakin, Ethel, *see* **Snowden**
Arnold Miss
1910–11, Finsbury WLL branch sec.
Arrowsmith, Mrs
1909, North Shields WLL branch sec.
Arthurton, Miss
1911, Ashton-in-Makerfield WLL branch sec.

Ayles, Bertha Winifred (née Batt)
1910, part-time organiser WLL; 1911, Bristol branch delegate to WLL conf; 1912, WLL EC.
Baker, Jennie H. (d. 1939)
1914–18, WLL EC; Finchley UDC; Hon. Sec. National Council for Unmarried Mothers; 192?, vice-pres. Finchley Divisional Labour Party and pres. women's section; pres. East Finchley Women's Co-operative Guild; Poor Law Guardian, Barnet; m. John Baker, Steel Smelters' Union.
Ball, Mrs C.
1910, St Helens WLL branch sec.
Banton, Mrs
1910, Leicester WLL branch sec; m. George, chair Leicester ILP; East Leicester MP 1924; 1913, Leicester Board of Guardians.
Barker, Ethell
1911 Abertillery WLL branch sec.; m. George, ex-miner, miners' agent, later MP Abertillery.
Barker, Mrs
1910 Manchester N. E. WLL branch sec.
Barnes, Edith
1906 Leicester WLL branch sec.
Bavington, Miss L. D.
WLL South London.
Beanland, Harriet
Suffragist; ILP; Board of Guardians 1913, Nelson WLL branch sec.
Bell, Edith
1906–07 WLL EC; Poor Law Guardian.
Bell, Florence Nightingale Harrison (b. 1865)
Cook, schoolmistress, lecturer, 1902 director Newcastle Co-operative Society; first sec. Newcastle LRC; sec. North East Society for Women's Suffrage; 1910 Newcastle WLL branch sec.; 1911 Newcastle branch delegate to WLL conf.; 1913 WLL EC; m. J. N. Bell, sec. National Amalgamated Union of Labour.
Bellamy, Mrs
WLL EC.
Bentham, Dr Ethel
Educated Royal Free Hospital, Royal Opthalmic Hospital, Rotunda Hospital, medical practitioner; Fabian; 1912–18 WLL EC; 192? Kensington Borough Council; 1918 Labour Party EC; 1922 Labour candidate, East Islington.
Birch, Mrs
1911 Hyde branch delegate to WLL conf.
Black, Clementina
1905 vice-pres. Women's Industrial Council; 1907 WLL.
Black, Lily
1910 Consett WLL.
Blacklock, Mrs
1911 Sunderland branch delegate to WLL conf.

Blair, Mrs
1911 Kirkdale WLL branch sec.
Bondfield, Margaret Grace
1910–12 WLL EC; 1912 WLL organiser: see *Dictionary of Labour Biography*, vol. II, pp. 39–45.
Booth, Clara
1911 Manchester North WLL branch sec.
Bradley, Sarah
1910 Hyde WLL branch sec.; 1911 Hyde branch delegate to WLL conf.
Brand, Mrs
1910 Glasgow Maryhill WLL branch sec.
Briggs, Mrs
1911 Leeds branch delegate to WLL conf.
Burrell, Alice
1912 Colne WLL branch sec.
Burt, Mrs
1910 St Helen's WLL branch sec.
Cairns, Waldie, Mrs
1911 N.E. District WLL.
Campbell, Mrs
1909 WLL EC.
Carnegie, Mrs
1911 Glasgow WLL branch sec.
Caswell, Mrs
1910 Hedbury Colliery WLL branch sec.
Cavey, Mrs
1911 Wigan no. 2 WLL branch sec.
Cawthorne, Mrs
1907–08 Hull WLL; WLL EC.
Chew, Ada Nield
1912 Rochdale WLL branch sec.; see *Dictionary of Labour Biography*, vol. V, pp. 57–64.
Conway, St John Katharine, *see* **Glasier**
Cooke, Mrs
1910 Newton Abbott branch sec.
Cooke, E., Mrs
1911 Penberth WLL branch sec.
Clynes, J.H., Mrs
1911 Oldham WLL branch sec.
Cooper, Annie
1913 Hyde WLL branch sec.
Cordery, Mrs
1908 Bromley by Bow branch sec.
Cruickshank, Mrs
1910 Leith WLL branch sec.
Curbison, Mrs
1911 South Shields WLL branch sec.

Curran, Marion (née Barry)
East London branch London Tailoring Union; WTUL asst. sec.; 1896 WTUL delegate to International Socialist Congress London; 1907 hon. pres. Jarrow WLL; 1908–09 WLL EC; 1911 Hackney Labour Exchange post: see *Dictionary of Labour Biography*, vol. IV, pp. 65–9, entry for husband Pete Curran.
Davies, Mrs
1910 Abertillery WLL branch sec.
Davies, Mrs
1910 Merthyr WLL branch sec.
Denny, Mrs
1912 West Ham South WLL branch sec.
Dideridge
1913 Wolverhampton WLL branch sec.
Donaldson, Louise
1912–18 Leicester WLL branch pres.; 1913–17 WLL EC; 1915–18 Leicester day nursery; m. Frederick Lewis Donaldson, Christian Socialist Church, later Canon of Westminster.
Duckett, Mrs
1911 Preston WLL branch sec.
Edwards, Mrs
1911 Ogmore Vale WLL branch sec.
Eldridge, Mrs
1913 Coventry WLL branch sec.
Ensor, Mrs
1910 Poplar WLL branch sec.
Evans, Miss
1911 Birmingham branch delegate to WLL conf.
Evans, Miss
1910 Nantyfflon WLL branch sec.
Fells, Joseph, Mrs
1909 WLL treas.
Fenton, Macpherson Mary, *see* **Macpherson**
Fey, Mrs
1906 Birmingham WLL branch chair.
Fiorci, Margaret
1906 Birmingham WLL branch sec.
Fleming, Mrs
1911 Shettleston WLL branch sec.; 1911 Shettleston branch delegate to WLL conf.
Flowers, Helena
1909 WLL; later sec. women's section, National and General Municipal workers, Manchester branch.
Foote, Miss Bessie
1911 Lochgelly WLL branch sec.
Forcey, Mrs
1910–11 Streatham WLL branch sec.

Ford, Isabella O. (d. 1924)
1903/4/5/6 ILP delegate to LRC conf.; 1903/4/5 ILP National Administration Committee; 1904 Parish Councillor, Adel, Leeds; 1906 WLL; 1912 Election Fighting Fund.
Fort, Mrs
1910 Lancaster WLL branch sec.
Frethey, Mrs
1911 Wood Green WLL branch pres.; 1912, Edmonton Board of Guardians.
Gasson, Mrs
1909 WLL EC.
Gawthorpe, Mary (b. 1881)
1906–11 WSPU National Committee; 1906 Leeds WLL branch sec.; 1906 WLL EC; ILP.
Gibbin, Mrs
1911 Benwell WLL branch sec.; 1911 Benwell Board of Guardians.
Gilliland, Mrs
1911 Birtley WLL branch sec.
Glasier, Katharine St John (née Conway, b. 1869, d. 1950)
Graduate Newnham College; Bristol teacher; Fabian lecturer; 1892 Cardiff Fabian Society; 1893 Bristol Socialist Society; 1893 ILP arrangements committee; 1893 ILP conf.; 1893 ILP NAC; 1893 speaker ILP and SDF; 1907–18 WLL EC; 1919–21 ed. *Labour Leader*, m. John Bruce Glasier, 1895: biography: Lawrence Thompson: *The Enthusiasts* (1979).
Glenn, Miss
1909 WLL.
Goddard, Miss D.
1910 Islington WLL branch sec.
Gossling, Nance (Ann Elizabeth) (née Tweed)
ILP; 1913 Kensington and Paddington WLL; Baby Clinic supporter; woman factory inspector; Wimbledon Labour Party women's section; local sec. anti-sweating League; 1931 Norfolk guest house; 1939–45 member war voluntary patrol; Women's National Housing and Town Planning Association; m. 'Arch', MP Birmingham 1929–31.
Gould, Mrs
1910–11 Hull WLL branch sec.
Graham, Mrs
1910 Manchester East WLL branch sec.
Griffiths, Mrs
1911 Coventry branch delegate to WLL conf.; 1912, Coventry Board of Guardians.
Grimwood, Miss E.
1910 Willesden WLL branch sec.
Halliday, Mrs H.
1910 Leeds WLL branch sec.
Hawley, Mrs
1910 Gorton WLL branch sec.
Hayman, Miss
1911 Burnley branch delegate to WLL conf.

Hedges, Louise
1909 WLL EC; sec. National Federation of Women Workers; sec. Dressmakers' Union.
Hewlett-Johnson, Mrs
1917 Altrincham WLL branch pres.
Holden, Dorothy
1907 Workington WLL branch sec.
Hope, Mabel
1906–08 WLL EC; sec. Postal Telegraph Clerks' Association.
Houston, Mrs
1910 Gateshead-on-Tyne WLL branch sec.
Howes, Mrs
1910/11 Birmingham East WLL branch sec.
Hughes, Mrs E. O.
1911 Ashton-in-Makerfield WLL sec.
Hughes, Mrs
WLL Birmingham.
Hume, Mrs
1910 Blackburn WLL branch sec.
Humphries, Mrs
1910 Tondu WLL branch sec.
Hunter, L., Mrs
1913 Shildon WLL branch sec.
James, Frances
1907 St Pancras WLL branch sec.
Johnson, Ellen
1913 Wood Green WLL branch sec.
Jones, Miss A.
1910 Swansea WLL branch sec.
Josling, Mrs
1911 Kensington WLL branch sec.
Kelly, J. A.
1906 Leeds WLL branch sec.
Kelly, Mrs
1911 Willesden branch delegate to WLL conf.; 1912, Willesden Board of Guardians.
Kelsall, Mrs
1910 Crewe WLL branch sec.
Kerrison, Edith (b. 1850)
Nurse, Sister, Seaman's Hospital Greenwich; 1894 ILP; West Ham Council; 1897 on West Ham Board of Guardians; 1907–17 WLL EC.
Kneeshaw, Miss
1911 Birmingham Bordesley WLL branch sec.
Lancaster, Bertha
1906–09 Wallasey WLL branch sec.
Lenn, Dorothy
1909 WLL organiser; 1910 Central London branch WLL sec.; 1911 Health Visitor, Leicester.

Lennon, Mrs
1911 Belfast WLL branch sec.
Lewis
1911 Barry WLL branch sec.
Lewis, Mrs
1911 Shildon Branch delegate to WLL conf.
Lloyd, Grace
1907–10 Jarrow WLL branch sec.
Lloyd, Grace
1908 Gateshead WLL branch sec.
Lloyd, Mrs
1910 Bristol WLL branch sec.
Longman, Mary
1910 Central London WLL branch sec.; 1915–16 WLL EC and general sec.
Lowe, Eveline Mary
1911 Islington delegate to WLL conf.; 1913–15 WLL EC; 1922 London County Council.
Lowe, Mrs
1911 Goldbourne WLL branch sec.
MacArthur, Mary (b. 6 August 1880, d. January 1921)
1906 National Federation of Women Workers; 1906 WLL EC; Women's Industrial Council; 1914–18 Standing Joint Committee of Women's Industrial Organisations; 1918 Labour Party parliamentary candidate; m. W. C. Anderson.
McCrory
1910 Sunderland WLL EC.
MacDonald, Margaret (née Gladstone, b. 20 July 1870, d. 8 September 1911) m. Ramsay MacDonald 1896; 1906 WLL pres.; 1911 WLL joint sec.: see *Dictionary of Labour Biography*, vol. IV, pp. 181–5.
McDonnell, Mrs
1910 Hebburn-on-Tyne WLL branch sec.
McKenzie, Mrs
1906/7 WLL EC; National Council of Adult Schools Assoc.
McNab, Clarice
1911 Leith branch delegate to WLL conf.; 1917–18 WLL EC; Nat. sec. Socialist Sunday Schools; m. Ben Shaw.
MacPherson, Mary Fenton, BA
Sec. Railway Women's Guild; ed. women's column *Railway Review*; 1906 founding sec. WLL; WLL EC; 1906 translator and interpreter Socialist Inter-Parliamentary committee (for *Labour Leader*); 1907 delegate Stuttgart International Socialist Conference; translator and interpreter Shop Assistants' International Conf.
Macrosty, Mrs
1910 WLL EC.
Martin, Mrs
1910 Wood Green WLL branch sec.
Martin, Miss E.
1911 Leicester WLL branch sec.

Mason, Mrs
1910–11 Birmingham Handsworth WLL branch sec.
Maugham, Mrs
1911 Crewe delegate to WLL conf.
Middleton, Mary (d. 24 April 1911)
1906 sec WLL; m. James, Asst Sec. LRC.
Miller, Mrs
1911 Altrincham WLL branch sec.
Miller, Miss L.
1910 Portsmouth WLL branch sec.
Mills, Mrs
1909 Gateshead WLL branch sec.
Mills, Mrs
1911 Barrow WLL branch sec.; 1912, Barrow Board of Guardians.
Millward, Mrs
1910 Newport WLL branch sec.
Mitchell, Cecilia
1908 Birmingham Handsworth WLL branch sec.
Moore, Mrs
1910 Dulwich WLL branch sec.
Moran, Miss S.
1910 Sutton WLL branch sec.
Morrice, Mrs
1911 Chatham, Gillingham and Rochester WLL branch sec.
Mottram, Mrs E.
1912 Leith WLL branch sec.
Muir, Mary
Bradford WLL; ILP; 1906–07 WLL EC.
Munro, Mrs
1911 Edinburgh WLL branch sec.
Munro, Mrs
1911 Manchester Middleton WLL branch sec.
Myles, Mrs M. M.
1916 Brixton WLL branch sec.
Nattress, Mrs
1911 Crook WLL branch sec.
Naughton, Mrs M. P.
1910 Partick WLL branch sec.
Naylor, Miss M.
1910–11 Wigan WLL branch sec.
Newell, Mrs E.
1913 St Helen's WLL branch sec.
Nodin, Minnie (d. 1936)
1906 Central London WLL branch sec.; 1907–18 WLL EC; 1911 WLL treas.; 1911 Baby Clinic Committee and Sewing Party; 1911 Central London branch delegate to WLL conf.
Norman, Mrs
1910 Fulham WLL branch sec.

Park, Miss Gretta
Singer; 1909 WLL.
Parker, Mrs
1911 Bristol branch delegate to WLL conf.
Pattenall, Mrs
1911 Goose Green WLL branch sec.
Peach, Mrs
1911 Leicester branch delegate to WLL conf.
Pease Mrs Margery
Poor Law Guardian; 1922 Labour candidate East Surrey; 192? Surrey County Council and Godstone Rural District Council; m. Edward Pease, Hon. Sec. Fabian Soc.
Pemberton, Miss
1911 Glasgow WLL branch sec.
Peters, Annie
1907 Barrow WLL branch sec.
Phillips, Marion, Dr (b. 1881, d. 1932)
Melbourne University; LSE; Poor Law Guardian Investigator; 1911 Kensington WLL branch sec.; 1911 Central London branch delegate to WLL conf.; 1912–18 WLL EC; 1912–18 Organising. Hon. Sec. WLL: see *Dictionary of Labour Biography*, vol. V, pp. 173–9.
Pimblott, Mrs W.
1910 Macclesfield WLL.
Pollitt, Mrs M. H.
1913 Swinton and Pendlebury WLL; m. James, ILP, Co-operator.
Potts, Miss
1907 Jarrow WLL branch sec.
Price, Mrs
1910 Stoke Newington WLL branch sec.; 1911 Stoke Newington branch delegate to WLL conf.
Price, Miriam
1913 Hackney WLL branch sec.
Rae, Mrs
1910 Clydebank WLL branch sec.
Ralphs, Kitty B.
1907 Preston WLL branch sec.
Read, Mrs
1911 Leicester branch delegate to WLL conf.
Relph, Mrs Elizabeth
1910 Workington WLL, branch sec.; 1912, Cockermouth Board of Guardians.
Rigby, Mrs Edith
1906 Preston WLL branch sec.; 1906 WLL EC; 1907 left WLL; sec. Preston WSPU; ILP.
Riley, Mrs
1911 Leicester branch delegate to WLL conf.
Robinson, Annot (née Wilkie, b. 1874, d. 1923)
1907 WSPU; ILP; 1910 WLL organiser; 1911 NUWSS organiser; 1911

Manchester Central branch delegate to WLL conf.; Chair, Women's Advisory Housing Committee Manchester; 1920 Women's International League for Peace and Freedom; m. Sam Robinson, 1909.
Robson, Miss
1911 Warrington WLL branch sec.
Salter, Ada (née Brown)
1897–1900 resident Bermondsey Settlement; 1912–18 WLL EC; 1912–18 treas. WLL; 1909–12 Bermondsey Metropolitan Borough Councillor; 1922–23 Mayor Bermondsey.
Sanderson-Furniss, Averil Dorothy (née Nicholl)
1925 Oxford Justice of the Peace; sec. Women's Housing Committee; member Housing Council, Ministry of Health; m. Henry, Ruskin College tutor 1907–16, Ruskin College Principal 1916–25.
Sangster, Miss S.
1909 WLL.
Scholefield, Mrs
1910 Cardiff WLL branch sec.; 1911 Cardiff branch delegate to WLL conf.; 1913 Swansea WLL branch sec.; 1913–18 WLL EC; 1913–18 South Wales organiser WLL.
Shuttleworth, Miss
1910 Birmingham WLL branch sec.
Simm, Lisbeth
1908–18 WLL organiser; 1908–18 WLL EC; NUWSS; m. M. T. Simm.
Slater, Mrs
1910 Manchester North WLL branch sec.
Smith, Miss
1911 Clitheroe WLL branch sec.
Smith, Miss H.
1911 Finsbury branch delegate to WLL conf.
Smith, Mrs
1910 Shildon WLL branch sec.
Smith, Margaret
1907–08 WLL EC.
Smith, Mrs 'Sam'
1911 Griffithstown WLL branch sec.
Smithson, Mrs
1911 North Shields delegate to WLL conf.
Snowden, Ethel (née Annakin, b. 1881, d. 1946)
Fabian Soc.; NUWSS; ILP; 1905 ILP delegate to LRC conf.; 1906 joined and resigned WLL; 1912 Election Fighting Fund; m. Philip Snowden 1905.
Stallybrass, Mrs
1907 Wallasey WLL branch sec.; 1911 Wallasey branch delegate to WLL conf.; 1912, Birkenhead Board of Guardians.
Stone, Mrs G.
1908 WLL EC.
Stuttland, Mrs
1911 Blackpool WLL EC.

Summabell, Mrs
1910 Bolden Colliery WLL branch sec.
Sutton, Mrs
1910 Ashton-in-Makerfield WLL branch pres.
Sykes, Mrs
1910 Brighouse WLL branch sec.; m. Albert Sykes.
Taggart, Mrs
1910 WLL branch sec.
Tasker, Mrs
1910 Wolverhampton WLL branch sec.
Taylor, Kate
1908 Glasgow WLL branch sec.
Thompson, Mrs
1910 Leeds Holbeck WLL branch sec.; 1912, Holbeck Board of Guardians.
Thompson, Miss
1911 Bishop Auckland WLL branch sec.
Thompson, Miss
1911 Barrow branch delegate to WLL conf.
Thorogood, Miss
1911 Central London branch delegate to WLL conf.
Turner, Mrs
1911 Glasgow WLL branch sec.
Wade, Miss
1910 Wallasey WLL branch sec.
Walker, Mrs
1911 Ecclestone WLL branch sec.
Walters, Miss
1910 Woolwich WLL branch sec.
Ward, Maud
1911 Rochester branch delegate to WLL conf.; 1911 Hendon WLL branch sec.; 1912 WLL EC; 1913 Chief Health Inspector, women's side.
Whitfield, Miss
1911 Haydock WLL branch sec.
Wilcox, Mrs A.
1911 Kensington WLL branch sec.
Wilkinson, Ellen Cicely (b. 1891)
Wesleyan; educated Manchester; 1912 ILP; 1913 Tyldesley WLL branch sec.; 1913–15 organiser NUWSS; 1913–25 National Organiser National Union Distributive and Allied Workers; 1923 Manchester City Councillor (Communist Party); Jarrow MP; 1945 Minister for Education; biography: Betty Vernon, *Ellen Wilkinson* (1982).
Williams, Miss
1910 Warrington WLL branch sec.
Willson, Laura
1907 Halifax WLL branch sec.
Young, Mrs
1911 Burnley WLL branch sec.

Appendix 2

Women's labour league branches

Branch record 1906–18, showing branches formed, secretary and other officers, branch history, whether the branch was active in 1910, whether executive committee members were drawn from the branch and whether the Labour Party fought a Parliamentary election in the constituency.

Sources

Women's Labour League Secretarial Correspondence and Related Papers; League Leaflet; Women's Labour League *Conference Reports*; Labour Party *Annual Reports* 1907–18.

Appendix 2: Women's Labour League branch record

Branch	*Secretary*	*Branch history*	*Active in 1910*	*Executive members drawn from*	*Parliamentary Labour Party candidature* (Successful = +)
Aberdare		Formed 1917			
Aberdeen		Formed 1911			
Abergavenny		Formed 1911	+		
Abertillery	1910 Mrs Davies 1911 Ethel Barker	Formed 1910 Re-formed 1911 Re-formed 1917			
Accrington		Closed 1917			
Altrincham	Mrs Miller Pres: Mrs Hewlett Johnson	Formed 1911 Closed 1917			
Annerley		Disaffiliated 1912			
Ardwick		Formed 1911			
Armley	Mrs Shore Treas: Mrs Sykes				
Ashton-in-Makerfield	Mrs Arthurton Pres. and Leader Mrs Sutton 1911 C. O. Hughes	Independent group resolved to join 1911			
Bargoed		Lapsed 1911			
Barrow	1906 Mrs Peters 1911 Mrs Mills	Formed 1906	+		1906 1910 January + 1910 December +
Barry	Mrs Lewis	Formed 1911 Re-formed 1917			
Battersea		Formed 1911			

Branch	*Secretary*	*Branch history*	*Active in 1910*	*Executive members drawn from*	*Parliamentary Labour Party candidature* (Successful = +)
Belfast	Mrs Lennon		+		1906 B. North
					1906 B. West
					1907
					1910 January
Benwell	Mrs Ainslie	Formed 1908	+		
	1911 Mrs Gibbon	Lapsed 1912			
Bermondsey		Formed 1911			1909
Birmingham	1906 Mrs Fiorci	Formed 1906	+		
	1908 Cecilia Mitchell	Re-formed 1908			
	1910 Miss Shuttleworth	Re-formed 1913			
Birmingham Bordesley	1911 Mrs Kneeshaw	1911	+		
Birmingham East	Mrs Holmes				1906
					1910 January
Birmingham Handsworth	1910 Mrs Mason	Difficulties 1915			
Birmingham Winson Green		Formed 1912			
Birtley	Mrs Gillard	Formed 1911			
Bishop Auckland	Miss Thompson	Formed 1911			1910 January
					1910 December
Blackburn	Mrs Hume	Formed 1910	+		1906
		Re-formed 1913			1910 January
					1910 December
Blackpool	Mrs Stuttland	1909	+		
Blyth	Mrs Auld	Formed 1909	+	Mrs Simm	
Boldon Colliery	Mrs Summabell	Formed 1910	+		
Bootle		Formed 1907			
Bow and Bromley	1908 Mrs Cordery	Formed 1908			1910 January
	Dolly Lansbury				1910 December +
					1912 G. Lansbury suffrage candidacy fails

Bowness		Formed 1914 Dead 1915			
Bradford Women's Central ILP	Formed 1914				Bradford West 1906 1910 January + 1910 December +
Brechin	Mrs Taggart	Formed 1909	+		
Bridgeton		Formed 1913 Closed 1916			
Brighouse	Mrs Albert Sykes	Formed 1910	+		
Bristol	1910 Mrs Lloyd 1910 Mrs Turner	Formed 1909	+	Mrs Ayles	Bristol East 1910 January
Briton Ferry		Formed 1913 Lapsed 1913			
Brixton	Mrs M. M. Myles	Formed 1913 Closed 1916			
Broughton		Formed 1917			
Burnley	1910 Miss Birley 1911 Mrs Young	Formed 1910 'severed connection' 1911. Marked SDP 1910 Closed 1916	+		
Bury		Formed 1911 Re-formed 1916			
Cardiff	Mrs Scholefield		+	Mrs Scholefield	
Central London	*see London Central*				
Chatham, Gillingham and Rochester	1911 Mrs Morrice	Formed 1910		Maud Ward	
Chiswick		Collapsed 1915			

Branch	*Secretary*	*Branch history*	*Active in 1910*	*Executive members drawn from*	*Parliamentary Labour Party candidature* (Successful = +)
Clitheroe	Mrs Smith		+		1906
					1910 January +
					1910 December +
Clydebank	Mrs Coe		+		
	1910 Mrs Rae		+		
Coalburn		Opened 1917			
Colne	Alice Burrell	Formed 1912			
Consett	Mrs Lily Black	Formed 1909	+		
Coventry	1910 Mrs Martin	Formed 1910	+		
	1913 Mrs Eldridge	Revived 1911			
Crewe	Mrs Kelsall	Formed 1909	+		1910 January
					1912
Crook	Mrs Natress	Formed 1908	+		
Croydon		Formed 1914			
		Closed 1915			
Cwmavon					
Darlington		Formed 1912			1906
Deptford		Formed 1914			1906
					1910 January +
					1910 December +
Derby		Formed 1913			1910 January +
					1910 December +
Douglas		Formed 1914			
Dulwich	Mrs Moore	Formed 1909	+		
Dulwich East		Formed 1913			

Dundee		'Gone' 1913		1906
		Re-opened 1917		1908
				1910 January +
				1910 December +
Earlestown		Formed 1913		
Ebbw Vale				
Eccles		Formed 1913		1906
				1910 January
Eccleston	Mrs Walker	Formed 1911		
Edinburgh	Mrs Munro	Formed 1911		
		Re-formed 1913		
Felling	Mrs Hutchinson	Formed 1910		
Finsbury	Miss Arnold	Formed 1910	+	
Forest of Dean		Formed 1911		
		'Lost' 1913		
Fulham	Miss Norman		+	
Gateshead	1908 Grace Lloyd	Formed 1908	+	1906 +
	1909 Mrs Mills			1910 January
	1910 Mrs Houston			
Gillingham	*see Chatham, Gillingham and Rochester*			
Girlington		Formed 1911		
Glasgow	Kate Taylor	Formed 1908		
	1911 Miss Carnegie		+	
	1911 Miss Pemberton			
Glasgow Maryhill	Mrs Brand	Formed 1910	+	
Golborne	*details unknown*			
Goose Green	Mrs Pattenhall	Formed 1911		
Gorseinon		Formed 1917		
Gorton	Mrs Hawley	Formed 1910		1910 January +
				1910 December +
Govanhill	Formed 1912			
	Difficulties 1915			
Griffithstown	1911 Mrs Sam Smith	Formed 1911		

Branch	Secretary	Branch history	Active in 1910	Executive members drawn from	Parliamentary Labour Party candidature (Successful = +)
Hackney	Miriam Price	Formed 1913 Suspended meetings 1917			
Halifax	Laura Wilson	Formed 1909 Ceased to exist 1911			1906 1910 January + 1910 December +
Hammersmith		Formed 1912 Merged with Fulham 1913			
Hampstead		Dead 1915			
Hanley		Formed 1912			1910 January + 1910 December + 1912
Haydock	Mrs Whitfield	Formed 1911			
Hebburn	Mrs McDonnell	Formed 1908	+		
Hebburn Colliery	Mrs Caswell	Formed 1910	+		
Heywood		Closed 1916	+		
Holbeach		Formed 1910	+		
Hull	Mrs Gould	Formed 1907 Dissolved 1910 Revived 1911 Difficulties 1915		Mrs Cawthorne	1906 (Central) 1907 (West)
Hutcheson		Formed 1913			1906
Hyde	1910 Mrs Bradley Annie Cooper	Formed 1910			1910 January

Ipswich		Formed 1912			
		Lapsed 1912			
		Re-formed 1913			
Islington	1911 Mrs Goddard	Formed 1910	+		
		Died 1917			
Jarrow	1907 Miss Potts	Formed 1907		Marion Curran	1906
	Grace Lloyd				1907 +
	Marion Curran				1910 January
					1910 December
Keighley		Dissolved 1914			1913
Kensington and	1911 Mrs Wilcox	Formed 1910	+	Marion Phillips	
Paddington	1912 Marion Phillips				
	1913 Nance Gossling				
Kilmarnock		Formed 1912			1910 (by)
		'Gone' 1913			
Kirkdale	Mrs A. Wilcox	Formed 1910			1906
	1911 Mrs Blair				1907
					1910 January
					1910 December
					1910 (by)
Kirkintilloch					
Lancaster	Mrs Fort	Formed 1910	+		
Larkhall		Formed 1913			
Lawton		Formed 1911			
Leeds	1906 Mrs Gawthorpe	Formed 1906	+	Mrs Gawthorpe	1906 (South)
	1906 J. A. Kelly				1908 (South)
	1910 Mrs Halliday				
Leeds Arnsley		Formed 1911			
Leeds East	Mrs Dighton	Formed 1910	+		1906
					1910 January +
					1910 December +
Leeds Farley		Formed 1915			

Branch	*Secretary*	*Branch history*	*Active in 1910*	*Executive members drawn from*	*Parliamentary Labour Party candidature (Successful = +)*
Leeds Harehill	Mrs Craven	1910 not a branch yet			
Leeds Holbeck	Mrs Thompson	Formed 1910	+		
Leeds New Wortley		Formed 1913 'Almost dead' 1915			
Leicester	1906 Edith Barnes 1910 Mrs Barton 1911 Miss E. Martin 1913 Mrs E. Banton	Formed 1906	+		1906 1910 January + 1910 December + 1910 December +
Leigh	Mrs G. Mottram	Formed 1912			1910 January +
Leigh West		Formed 1915			
Leith	Mrs Cruickshank	Formed 1910			1910 January
Lincoln	*details unknown*				
Liskeard		Formed 1906			
Liverpool Edgehill		Formed 1913 Collapsed 1914			
Lochgelly	Bessie Foot	Formed 1911			
London Central	1906 Minnie Nodin 1910 Dorothy Lenn 1910 Mary Longman 1911 Mrs E. Pearse	Formed 1906	+	Margaret MacDonald Mary Macpherson Mrs Macrosty Mary Middleton Minnie Nodin Ada Salter Jennie Baker	
Long Eaton		Formed 1913 'Dead' 1915			

Macclesfield	Mrs Pimblott	Formed 1910 'Dead' 1915			
Manchester Central	Mrs Russell	Formed 1909 Dissolved 1912 Re-formed 1913	+		
Manchester East	Mrs Graham	Formed 1910	+		1910 January 1910 December +
Manchester Middleton	1908 Mrs Hilton Mrs Munro	Formed 1908 Lapsed 1914	+		
Manchester North	Mrs Slater 1911 Clara Booth	Formed 1910			
Manchester	Mrs Barker	Formed 1910	+		1906 1910 January + 1910 December +
Marylebone		'Almost dead' 1915			
Merthyr Tydfil	Mrs Davies	Formed 1910 'Dead' 1912			1906 1910 January 1910 December
Middlesbrough		Formed 1913 Suspended meetings 1915			1910 January
Nantyfflon	Mrs Evans	Formed 1910	+		
Nelson	Mrs Acton 1913 Harriet Beanland	Formed 1907 Re-lapsed 1913			
Newburn		Formed 1908			
Newcastle upon Tyne	Mrs Harrison Bell	1910	+	Mrs Harrison Bell	1906 1910 January + 1910 December +
Newport	Mrs Milward	Formed 1910	+		
Newton Abbot	Mrs Cooke	Formed 1909	+		1906
North Ashton		Formed 1911			

Branch	*Secretary*	*Branch history*	*Active in 1910*	*Executive members drawn from*	*Parliamentary Labour Party candidature* (Successful = +)
North Shields	1909 Mrs Arrowsmith 1911 Mrs Martin	Formed 1909	+		
Norwich		Formed 1911			1906 1910 January + 1910 December
Nottingham		Formed 1912 'Lost' 1913			
Ogmore Vale	Mrs Edwards	Formed 1911			
Oldham	Mrs Clynes	Formed 1911			
Partick	Miss F. N. Naughton	Formed 1910	+		
Patricroft		Difficulties 1915			
Pemberth	Miss E. Cooke	Formed 1911			
Penketh and Warrington		Formed 1911 Re-formed 1916			
Pontypool		Opened 1916			
Poplar	Mrs Ensor	Formed 1910	+		
Portsmouth	1907 Mrs Colley Priest 1910 Mrs L. Miller	Formed 1907	+		1906 1910 January
Preston	1906 Mrs Rigby 1907 Kitty Ralphs 1911 Mrs Duckett	Formed 1906 Split 1907 Re-formed 1907 Re-formed 1911		Mrs Rigby	1906 + 1910 January 1910 December
Rochdale	1912 Ada Nield Chew	Formed 1913 'Dead' 1915			
Rochester	*see Chatham, Gillingham and Rochester*		+		
Rotherhithe		Formed 1913			

Rowtynm		Formed 1911			
St Helen's	1909 Mrs Bell 1913 Mrs E. Newell	Formed 1909 Merged 1913 with St Helen's E.M. Separated again 1913	+		1906 + 1910 January + 1910 December
St Helen's Ellen Martin	Mrs Burt	Seceded from St Helen's 1910 Merged 1913 Separated again 1913	+		
St Pancras	Frances James	Formed 1907			
Selbourne		Formed 1911			
Sheffield		Formed 1912			
Shettleston	Mrs Sims 1911 Miss Fleming	Formed 1910 Re-formed 1911	+		
Shildon	1908 Mrs Smith 1911 Mrs L. Hunter	Formed 1908	+		
Shipley		Formed 1917			
Shoreditch		Formed 1916			
Smethwick		Formed 1913 Re-formed 1912 'Dead' 1915			
South Shields	Mrs Curbison	Formed 1911			
Stanhope		Formed 1911 Closed 1915			
Stanley	Mrs F. James	Formed 1910 Re-formed 1914	+	Mrs James	
Stoke Newington	Miss Price	Formed 1910	+		
Streatham	Miss Forcey	Formed 1910	+		
Stublands Cross		Formed 1913			
Sunderland	Mrs M. Mcrory	Formed 1910	+		1906 + 1910 January 1910 December +

Branch	*Secretary*	*Branch history*	*Active in 1910*	*Executive members drawn from*	*Parliamentary Labour Party candidature* (Successful = +)
Sutton	Mrs Moran	Formed 1910	+		
Swansea	1909 Miss Jones	Formed 1909	+		
	1913 Mrs Scholefield				
Swinton and Pendlebury					
Taunton		Formed 1909			1909
		Ceased to exist 1912			
Thornton Heath	Mrs Pimblott	Formed 1910	+		
		Dissolved 1912			
Throckley		Formed 1908			
Tondu	Mrs Humphries	'Gone' 1913			
Tyldesley	1913 Ellen Wilkinson	Formed 1912			
Walkden		Re-formed 1913			
Wallasey	1906 Bertha Lancaster	Formed 1906	+	Katharine Bruce Glasier	
	1907 Mrs Stallybrass				
	1910 Mrs Wade				
Walsingham		Formed 1911			
Warrington	Miss Rolson	Formed 1909			
	1911 Miss Williams				
West Bromwich		Formed 1911			
West Ham South	Mrs Denny	Formed 1912			1906
					1910 January +
					1910 December +
Wigan	Miss Naylor	Formed 1910	+		1910 January +
Wigan 2	Miss Cavey	Formed 1911			1910 December +

Wigan 3		Formed 1911 (Became one branch 1913. Lapsed 1914)		
Willesden	Mrs Greenwood	Formed 1910 'Gone' 1913	+	
Windy Nook		Formed 1910		
Wolverhampton	1910 Mrs Tasker 1913 A. Dideridge	Formed 1910	+	1906 (Wol. West) + 1910 January
Wood Green	1906 Mrs Martin 1911 Mrs Frethes 1913 Ellen Johnson	Formed 1906	+	
Woolwich	Mrs Walters	Formed 1910	+	1906 + 1910 January 1910 December +
Workington	1907 Dorothy Holden 1910 Mrs Relph 1911 Miss Rolson	Formed 1907	+	
Wrexham		Formed 1913	+	
Ystalyfera		Closing 1915		

Bibliography

Primary sources

Unpublished material

Women's Labour League Secretarial Correspondence and Related Papers (Labour Party Headquarters Archives, Walworth Road, London)

Labour Representation Committee Papers; Labour Party *General Correspondence*; Labour Party *Subject Files* (Labour Party Headquarters Archives, Walworth Road, London)

J. R. MacDonald and M. E. MacDonald Papers, PRO/30/69; *Political Party*, Correspondence, Margaret MacDonald, papers relating to her Political and Social Work; *Personal*, Correspondence, General, Family and Personal Papers of M. E. MacDonald; *Political and Public*, Pamphlets (Public Records Office, London)

Margaret MacDonald Papers; Infancy of the Labour Party; Coll. Misc. 196 I and II (British Library of Political and Social Science, London)

The Gertrude Tuckwell Collection 1890–1920 (microfilm) (Trades Union Congress Library, London)

Independent Labour Party: *National Administration Committee Minutes and Related Records* (microfilm); *Francis Johnson Correspondence* (microfilm) (Labour Party Headquarters Archives, London)

Central Manchester Independent Labour Party *Minutes* (Manchester Central Library)

Annot Robinson Papers (the property of Mrs H. Wilson, Altrincham) (Manchester Central Library)

James and Lucy Middleton Papers: The Ruskin Collection; Walter Ayles' Papers; Pete Curran by-election papers (Ruskin College, Oxford)

Books

Aberdeen, Countess of (ed.), International Congress of Women, 1899, *Transactions* (London, 1899)

Bax, Belfort, *Essays in Socialism New and Old* (London, 1906)

Black, Clementina, *Married Women's Work* (London, 1984)

Bondfield, Margaret, *A Life's Work* (London, 1949)
Brittain, Vera, *Lady into Woman* (London, 1953)
Buckley, M. E., *The Feeding of Schoolchildren* (London, 1914)
Clapperton, Jane Hume, *Margaret Dunmore, or a Socialist Home* (London 1888)—*Scientific Meliorism and the Evolution of Happiness* (London, 1899)
Collett, Clara, *The Economic Position of Educated Working Women* (London, 1890)
Drake, Barbara, *Women in Trades Unions* (London, 1920)
Fairfield, Zoe, *Some Aspects of the Women's Movement* (London, 1915)
Ford, Isabella O., *Women's Wages and the Conditions under which they are Earned* (London, 1893)
—*Industrial Women and How to Help Them* (London, 1903)
—*Women and Socialism* (London, 1904)
—*Miss Blake of Markshalton* (London, 1890)
—*On the Threshold* (London, 1895)
—*Mr Elliot* (London, 1901)
Greig, Theresa Billington, *The Consumer in Revolt* (London, *c.* 1912)
Labour Party Publishing Co., *The Book of the Labour Party: Its History, Growth, Policy and Leaders* (London, 1925)
—*Labour's Who's Who* (London, 1924–29)
Llewellyn Davies, Margaret (ed.), *Maternity: Letters from Working Women* (London, 1915)
MacDonald, James Ramsay, *Margaret Ethel MacDonald* (London, 1911)
Mitchell, Hannah, *The Hard Way Up* (London, 1968)
Montefiore, Dora B., *From a Victorian to a Modern* (London, 1927)
National Union of Women's Suffrage Societies, *The Election Fighting Fund: What it has achieved* (Birmingham, 1927)
Pember Reeves, Maud, *Round About a Pound a Week* (London, 1914)
Phillips, Marion, *Women and the Labour Party* (London, *c.* 1918)
Schreiner, Olive, *Women and Labour* (London, 1911)
Snowden, Ethel, *The Woman Socialist* (London, 1914)
—*The Feminist Movement* (London, 1915)
Stead, W. T. (ed.), *Coming Men on Coming Questions* (London, 1909)
Webb, Beatrice, *My Apprenticeship*, vol. I (Pelican, 1938)
Wilkinson, Lily Gair, *Revolutionary Socialism and the Women's Movement* (Glasgow, 1910)
—'Women's freedom', in S. Fleming (ed.), *Women in Rebellion*, Square One Pamphlets, no. 6 (Independent Labour Party, 1973)

Reports

Hansard's Parliamentary Debates, 4th Series (1906)
Royal Commission on Labour, PP, 1892, c. 6894
Labour Party *Annual Reports*
The Labour Party Year Book, 1916 (Co-operative Press, 1916)
Women's Labour League *Conference Reports*

Newspapers

Clarion
Justice
Labour Leader
Labour Woman
League Leaflet
Northern Democrat
Woman Worker

Articles

Collette, Christine, 'Socialism and scandal in 1900', *History Workshop Journal*, 23, Spring 1987
—'An independent voice', *North West Labour History*, 12, 1987
Dyhouse, Carol, 'Working-class mothers and infant mortality in England 1895–1914', *Journal of Social History*, XII, 2, winter 1978
Hakim, Catherine, 'Census reports as documentary evidence', *Sociological Review*, XXVIII, 3, August, 1980
Kirk, Neville (ed.), 'Women and the Labour Movement', *North West History*, 7, 1980–81
McKibbin, Ross, 'James Ramsay MacDonald and the problems of the independence of the Labour Party 1910–1914', *Journal of Modern History*, 42, 1970
—'Why was there Marxism in Great Britain?', *English Historical Review*, 39, April 1984
Marwick, Arthur, 'The Labour Party and the Welfare State in Britain 1900–1948', *American Historical Review*, LXIII, December 1967
Pugh, Martin D., 'Politicians and the women's vote 1914–18', *History*, LIX, 197, October 1974
Rowan, Caroline, 'Women in the Labour Party 1906–1920', *Feminist Review*, 12, 1982
'Socialist feminism out of the blue', *Feminist Review*, 23, summer 1986
Yeo, Stephen, 'A new life: the religion of socialism in Britain 1883–1896', *History Workshop Journal*, 4, autumn 1977

Secondary sources

Books

Anderson, Dame Adelaide, *Women in the Factory* (Murray, 1922)
Bagwell, Philip S., *The Railwaymen* (London, 1963)
Banks, Olive, *Faces Of Feminism* (Martin Robertson, 1981)
Bellamy, J. and Saville, J. *Dictionary of Labour Biography*, (eds.), vols. I–VII
Bunbury, Sir H. N. (ed.), *Lloyd George's Ambulance Wagon: the memoirs of A. J. Braithwaite* (Methuen, 1957)
Crow, Duncan, *The Victorian Woman* (Allen & Unwin, 1978)

Engels, F., *The Origin of the Family, Private Property and the State*, in *Selected Works* (Lawrence & Wishart, 1968)
Halévy, E., *A History of the English People*, Epilogue, vol. II, 1905–15 (Ernest Benn, London, 1934)
Hamilton, Mary Agnes, *Margaret Bondfield* (London, 1924)
Harrison, Brian, *Separate Spheres, The Opposition to Women's Suffrage in Britain* (Croom Helm, 1978)
Herbert, Lucy, *Mrs Ramsay MacDonald* (London, 1924)
Kendall, Walter, *The Revolutionary Movement in Britain 1900–21* (Weidenfeld & Nicholson, 1969)
Liddington, Jill, *The Life and Times of a Respectable Rebel: Selina Cooper, 1864–1946* (Virago, 1984)
Liddington, Jill and Norris, Jill, *One Hand Tied Behind Us: The Rise of the Women's Suffrage Movement* (Virago, 1978)
Mappen, Ellen, 'Strategies for change: social feminist approaches to the problem of women's work' in Angela John (ed.); *Unequal Opportunities: Women's Employment in England 1800–1914* (Blackwell, 1986)
Markham, Violet, *May Tennant* (Falcon Press, 1949)
Middleton, Lucy (ed.), *Women in the Labour Movement* (Medwood Burn, 1977)
Pankhurst, Sylvia E., *The Suffragette Movement: An Intimate Account of Persons and Ideals* (London, 1931)
Pelling, Henry, *Origins of the Labour Party* (2nd ed., Oxford University Press, 1963)
Porter, Cathy, *Alexandra Kollantai* (Virago, 1980)
Rowbotham, Sheila and Weeks, Jeffrey, *Socialism and the New Life: The Personal and Sexual Politics of Edward Carpenter and Havelock Ellis* (Pluto Press, 1977)
Rowbotham, Sheila, Segal, Lynne and Wainwright, Hilary, *Beyond the Fragments: Feminism and the Making of Socialism* (Merlin Press, 1979)
Rudé, C., *Ideology and Popular Protest* (Lawrence & Wishart, 1980)
Sanderson-Furniss, A. D. and Phillips, Marion, *The Working Woman's House* (London, 1920)
Strachey, Ray, *The Cause: A Short History of the Women's Movement in Great Britain* (1928, reprinted Virago, 1980)
Thompson, Lawrence, *The Enthusiasts: A Biography of John and Katharine Bruce Glasier* (Victor Gollancz, 1979)
Vernon, Betty, *Ellen Wilkinson* (Croom Helm, 1982)
Vicinus, Martha, (ed.), *A Widening Sphere* (Methuen, 1980)
Wilkinson, Ellen, *The Town that was Murdered* (Gollancz, 1937)

Index